AMSTERDAMER PUBLIKATIONEN ZUR SPRACHE UND LITERATUR

herausgegeben von

COLA MINIS

15.BAND

RODOPI N.V.

AMSTERDAM 1974

German – Romance Contact: Name-giving in Walser Settlements

von

Peter Nichols Richardson

RODOPI N.V.

AMSTERDAM 1974

Library of Congress Catalog Card Number: 74-79043

ISBN: 90–6203–221–4

FOREWORD

I wish to thank Professor Konstantin Reichardt
for undertaking the wearisome task of overseeing the
development and progress of this study. Professors
Herwig G. Zauchenberger of the Claremont Graduate
School and William G. Moulton of Princeton University
and Dr. Andrea Schorta of the Dicziunari Rumantsch
Grischun in Chur gave me valuable help and advice in
the initial stages of the investigation.

Staatsarchivar Dr. Rudolf Jenny kindly invited
me to conduct my work in the Staatsarchiv Graubünden;
Fräulein Dr. Elsbeth Cathomas and Herr Gaudenz Vonzun
in the Staatsarchiv and Fräulein Linda Riffel and Herr
Raimund Riedi in the Kantonsbibliothek gave me valuable
assistance throughout the year in Chur.

Dr. Lukas Burckardt of the Swiss Embassy in Wash-
ington helped me to establish contact with the foundation Pro Helvetia and its director, Herr Luc Boissonnas,
who generously supplied me with essential research
materials. I must also record my indebtedness to the
many teachers, ministers, and public officials who
granted me access to the individual community archives
throughout Graubünden.

i

To no one do I owe more gratitude than to my
wife, whose devotion, patience, and untiring assistance enabled me to overcome the many difficulties
which the project entailed. A mia chara duonna saja
dedichada quaista lavur.

Danusa im Prättigau
July 8, 1970

ii

CONTENTS

iii

ABBREVIATIONS

ASG: Archiv für schweizerische Geschichte. Zürich, 1843-1874.

ASV: Geiger, Paul and Weiss, Richard. Atlas der schweizerischen Volkskunde. Basel, 1962.

BM: Bündnerisches Monatsblatt. Chur, 1850ff.

BNF: Beiträge zur Namenforschung. Heidelberg, 1949ff.

BSG: Bachmann, Albert, ed. Beiträge zur schweizer-deutschen Grammatik. Frauenfeld, 1910ff.

BSM: Hotzenköcherle, Rudolf, ed. Beiträge zur schweizer-deutschen Mundartforschung. Frauenfeld, 1949ff.

BUB: Meyer-Marthaler, Elisabeth and Perret, Franz, ed. Bündner Urkundenbuch. I. Chur, 1955.

CD: Mohr, Theodor von. Codex Diplomaticus. 4 vols. Chur, 1848-61.

GLS: Geographisches Lexikon der Schweiz. 6 vols. Neuenburg, 1902-1910.

Gremaud: Gremaud, J. Documents relatifs à l'histoire du Vallais. I (300-1255) Lausanne, 1875; II (1255-1300) Lausanne, 1876. (also DV)

HBLS: Historisch-Biographisches Lexikon der Schweiz. 7 vols. and supplement. Neuenburg, 1921-1934.

JHGG: Jahresberichte der Historisch-antiquarischen Gesellschaft von Graubünden. Chur, 1871ff.

JSG: Jahrbuch für schweizerische Geschichte. Zürich, 1876ff.

LV: Drosdowski, Günther. Duden Lexikon der Vornamen. (Duden Taschenbücher no. 4) Mannheim/Zürich, 1968.

QSG: Quellen zur schweizer Geschichte. Basel, 1877ff.

RLR: Revue de linguistique romane. Paris, 1925ff.

RNB: Planta, Robert von and Schorta, Andrea. Rätisches
Namenbuch. I. Zürich/Leipzig, 1939; II. Bern,
1964.

Schw. Id.: Schweizerisches Idiotikon. Frauenfeld, 1881ff.

SDS: Hotzenköcherle, Rudolf and Trüb, Rudolf. Sprach-
atlas der deutschen Schweiz. I. Bern, 1962; II.
Bern, 1965.

SZG: Schweizerische Zeitschrift für Geschichte.
Zürich, 1951ff.

VR: Vox Romanica. Zürich, 1936ff.

ZfrPh: Zeitschrift für romanische Philologie. Halle,
1877ff.

ZNF: Zeitschrift für Namenforschung. Berlin, 1938ff.

ZMF: Zeitschrift für Mundartforschung. Halle, 1935ff.

ZSG: Zeitschrift für Schweizerische Geschichte.
Zürich, 1921ff.

ZSK: Zeitschrift für schweizerische Kirchengeschichte.
Freiburg, 1907ff.

CHRONOLOGICAL TABLE

4th cent. B.C.: Etruscan-Celtic contact in eastern
 Switzerland

2nd-1st cent. B.C.: Celts throughout Switzerland

58 B.C.: Helvetii defeated by Caesar

58 B.C.-454 A.D.: Roman rule in Switzerland

16-13 B.C.: Beginning of Roman influence in eastern
 Switzerland (Raetia)

1st cent. A.D.: Construction of Roman _limes_ in Transalpine Gaul

3rd cent.: _limes_ overrun by Alemanni

ca. 200: Scattered Alemannic penetration over Italian
 Alps

300: Raetia divided into Raetia Prima and Raetia Secunda

401: Roman army recalled into Italy

406: Germanic tribes (Vandals, Suebi, Alani, Burgundians)
 in Palatinate and Alsace.

431: Burgundians settled south of Geneva by Aetius.

451: Huns attack Burgundians near Geneva

453: First mention of Bishop of Chur

454: Aetius murdered; Alemanni invade south of Rhine

493: Theoderic conquers Italy

496: Alemanni seek refuge with Theoderic

526: Death of Theoderic; Raetia becomes part of Frankish
 state

ca. 700: Last Romance speakers around Lake Constance

800: Alemanni in Upper Bernese area

806:     Frankish system of government in Raetia

9th-10th cent.:   Alemanni enter Valais

843:     Chur bishopric transferred from Milan to Mainz

9th-14th cent.:   Germanization of Rhine Valley from St.
         Gallen to Maienfeld; some Germanizing activity in
         Prättigau and Schanfigg

1100-1150:   Walser in the Urserntal

ca. 1200:   Walser migrate to Italian Piedmont and head-
         waters of the Rhine

ca. 1260:   Rheinwald colony established

ca. 1280:   Davos colony established

1396:   Gotteshausbund

1424:   Oberer (Grauer) Bund

1436:   Death of Friedrich VII von Toggenburg;
         Zehngerichtenbund

1471:   Merger of three alliances

1300-1600:   Walser Germanize Prättigau and Schanfigg

1538:   Aegidius (Gilg) Tschudi, Die uralt warhafftig
         Alpisch Rhetia

1582:   Ulrich Campell, Raetiae alpestris topographica
         descriptio

16th cent.:   Final Germanization of Chur

1742:   Nicolin Sererhard, Einfalte Delineation . . .

1803:   Graubünden joins Swiss Confederation

MAP ONE

LANGUAGE DISTRIBUTION
IN
PRESENT — DAY GRAUBÜNDEN

(cf. Carigelli GB 19)

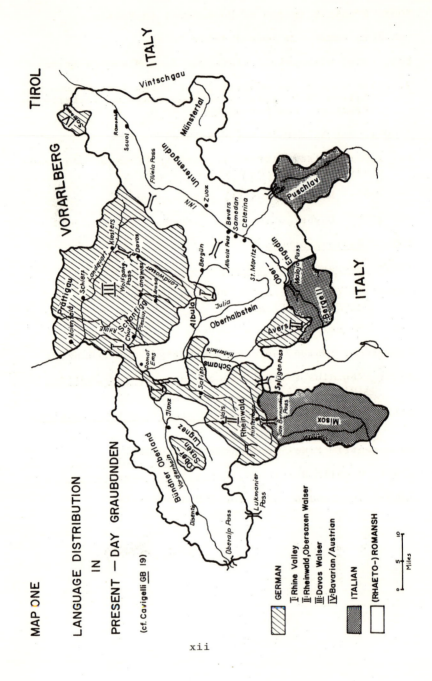

GERMAN

Ⅰ: Rhine Valley
Ⅱ: Rheinwald, Obersaxen Walser
Ⅲ: Davos Walser
Ⅳ: Bavarian / Austrian

ITALIAN

(RHAETO-) ROMANSH

0   5   10
Miles

TIROL
ITALY
VORARLBERG
ITALY

Vintschgau
Münstertal
Unterengadin
Ramosch
Scuol
Flüela Pass
INN
Zuoz
Bevers
Samedan
Celerina
Klosters
Landquart
Schiers
Prättigau
Wolfgang Pass
Davos
Landwasser
Langwies
Bergün
Albula Pass
St. Moritz
Engadin
Maladers
Schanfigg
Plessur
RHINE
Chur
Monstein
Julia
Albula
Oberhalbstein
Oden
Maloja Pass
Puschlav
Bergell
Avers
Domat / Ems
Hinterrhein
Safien
Schams
Bündner Oberland
Vorderrhein
Ilanz
Lugnez
Ober Saxen
Vals
Rheinwald
Hinterrhein
Splügen Pass
San Bernardino Pass
Misox
Disentis
Oberalp Pass
Lukmanier Pass

xii

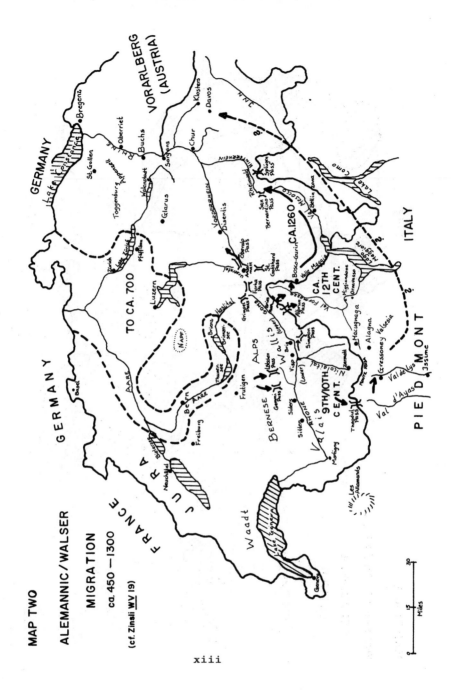

MAP TWO

ALEMANNIC/WALSER

MIGRATION

ca. 450 – 1300

(cf. Zinsli WV 19)

GERMANY

VORARLBERG (AUSTRIA)

FRANCE

GERMANY

JURA

TO CA. 700

AARE

ITALY

PIEDMONT

Bregenz
Oberriet
Buchs
St. Gallen
Toggenburg
Werdenberg
Rhine
Sargans
Chur
Glarus
Disentis
Klosters
Davos
Inn
VORDERRHEIN
HINTERRHEIN
Rheinwald
Spluegen Pass
San Bernardino Pass
Bellinzona
CA. 1260
Bosco-Gurin
Valle Maggia
Lake Como
Lugano
Maggia
Zurich
Lake of Zurich
Pfäffikon
Napf
Luzern
Alpnach
Jagerbach
Obwalden
Disentis
Vogelsberg
St. Gotthard Pass
Furka Pass
Grimsel Pass
Oberalp Pass
CA. 12TH CENT.
Maggiandone
Ornavasso
Briens
Brienzersee
Thunersee
Frutigen
Bern
Freiburg
Neuchâtel
Aare
BERNESE
ALPS
Wallis
Aletsch Pass
Gemmi Pass
Goms
Simplon Pass
Visp Br.
Visp (Lower)
Macugnaga
Alagna
Gressoney Valsesia
Zermatt
Monte Rosa
Sitten
Siders
VALAIS
RHONE
9TH/10TH CENT.
Nicolaital
Theodul Pass
Martigny
Les Allemands
Val d'Ayass
Val de Lys
Issime
Val de Gressoney
Waadt
Lake Geneva
Geneva

0   15   30
Miles

xiii

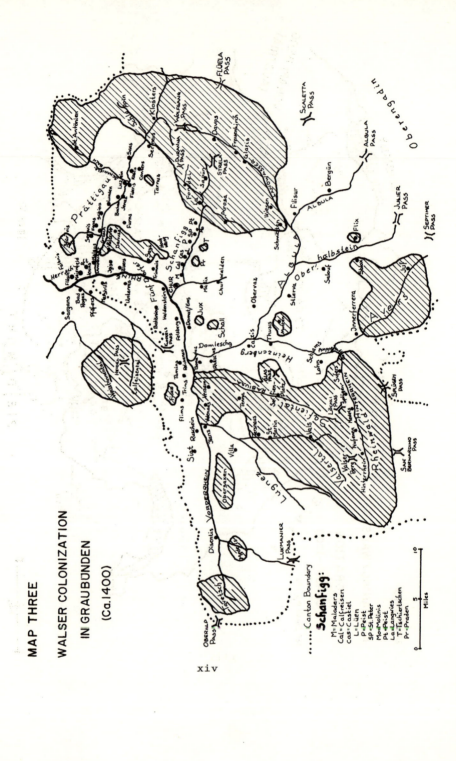

MAP THREE

WALSER COLONIZATION

IN GRAUBÜNDEN

(Ca. 1400)

Schanfigg:
M=Maladers
Cal=Calfreisen
Cas=Castiel
L=Lüen
P=Peist
SP=St. Peter
Mon=Molinis
Pt=Pagig
La=Langwies
T=Tschiertschen
Pr=Praden

······· Canton Boundary

xiv

INTRODUCTION

I. The Problem

This study concerns the phenomenon of cultural contact, or the mutual influence of two neighboring cultures.
The investigation treats one contact situation from both
synchronic and diachronic perspectives: Each stage of
the cultural symbiosis is examined by itself, and the
historical development of the whole is seen in a comparison of these various stages. The two groups in question
are, roughly stated, the German-speaking and Romansh-
speaking populations of the Swiss canton of Graubünden.

The contact between two separate language groups may
be manifested in several ways. As Weinreich (LC),
Moulton (SG), Jud (GR),[1] and others have pointed out,
several aspects of linguistic contact ranging from phono-
logical to syntactic interference may readily be measured
in bilingual areas of this type. Comparative folklore
studies have revealed the delicate interweaving of con-
trastive cultural phenomena in this German-Romance contact zone (cf. Weiss AG, DvS).

No investigation of cultural contact would be complete, however, without a thorough study of the traditions of name-giving in each culture. Students of early
Germanic civilization rely largely on onomastic forms

xv

for clues to the geographic and temporal distribution of
linguistic phenomena; indeed, many of the earliest runic
inscriptions record little more than a single name.
There could hardly be a more convincing indication of
the importance of this most personal aspect of language.
The individual, as Weinreich notes (LC 71), is the ultimate locus of linguistic interference. Because the individual is also the immediate source of name-giving,
the study of personal names should perhaps best indicate
the extent of interpenetration of two cultures in contact.

*   *   *

"What's in a name?" asks Juliet in her balcony soli-
loquy. Her anguish in this scene (II.ii.) is caused by
Romeo's membership in a family hostile to her own; if
Romeo were not associated with the name Montague--if the
identity of his name with that of a hated clan did not
exist--the tragedy of Shakespeare's drama would be un-
founded.

This is only one instance in which a person's name
is decisive in the fate of its bearer. In other well-
known cases Hildebrand asks his son Hadubrand to identify
himself--and therefore his family--on the battlefield;
and Sigurð refuses to tell the dying Fafnir his name for
fear that the dragon might lay a curse upon him. In
these situations the knowledge of a name itself is of

xvi

such singular importance that it could spare the life or hasten the death of the person whom it identifies.

Often a name is considered to be virtually identical with its bearer. In the valley of Prättigau in Graubünden the very mention of white snakes was once thought to make them appear,[2] and taboos in many primitive societies prohibit the calling of the sun, moon, and other mystical objects by name. Personal names are believed by the Navahos to be powers in themselves; they can be worn out with too much use, but as long as they are "fresh" they can give their bearers additional powers in dangerous situations.[3] Most important to all peoples is the relationship between the individual and the label which identifies him to his fellows:

> This psychological impact of name-bearing upon the bearer is of the greatest importance. It is responsible for all the magic powers ascribed to names, for the solemnity with which Christian baptism and non-Christian name-giving ceremonies are performed, for name taboos, for the intangible honor, pride, value, and sometimes shame, attached to one's name, and conversely, for the fear and opprobrium of namelessness. (Pulgram TN 165 note 59)

For this reason the choice of a name is one of the greatest responsibilities of parenthood. The recent wave of popular names from the world of politics, entertainment, and sport has placed the task of name-giving squarely on the parents of a child. In times of more

cultural stability, however, the consensus of other family members was often sought for the approval of a name.
In Graubünden, and undoubtedly elsewhere as well, a
firmly established pattern often determined the names
of children long before they were born: The first son
was named after the father's father, the first daughter
after the mother's mother, and so on (cf. Geiger-Weiss
ASV map 207 and ASVKo 351ff.).

The very act of name-giving has thus been of central importance to the maintenance of ties with the past,
to the perpetuation of a cultural tradition. If this
onomastic heritage has been altered in any way by external affairs, these affairs must be understood to have
had other cultural consequences before their effects became manifested in a change in name-giving practices.
In short, name-giving would seem to be one of the least
changeable elements of a cultural group; as such it
should reflect the most thorough interpenetration of
two cultures in contact.

*   *   *

The present study has grown from a preliminary
investigation of name-giving practices among Catholics
and Protestants in Graubünden, in which onomastic traditions were found to vary considerably between the
confessional groups. Yet the possibility existed that

the onomastic differences between communities might have their origin in a more basic cultural phenomenon, namely that of the Medieval division of the canton into German-speaking and Romansh-speaking sectors.

After a brief introductory history of Graubünden (Chapter I), this study examines name-giving traditions in both German and Romance regions for the pre-Reformation period (Chapters II and III); the results are then compared with those of post-Reformation sources (Chapter IV) in order to measure the effect of the religious realignment on German and Romance communities. A survey of German-Romance contact in Graubünden (Chapter V) helps to reinforce the conclusions which are reached throughout the study and which are summarized in Chapter VI.

II. Graubünden

With an area of 2743 square miles and a population of 147,458, Graubünden forms the largest and most sparsely populated canton of Switzerland.[4] It is also the only officially trilingual canton: Approximately 57% of the population declare German as their first language; Romansh, or Rhaeto-Romansh, is the first language of 26%, and Italian is the mother tongue of 16% of the population.[5] Many citizens of Graubünden, or **Bündner**, are

bi- or trilingual: hardly surprising considering that
the three languages are spoken in an area about half
the size of Yellowstone National Park.

Roughly speaking, the dialects of Romansh are spoken in the Bündner Oberland between the Oberalp Pass and
Domat/Ems, in Domleschg between Rhäzüns and Thusis, in
Schams, in the Albula Valley, in Oberhalbstein, and in
the Ober- and Unterengadin (see map I). Italian is used
in the Misox, the Bergell, and the Puschlav. Elsewhere
two German dialects are found: the east Alemannic dialect
of the Rhine Valley ("Hochalemannisch") and the archaic
west Alemannic Walser dialect of Obersaxen, the Rheinwald,
Davos, and their daughter colonies throughout the canton
("Höchstalemannisch").

The confessional division of Graubünden is approximately equal between Catholic and Evangelical Reformed
(Protestant). Confessional lines do not generally correspond to linguistic lines.

Nearly one-third of the land area of Graubünden is
too mountainous to be cultivated or used as pasture, yet
until the recent surge of tourism the main industry of
the canton was agriculture. At the highest elevations
(above 1000 meters) the farmers are chiefly herdsmen; in
lower valleys grain crops, vegetables, and fruit are
grown. Not surprisingly, the highest permanently occupied town in Europe (Juf = 2133m) is located in

Graubünden (Zermatt = 1620m, Garmisch = 692m).

The frequent reference to "Passland Graubünden" is well grounded in historical fact. The shortest route from Swabia to Italy led from Ulm to Bregenz to Chur, then up the valley of the Hinterrhein to a) the Splügen Pass and Chiavenna or b) the San Bernardino Pass and Bellinzona/Locarno. The east-west route heavily traveled in Roman times led from Lake Geneva through the Rhone Valley (the present canton of Valais) to the Furka Pass, then from Andermatt over the Oberalp Pass to the head-waters of the Rhine in Graubünden. From Chur the route extended eastward over the Strela Pass to Davos and from there over the Flüela Pass into the Unterengadin and Tirol.

These passes and others (Lukmanier, Septimer, Maloja, Julier, Bernina) combine with the strategic location of Graubünden between north and south, east and west to make this "land of 150 valleys" an area of extraordinary historical and cultural complexity.

III. The Sources

Both published and unpublished sources are examined for their name content. For the pre-Reformation period all material is published (usually in BM or JHGG[6]) with the exception of a) the Tavetsch and Pleif Jahrzeitbücher, which are photocopied and preserved in the Staatsarchiv Graubünden in Chur, and b) miscellaneous community documents found either in the original in the 224 individual Gemeindearchive throughout Graubünden or in photocopies in the Staatsarchiv.

These early sources appear in several forms. The most important are:

1) The Latin records of property transfer and other legal matters in thirteenth century Valais published by Gremaud (DV). The following sample document from June 16, 1276, in Raron is taken from volume II (no. 840):

> Notum sit omnibus presentem paginam inspecturis quod ego Willermus sub Saxo, filius quondam Warneri de Raronia, laudatione Beatricis vxoris mee et filiarum mearum Salome et Odilie, uendidi et finaui pro XX et I lb. ,solutis et VI d. seruicii ad festum b. Martini et XII placiti, omni exactione remota, Ro. uicedomino de Raronia et heredibus suis et cui dare uel uendere uoluerit, uineam meam in der Stegebundum et agrum ante iacentem cum uia et aqua et omnibus pertinentiis suis; pro quo seruicio et placito ego et heredes mei et hereditas mea tenemur sibi et heredibus eius et cui dare uel ueldere uoluerit, predictam uenditionem firmiter gerentire. Inde rogauimus literam fieri et testes aponi qui sic uocantur: Olricus domicellus de Rarun, Bertoldus frater eius, Jo. minister et multi alii. Actum in platea de Rarun, M.CC.LXX.VI, XVI kl. julii.

2) <u>Jahrzeitbücher</u>: books which contain records of church celebrations as well as lists of masses to be said in memory of the deceased (<u>Seelenmessen</u> or <u>Jahrzeiten</u>). The church is given money from a specified piece of property; the priest is thereby obligated to say one or more daily masses depending on the number of people deceased on a given day and on the amount of money given. Examples follow from Tavetsch (ca. 1450), Maienfeld (1475), and Langwies (1488-1500):

<u>Tavetsch</u> (Staatsarchiv Graubünden AB IV 6/119):

Jẽcklin perchten johēs p̄r sug. peꞇ p̄r sug Greta
nn uxor p̄dcti jãklin⁊ omj ancestor__ ⁊successor__ ...
(Jẽcklin perchten johannes pater suus petrus pater
suus Greta nec non uxor praedicti jãklin et omnes
ancestores et successores ...)

It [em] Anshelm giss   filia sua Nesa gstatuẽrꞇ [con-
statuerunt] plb̄n̄o iiij °ᵒʳ. . . . die nẽchsten obgeschr
iiij jarzit vnd guꞇ hand jnne die er nach ōsthr
eliche brũd. pet. marth jaklin jeñi Anshelm Durrich
die sind gewesen des jūgen jeñi percht eliche sũn ...

<u>Maienfeld</u> (Jecklin <u>SA</u> 38f.):

Item Wilhelm Folmãr von Flãsch und Aelli Brãgentzerin
sin elich hussfrow hand gelãssen bi lebendigem lib ain
ewig iartzit für sich selbs und ir baider fordren und
nachkomen und besunder fũr Wilhelms vatter und ouch
mõter und zwayer siner husfrŏwen Margaretan und Annen
und ouch der Aellinen man **Haintzen**, den si vor

Wilhelmen hat gehept und iro baider tochter Greth und ouch Gilgen der Haintzen brüder gewesen ist.

Langwies (Jecklin JK 16f.):

Item Margaretha, Hänsli Pregentzers husfröw haut gemacht ain ewig iartzit, ir und iren kinden, dominica proxima post epiphania cum dominicale commemoracione mit xviij d. ab irs sons Hans güt, lit in Phandey, stost inwert an Hungersbach, abwert an landtwasser, usna an Henslis Jos güt, obna an die strass.

3) **Zinsbücher**: tax lists, in which yearly property taxes were set to be collected on specific days. Taxes could be paid with cheese, lard, grain, (later) coinage, or in special cases with other commodities such as fish or cloth. The following sample is taken from the tax register of the Churwalden cloister (Jecklin ZP 24):

Item Dysch Ryschen erben, Jann Talpen erben zinsent von irem erblehen. -- Zins xvij werd käs und iij kr. und v schöffel iij f. ij qrt. korn. -- Zinsszyl, hoffal. Uff Galli käs, Purificationis korn, acht tag darnach hoffal.

(In this entry the descendants of Dysch Rysch and Jann Talp pay the following yearly tax on part of their property: 17 Wertkäs (about 71 lbs. of cheese), three **Krinen** (18 spoonfuls) of lard, and $5^7/8$ bushels of grain. The cheese is to be paid on October 16, the grain is to be paid on February 2, and the tax on the entire property is due on February 10.)

4) Spendbücher: registers containing the gifts by specific individuals to the church, originally for the purpose of financing the donation of food, clothing, and money to the poor. The gifts were taken in part from the money from Jahrzeiten and from private donations. Each landowner seems to have been required to give in proportion to the value of his property, whose borders were defined in relation to the land owned by other citizens. The following is taken from the Davos Spendbuch of 1562 (Jecklin DS 35):

> Meretta Brangery sol fünf schilig und siben
> pfenig ab dem huss und gůt, so ires vatters
> gesin ist, gelegen in der Spinen, genant das
> Bort. Stost ufwert an Flury Rüschs gůt, ab-
> wert an Elsi Brangeri gůt, usswert an den
> kilichweg, so gán sandt Nicklaus gat, inwert
> an Hans Ambůls gůt.

*   *   *

The only published source consulted for the post-Reformation period is a list of the male voters in the Zehngerichtenbund from 1623 (Gillardon BG). All other material consists of the Latin (Catholic) and German (Protestant) birth, marriage, and death records kept in church registers in the individual church archives of Graubünden. Because each of the canton's 224 communities

xxv

has its own archives, the collection of this material involved considerably more work than did the evaluation of pre-Reformation published documents. The church registers vary in their state of preservation. In some cases local officials (community presidents, ministers, teachers) have taken an active interest in the preservation of their documents, and their efforts must be commended (cf. Flims, Küblis, the Rheinwald); in other cases valuable records are simply exposed in damp cellars (Castiel) or in fire hazards such as the attics of wooden houses (Siat). Too often the elements have taken their toll: The entire village of Obermutten, including its wooden church, burned in the 1940's; and too often man himself is to blame: The church books of Maladers can no longer even be found.

The terminal date of the investigation is arbitrarily set at 1700. By this time the contact and mixture of Walser and Romance populations was complete. Some important communities, such as Vals and Tavetsch, could not be examined because their records begin after 1700; yet the sources which are available for the 1500's and 1600's in Walser and Walser-Romance contact zones alone yield over 16,400 names and assure a reliable statistical survey of the post-Reformation onomastic relationships in these areas.

*   *   *

This study represents the first investigation of personal names in Graubünden since Professor Muoth's survey of 1892 (BG). This early work considers only the development of family names from first names, and thus does not provide the perspective necessary for an understanding of name-giving practices as a whole. Most of the pre-Reformation material covered in the present investigation came to light long after Professor Muoth's work was completed; also, no church records of the post-Reformation era were examined by him.

Name study is hardly new to the history-conscious Bündner, yet has been conducted on a scientific basis only for the vast numbers of place and field names in the canton. The exhaustive work of the Romanists Robert von Planta and Andrea Schorta in this area of investigation has resulted in the incomparable two-volume Rätisches Namenbuch (RNB). A third volume of this study is planned for personal names, and it is hoped that the present investigation will in some way ease the burden of name collection and evaluation which this ambitious project entails.

IV. Footnotes

[1] See abbreviations in the bibliography.

[2] G. Fient, _Das Prättigau_. Davos, 1897, 240.

[3] Frederik Hetmann, _Die Spur der Navahos_. Recklinghausen, 1969, 67.

[4] _Statistisches Jahrbuch der Schweiz_. Bern, 1969, 13 and 93.

[5] _Eidgenössische Volkszählung 1. Dez. 1960. XI: Kanton Graubünden_. Bern, 1964, 53.

[6] See list of abbreviations, p. viii.

CHAPTER ONE

THE HISTORICAL BACKGROUND

In the fifth century A.D. much of the Romance-
speaking area of what is now northern Switzerland was
settled by Germanic invaders from the north. In the
following centuries this initial thrust continued south
as far as the Rhone Valley, a former Roman stronghold,
which became almost completely Germanized. By the thirteenth century this area, today called Valais, was so
overpopulated that many of its inhabitants, called Walser, migrated to the Italian Piedmont, then east to what
is today the canton of Graubünden. In doing so they
once again settled as a Germanic superstratum in a
Romance-speaking area.

The language and customs of the Romance speakers
whom the Walser encountered in Graubünden had been well
established there since the early centuries of the
Christian era. Nevertheless, these "natives" showed
little cultural evidence of the original population.

I. <u>Pre-Christian Switzerland</u>

Switzerland has always been densely populated,
even in prehistoric times. The eastern regions where
the Walser settled in the late 1200's had already been

occupied some seventeen centuries before by a tribe
known as the Raetii, whose origin is still unclear.[1]
Were the Raetii Etruscans? Illyrians? Celts? Were
they even Indo-European? This is difficult to determine from the available evidence (Stähelin SR 16ff.).
Livy and Pliny believed the Raetii were Etruscans (HBLS
V, 602), and the appearance of Etruscan helmets in the
villages of Obersaxen and Igis indicates that this may
have been true.[2]

In the fourth century B.C. the northern Etruscans
were forced by Celtic tribes from the northeast to retreat into the periphery of what is now eastern Switzerland. It seems likely that Etruscans and Celts
somehow combined in the zone of contact to become the
Raetii, but how this may have happened is uncertain.
We may only postulate that the distinction between conquerors and conquered became obscured in the synthesis
of the two cultures so that neither tribe predominated.
In any case, the Raetii never constituted a single political unit, but were composed of several small tribes:
the Rigusci in the Engadin, the Suanetes on the headwaters of the Rhine, the Calucones in the Rhine Valley
between present-day Chur and Sargans, and the Brixantes
and the Vennonetes farther north around Lake Constance
(Stähelin SR 19).

Shortly before the beginning of the Christian era
the rest of what is now Switzerland was inhabited by

Celtic, or Gaulish, peoples. The Helvetii alone occupied more than one-half of present-day Switzerland,
from the Rhine in the north to the Rhone in the south
and from the Bernese Alps to the Jura in the west. At
the same time the Raetii occupied the eastern regions
from the northern slopes of the Italian Alps to Lake
Constance, and countless other Celtic peoples lived
adjacent to the territory settled by these two powerful tribes (HBLS V, 667).

II.   The Romans in Switzerland

As securely as they held this territory, the Celtic inhabitants of Switzerland were soon made to feel
the pressure of the expanding Roman Empire. As early
as 58 B.C. the Helvetii were defeated by Julius Caesar.
In 16-13 B.C. the stepsons of Caesar Augustus conquered
the Raetii, and the Romanization of eastern Switzerland
began. The Romans extended the lands held by the Raetian tribes to form the boundaries of the new province
of Raetia. In the west Raetia reached from the St.
Gotthard northward to Sigmaringen, and the Danube from
Sigmaringen to Passau (Batavis) formed its northern limits. In the east the border ran along the Inn (Oenus)
to just east of Innsbruck, then south to Bozen (Pons
Drusi). The southern border extended through Bellinzona to the area of the Simplon Pass, then north to

the St. Gotthard (Planta <u>DaR</u>, Appendix 1). This territory was supplemented by the addition of Valais
(Vallis Poenina) and the area immediately south of
Lake Geneva. In 300 A.D. Raetia was divided into the
southern Raetia I (<u>Raetia Prima</u>) and the northern
Raetia II (<u>Raetia Secunda</u>) by a line extending due
east from Lake Constance through Partenkirch (Parta-
num) to the Inn.

Raetia was one of two chief administrative districts formed by the Romans in Switzerland. The second,
Gallia Belgica to the west, clearly commanded more attention from the Romans. The many ruins and inscriptions found in the southwest attest to intense Romanization there; in the northeast very little such evidence has been found, indicating only superficial Romanization. On the whole it is understandable that the
penetration of Roman ideas and customs proceeded more
slowly in Raetia than in any other province. Herrling
attributes this in part to the fact that the inhabitants, although self-supporting, were poor, and were
neither consumers of Roman goods nor suppliers of materials vital to the Roman economy. The terrain in
the south of Raetia I was altogether forbidding, pro-
viding an all-important buffer zone between Italy and
the barbarian lands in the north (Herrling <u>RR</u> 161f.).
The chief carrier of Roman culture here was the army,

assigned to guard the frontier in Raetia II as well
as the strategic passes in Raetia I.

III. <u>Germanic Tribes in Switzerland</u>

The Romans were eager to recruit soldiers for
this army, for their hold on Transalpine Gaul was tenuous at best. The <u>limes</u>, fortifications established
along the northern frontier at the end of the first
century A.D., were destroyed or occupied by the advancing Alemanni in the middle of the third century. The
Roman occupation army could no longer defend the <u>limes</u>
and was gradually forced to retreat. By the end of
the fourth century the right bank of the Rhine was
lost, and in 401 the Roman legions were ordered to
fall back across the Alps to defend their homeland
against Alaric and his Visigoths. Raetia, Gaul, and
Britain were left to the conquering barbarians (Stähelin <u>SR</u> 259).

In the west the Vandals, Suebi, Alani, and Burgundians occupied the Palatinate and lower Alsace by
406. In 431 the Roman Aetius settled Burgundians south
of Geneva[3] to protect him against attack from the north,
which came from Attila's Huns in 451. In 454 Aetius
was murdered, and the Burgundians moved eastward into
modern Valais, Neuchâtel, Freiburg, and the Bernese
Jura (Stähelin <u>SR</u> 320; Büttner <u>GG</u> 194f.).

In the north and east the Alemanni, who in scattered groups had already penetrated over the Alps into Italy about 200, now poured south over the Rhine to stay. Their former homeland had included the area between the Rhine and a line continued north from the Lech, and extended from the Main in the north to Lake Constance in the south. This vast territory supplied streams of Germanic colonists to the newly occupied land south of the Rhine (Oechsli NB 245).[4] By the beginning of the Merovingian period nearly a century after Aetius' death, the Alemanni had settled among Gallo-Romans as far south as the Bernese Alps. Some German speakers pressed on as far south as the Italian Piedmont, following the route from Bregenz to Chur and over the Splügen Pass, but they did not establish colonies at the time and left no linguistic traces (HBLS I, 198f. (maps)). For the present, Raetia I remained thoroughly Romance (Schmidt GB 373).

The final borders of Alemannic territory still remained to be determined. In 506 the Alemanni, defeated across the Rhine by the Frank Chlodwig, fled to Theodoric, who had conquered Italy in 493 and regarded himself as ruler of Raetia I and II as well. The refugees were settled in the Raetian provinces, largely in Raetia II and the northernmost reaches of Raetia I. Yet they were still unable to escape the powerful Franks to the north.

With the death of Theodoric Alemannia came under the
rule of the Merovingian king Theudebert and in 538
yielded its autonomy to the dominion of the Frankish
state.

IV.   Language Relationships in Switzerland
         during the Roman Occupation

   This astounding series of confrontations between
Gaulish and Romance and, later, Germanic speakers produced a varied linguistic picture in the Alpine provinces.

   Latin was the language of the Roman conquerors,
whose military administration could hardly tolerate
the use of the native Gaulish idiom in civil affairs.
As tolerant as the Romans were of local tradition, they
were committed to the establishment of a firmly Romanized link with the Empire. They never tried to stamp
out the native language (Herrling RR 153), but also
probably did not encourage its use in matters of interest to Rome. On the other hand, Latin seems to have
achieved widespread use among the natives, possibly for
economic or social reasons (Planta DaR 219). We may
assume that anyone used Latin who stood to gain by doing
so, whether it was the merchant who desired contact with
other parts of the Empire or the common man who admired

the uniformed Roman soldier and may have aspired to
call this part of the Roman culture his own (Herrling
RR 158). During the five centuries of uninterrupted
Roman rule in Switzerland from 58 B.C. to 454 A.D.
many Gaulish speakers were called to military service
in the Roman legions, and the native contact with Latin,
already begun by Roman officials, merchants, and colonists, was intensified (Stähelin SR 332f.).

The language spoken at the end of the Roman occupation of Switzerland contained elements of both Vulgar Latin and the various Gaulish idioms used by the
pre-Roman population there. It is generally called
Gallo-Romance.

The invasion of Germanic tribes into Switzerland
posed a threat to the continued existence of the Gallo-
Romance idiom. Walther v. Wartburg believes that the
Alemannic invasion in the fifth century probably caused
the initial differentiation of the Gallo-Romance dialects. To the west of the Alemanni the Franco-Provençal group developed, while Romansh flourished in the
east (ZfrPh LVI, 16 and 25ff.).[5] The success of the
Germanic dialects in Switzerland depended on both the
relative numerical strength of the Germanic and Gallo-
Roman populations and the manner in which the Germanic
conquerors approached the natives whose land they occupied. Thus it is hardly surprising that Switzerland

was not uniformly Germanized.

In the southwest the Burgundians accepted Christianity and intermarried with the native inhabitants, who had been thoroughly Romanized after the five centuries of Roman rule (Moulton SG 22ff.).[6] By extending its dominion over Valais as well as the area in the northwest, the Burgundian ruling stratum spread itself too thin and eventually dissolved and became Romanized. Linguistic evidence of Burgundian rule in this area is now to be found chiefly in place names in -inges, -enges, -ange, -ins, or -ens (< -ingōs).[7]

The Germanization of north central and eastern Switzerland took place under totally different conditions. Partly because Raetia had not been so intensively Romanized as Gallia Belgica (Mommsen SR 372f.), the Alemanni had little difficulty maintaining their cultural and linguistic integrity after they settled there. Their contact with the Ostrogoths and later subjugation under Frankish rule virtually assured the continued existence of their language, however much it may have been influenced by the other Germanic dialects.

Even after the nominal end of the tribal migrations in the sixth century, much of modern Switzerland was inhabited by Gallo-Romans. Romance dialects were still dominant southwest of the Aare River as well as south of the Bernese Alps in Valais, which had been completely

Romanized. In addition, many of the Gallo-Romans who had occupied north central Switzerland probably took refuge from the invading Alemanni in the Raetian Alps, thus intensifying the Romanization there which before the middle of the fifth century had been superficial at best (Stähelin SR 333). Romance dialects--and a tenacious Gaulish substratum[8]--were indeed widespread, but remained largely on the periphery of the compara- tively rich north central area occupied by German speakers. It was the descendants of the Alemanni who directed the further linguistic development of south central and eastern Switzerland.

V. German Political Influence in Raetia

As we have seen, Raetia[9] was still completely Roman at the end of the fifth century. Religious au- thority in Raetia was vested in the Bishop of Chur (first mentioned in 453), an appointee of the arch- diocese of Milan. Secular affairs were directed by praesides. Tello (died 773), the last of a powerful native ruling family, combined both secular and reli- gious offices as praeses and Bishop.

Shortly after Raetia came under Frankish rule in 538 the region north of the Hirschensprung near Ober- riet was separated politically from the Romance area to the south and divided among Frankish administrative

districts (Pult <u>HU</u> 162). Thus throughout its early
post-Roman history Raetia belonged to the Frankish
kingdom but, partly because the Chur bishopric belonged to Milan, managed to maintain its autonomy as
a kind of church-state. Germans represented a very
small proportion of the Raetian population until the
beginning of the ninth century, and it was probably
for this reason that the Frankish kings allowed the
Raetians to keep their Roman laws and traditions.

After the death of Bishop Remedius in 806, however, Charlemagne decided to establish the Frankish
system of government in Raetia. He separated the highest secular authority from that of the Bishop and formed
the duchy of Raetia Curiensis, or Curraetia, consisting
of Lower (northern) and Upper (southern) Raetia, which
were divided by the Landquart River (Planta <u>DaR</u> 357f.).
The final change from Roman to Frankish rule took place
when the Treaty of Verdun in 843 transferred authority
over the bishopric of Chur from Milan to Mainz (<u>HBLS</u>
II, 585). Now Curraetia was geographically, politically, and religiously independent of Italy and became
an organic part of the Frankish kingdom.

VI. <u>German Linguistic Influence in Raetia</u>

Robert von Planta (<u>OS</u> 89ff. and map 4) sees four
kinds of place-name evidence of German influence in

Romansh-speaking Raetia during the Franconian period:
place names 1) of Valais origin from the Oberalp Pass
to Obersaxen; 2) from Bavaria and Tirol in the Unterengadin; 3) from the Langobards in the Misox south of
the San Bernardino Pass; and 4) of east Alemannic origin in a large area extending from Obersaxen up the
Rhine Valley through Chur to Ragaz, down the Hinterrhein to the Roffnaschlucht, and in Prättigau as far
east as Küblis. This last group of place names records
the gradual progress of German speakers from Lake Constance up the Rhine Valley toward Chur, and their distribution shows that this was the most significant period of Germanization before the late Middle Ages.

The final integration of Raetia into the Frankish
kingdom in 806 led to a long period of peaceful Germanization.[10] Commerce between Curraetia and the political centers in the north and immigration of German
speakers into the area steadily moved the boundary between German and Romansh south from the Hirschensprung.
In spite of the Germanization of northern Raetia, some
Romance speakers seem to have remained around Lake Constance until about 700 (Pult HU 201). Raetia, whose
Gaulish speakers had once become Romanized, now experienced a second change of language and culture.

German influence in Curraetia came with two main
classes of settlers from southern Germany, aristocrats

and laborers.[11] The new Frankish political system
brought administrators into the land: nobles and rich
property seekers as well as the clerics and lawyers
who made up their following. These secular and religious aristocrats were granted fiefs and offices, and
the ruling class in Curraetia eventually became mostly
German. It is significant that the overwhelming majority of sales documents from the early centuries of
German rule record the transfer of property from Romance-speaking natives to Germans.[12] After land had
been acquired it had to be settled, and the landowners
brought in large numbers of German laborers to clear
and till their new property. On the whole, the appearance of German place names indicates that the majority
of the Germans in the area may have been unskilled laborers (Planta OS 90). For example, OHG wald replaced
silva, foresta, and bosco in the Romansh of the area,
and many names in runcu, runcalia, etc., (< Latin
runcare 'weed' RNB II, 292ff.) date from this period.[13]

It is difficult to assess the linguistic effect
which these German speakers had on the native Romance
population. The Germans certainly represented a considerable part of the population, and many were undoubtedly bilingual. Nevertheless, it must be remembered that during the initial stages of Germanization
Germans and Romance natives were legally separated:

The latter maintained their obeisance to Roman law and customs, and the newcomers were subjects of the Frankish throne. Also, the Germans were not evenly distributed among the native populace, but rather lived in small groups in estates scattered mostly along the valley trade routes (Planta OS 95f.).[14] Chur, the center of religious and political authority in Curraetia, was the largest and most influential of these estates and to a great extent must have exerted a normalizing influence on the German spoken within the limits of its authority.

Just as many Germans must have been bilingual, so, too, were there Romance speakers who by desire or necessity learned the language of their overlords.[15] The upper stratum of Germans in Curraetia was in a position to hire domestic help, and natives certainly were employed in Chur, where contact with members of the German ruling estate was inevitable.[16]

Of course, not all Germans associated with the estates were nobles. Aristocrats were surrounded by their lawyers, advisers, bodyguards, and messengers; coachmen, cooks, and servants, while not directly involved in official affairs, attended to the comfort of their masters. One may safely assume that nearly every member of the ruling stratum maintained a degree of contact with Romance speakers, and that many of the people on

each side learned to understand the language of the
other, and probably to speak it with some degree of
fluency. As Germanization progressed into the late
Middle Ages, however, it seemed less essential that
the German landowners maintain communication with the
Raetians. Since Germans owned most of the land, they
conducted important business with their own kind and
did not need to know Romansh. Germanization was especially strong where the Bishop owned large pieces
of property administered by magistrates, stewards, and
other minor officials.

In spite of the inroads made by German in Romance
territory, Curraetia remained largely Romance throughout the Middle Ages. The political innovations of the
Carolingian period greatly affected only the administrative center of Chur and hardly disturbed the linguistic balance of the entire area.[17] Except for the
regions which bordered directly on the Alemannic territory in the Urserntal across the Oberalp Pass, Romance speakers retained their idiom for centuries. It
is important to remember that German was not a fully
developed literary language during the first centuries
of Frankish rule in Curraetia, and that both German
and Romansh yielded to Latin in churches and schools.
The use of Latin as a literary idiom undoubtedly helped
Romansh survive as long as it did (Meinherz MBH 208).

If the progress of Germanization from the north
and east was slow, it was also unrelenting.[18] The
canton of Glarus was not fully Germanized before the
eleventh century (Pult HU 210).[19] Liechtenstein was
heavily German in the thirteenth century, but Sargans
and Ragaz-Pfäfers, only a short distance to the south,
were almost entirely Romance until about 1300 and did
not become fully Germanized until over a century later
(Pult HU 195). The two languages were not used equally
in the Bündner Herrschaft (the towns which comprise the
present Kreis Maienfeld) until about 1300 (Meinherz MBH
225f.). Romansh, due largely to the close ties between
the Herrschaft and Chur, held out there for over two
hundred years until after the Reformation. Ulrich
Campell's Raetiae alpestris topographica descriptio of
1582 reported that the Raetica lingua was spoken by
elderly people in Malans as late as 1540 (Pult HU 184).

Malans is located on the east bank of the Rhine
where the Landquart River flows west out of Prättigau,
a long valley reaching southeast toward Davos. Isolated discoveries of Roman coins in Prättigau indicate
that Roman settlement, which occurred far back from the
dangerous flood plain of the river, was quite sparse
(HBLS V, 478). Planta (OS 89ff. and map 4) records
east Alemannic place names as far east as Küblis during
the Franconian period, but the careful morphological

studies of R. Hotzenköcherle show that Germanization
from the Rhine Valley probably proceeded only as far
as the present town of Lunden between Schiers and
Jenaz (BV 501).

Prättigau was Germanized before Schanfigg, the
valley to the east of Chur formed by the Plessur River.
Swabian nobles may have introduced German in Schanfigg
as early as the ninth century, but seem to have left a
negligible linguistic impression on the native Romance
population (Kessler MS 176). The German of the Rhine
Valley entered Schanfigg from Chur and was used first
in Maladers, possibly extending as far east as Calfreisen, Castiel, and Lüen in the fourteenth century. It
proceeded no farther into inner Schanfigg.

The Germanization of Chur seems to have been my-
steriously slow. Because of its early position as political and religious center of Curraetia, Chur had attracted large numbers of the German-speaking secular
and religious aristocracy. Nevertheless, the majority
of Chur, located at present on the northern edge of Romansh territory, was Romance-speaking through most of
the fifteenth century (Planta OS 96).[20] Campell's de-
scription of Raetia recorded the triumph of German during his lifetime. The Rhaetica lingua, he said, had
been spoken in Chur until the beginning of the sixteenth century. Within the last hundred years it had

fallen _in obsolescente_ and German had become the only language used in daily commerce. The citizens of Chur now (1582) understood Romansh, but did not like to speak it in public. Very few families spoke only Romansh at home (Kessler <u>MS</u> 171f.).

As has been mentioned, German was used extensively in Chur from the time the bishopric was transferred from Milan to Mainz in 843. In spite of this, it has been seen above that Romansh was spoken by the majority of the common people in northern Raetia until about 1300, and small concentrations of Romance speakers were still present over two hundred years later. It is probable that the language balance in Raetia prior to the end of the Middle Ages was not significantly disturbed by the Low Alemannic dialects imported into Chur by officials of the Frankish state. On the popular level, German could triumph in the Rhine Valley only after its introduction by the descendants of the Alemanni who gradually spread into Raetia from the north (St. Gallen --Lake Constance) and west (Toggenburg--Glarnerland). The Rhine Valley was for the most part Germanized not from Germany, but from Switzerland itself.

VII.   <u>German Influence in Central Switzerland</u>

In central Switzerland the Alemanni continued south to the Bernese Alps and beyond to Valais.

Linguistic evidence of their settlement in the Upper
Bernese area shows that they neither totally dominated
nor were dominated by the Gallo-Roman culture which
they encountered.[21] Germanized place names and agri-
cultural terms of Gallo-Roman origin suggest that a
long period of bilingualism existed before German finally prevailed (Moulton SG 26f.; Zinsli BO 349).

    The extent of the Alemannic settlement of central
Switzerland may be judged by many linguistic criteria.[22]
The presence of the Old High German sound shift and of
Germanic word initial accent in Gallo-Roman place names
(Cappini'acum ⟩ 'Chäpfnach; Tu'ricum ⟩ 'Zürich)[23] and the
composition of German place names[24] show that German
speakers had made contact with the following areas by
800 at the latest (Sonderegger AS 33ff.): the lower
Rhine Valley near St. Gallen; the foothills of Appen-
zell; lower Toggenburg and the Neckertal; the southern
edge of Lake Zurich around Pfäffikon; parts of the
Glarnerland; the Vierwaldstättersee; the fringes of
the Napf area between Luzern and Bern; the valley of
the Aare, which they had entered as early as the middle
of the sixth century (Büttner GG 196), to the Thunersee and Brienzersee; the entrance to the alpine valleys
of the Upper Bernese area; the valley of the Saane; the
Bielersee; and parts of the Jura Mountains, where they
had already made contact with Romance speakers in the

first half of the sixth century (Büttner GG 198).

VIII. Germans in Valais

It is not certain how German colonizing activity extended this area to Valais in the south, for reliable sources concerning Alemannic influence in Valais are not available until far into the twelfth century. The Alemanni may have moved slowly up the Haslital and over the Grimsel Pass into Upper Wallis.[25] Yet for lack of convincing historical documentation the Grimsel route is open to question, and it seems likely that some Alemanni initially came into Wallis over one of the passes to the west.[26]

The pioneering work of R. Hotzenköcherle (SD) and H.U. Rübel (VO 137ff.) has revealed two distinct dialect groups in German-speaking Valais: one extending from around Visp to the head of the Rhone Valley, and another reaching west to the French language border at Siders/Sierre. Most important here are the correspondences between these dialects and those spoken to the north of the Upper Bernese passes. The dialect of Goms is similar to that spoken to the north of the Grimsel, and features of the language of Lower Wallis (below Visp) are found again immediately to the north of the Gemmi. For example, the umlaut of OHG $\bar{a}$ is treated

differently in the two areas: OHG <u>swāri</u> becomes
closed [ʃveːr] in the west, but open [ʃväːr] in the
east (cf. <u>SDS</u> I, 73-81). Such correspondences suggest
that the settlers of the western dialect group in Lower
Wallis came chiefly from the area directly to the north,
probably over the Gemmi, and that the first German speakers in Upper Wallis came over the Grimsel.

Let us then assume that a large number of German
speakers came over the Gemmi Pass, perhaps in the ninth
century. Unable to establish colonies in the region
around Sitten/Sion, the political and religious center
of the valley, they were forced eastward toward the
sparsely populated headwaters of the Rhone. At first
they settled on the mountainsides above Romance-speaking
areas, but several generations later their influence
extended to Upper Wallis.[27] By the middle of the thirteenth century Goms must have been thoroughly settled,
chiefly by those Alemanni who entered Wallis by way of
the Grimsel Pass.[28]

IX. The Beginning of the
Walser Migration from Wallis

Shortly after the turn of the thirteenth century
Germans from the Nicolaital in Wallis crossed the Theo-
dul Pass into northern Italy, where they settled in the
Val d'Ayas and the Val de Lys after about 1220. Walser

are mentioned in the neighboring Valsesia by the mid-
1200's, and upper Sermenza was also colonized at this
time. Settlers from the Saastal came to Macugnaga,
the chief Walser colony in the Valle d'Anzasca, between 1261 and 1291 (Joos WW 295).

Within the present canton of Valais, but connected to the Rhone valley only by the Simplon Pass, are
the two Walser settlements of Simpeln and Zwischen-
bergen, founded about 1200. These colonies, as well
as those in Italy just mentioned, were established by
settlers from Lower Wallis.

In the early 1200's Walser from Upper Wallis
crossed the Albrun Pass from the Binntal as well as the
Gries Pass from the Eginental and settled in the upper
Val Formazza (Joos WW 295). From here they colonized
Bosco-Gurin in 1244, the only German-speaking town in
the present canton of Ticino. Ornavasso and Miggian-
done were then settled late, after 1275 (Kreis DW 47ff.).

Walser migrated north and west as well. They settled in the French villages of Vallorcine and Les Ala-
mands in the middle of the 1200's. At the same time
they pushed north from the Lötschental to the Lauter-
brunnental, resettling the land which their Alemannic
ancestors had occupied centuries before. Their migration took them as far north as Planalp, to the north
of modern Brienz, in about 1300 (Kreis DW 59-63;

Joos **WW** 296f.).

The Urserntal, which is bounded by the Furka Pass
in the west, the Oberalp Pass on the east, and the St.
Gotthard Pass on the south, was the first area to be
settled by the German speakers emigrating over the
Furka Pass from Upper ·Wallis. It is probable that
Walser first came to the valley in the first half of
the twelfth century (Müller **WW** 356; Joos **WW** 297), and
it is significant that they took this first early step
toward reactivating an ancient line of communication
between the Rhone and Rhine valleys which had been
established at least as early as the time of Augustus
(Stähelin **SR** 112f.).

X.   The Walser in Graubünden

a) The Migration over the Oberalp

When the Walser crossed the Furka Pass, the Urserntal was already closely allied with the church in
Disentis and, therefore, with the bishopric of Chur as
well. Soon Walser from the Urserntal penetrated over
the Oberalp Pass into Tavetsch and Medels.[29] A Disentis document from 1203 shows that at least two German
speakers, Walterus prelatus de Ursaria and Olricus de
Prato, held positions of authority there (Büttner **MS**
203); it also makes it seem probable that because of

their respected office they represented a well-established community in the Urserntal.

The Walser who colonized Tavetsch and Medels in
the late 1100's pushed farther down the Rhine toward
Chur and established themselves in Obersaxen as well,
probably arriving no earlier than 1200. Today Obersaxen, situated on a high terrace above the Rhine, is
a German island in Romansh territory and probably represents the last stage of the Walser migration over
Furka-Oberalp which began in the early 1100's.[30]

The farther the Walser penetrated into Graubünden, the less is known about the routes they followed.
Of the two large primary settlements of Rheinwald and
Davos, we are better informed about the colonization
of the former.

b) The Rheinwald Settlements

The Rheinwald was the next area to be settled
after Tavetsch, Medels, and Obersaxen, but the colonists were not of the same group. The first Walser
contact with Graubünden took place from the Urserntal,
but the Rheinwald was colonized from the Val Formazza
(Pomat), which forms the northernmost end of the Val
d'Antigorio, by way of the Val Mesolcina (Misox) and
the San Bernardino Pass. In a document from 1274

two Walser[31] became the vassals of the baron of Sax-
Misox; because they seem to have been well established
in the area, Kreis (DW 69f.) assumes that they came to
the Rheinwald about 1260. In 1286 land was given in
fief to nine Walser from the Val Formazza and to eight
from Simpeln, one from Brig in Wallis, and one from
the Maggiatal (Joos WW 318). Thus one of the most important Walser strongholds in Graubünden seems to have
been founded primarily from earlier Walser colonies,
and may be termed a secondary settlement. The path
taken from the Val Formazza probably traversed the Gu-
riner Furka from Foppiano, then descended from Bosco-
Gurin down the Valle Maggia to present-day Locarno and
Bellinzona to the Val Mesolcina (Misox).

At that time the inner valley directly north of
the San Bernardino Pass was probably uninhabited. The
Walser colony in the Rheinwald soon expanded to include
the Romansh towns of Medels, Splügen, and Sufers. Germanization was rapid at least as far as Splügen, for in
the early 1300's Walser crossed from here into the Safiental to the north by way of the Safier (Löchli) Pass.
The Walser encountered little resistance there, and the
Safiental seems to have been heavily German after two
generations. From Safien-Platz a trail leads east up
the Heinzenberg to Tschappina, first mentioned as a
Walser colony in 1396. Tschappina is near the Glas

Pass, which for a long time was the most convenient
entrance to the Safiental from the Rhine Valley by
way of the Domleschg. The mouth of the Safiental is
very narrow and hindered access to the valley from
the Vorderrhein until a bridge was built across the
Rabiusa River in the fifteenth century. For this
reason Szadrowsky (Wd 164), Brun (MO 200), Zinsli (WV
29), and others have believed that the Walser settlements Versam and Valendas, in the valley of the Vorderrhein, were established from Obersaxen. There may well
have been some colonists from Obersaxen, but one may
also reasonably suppose that many Walser in Versam and
Valendas came from the Safiental as well as the adjacent Valsertal, which had been settled from Hinterrhein
about 1350 (Joos WW 321; Kreis DW 82ff.).[32]

East of the Rheinwald colonies is the valley of
Avers, a tributary of the Hinterrhein. The region
above Innerferrera in Avers was sparsely settled by
Romance speakers, and they were quickly Germanized by
the Walser around the middle of the fourteenth century.
The dialect of Avers shows that the colonists came from
the Rheinwald (cf. Clavadetscher GA).

From Juf, the highest permanently occupied settlement in Europe, Walser soon crossed into Oberhalbstein.
Here, on this important trade route north of the Septimer and Julier passes, Romanization had been intensive.

and only the alpine regions of Sblox and Flix could
be even temporarily Germanized (Joos **WW** 323ff.; Kreis
DW 86f.; Zinsli **WV** 244).

The last major town settled by Walser from the
Rheinwald was Mutten. Although the direction of colonization is not certain, dialect studies have shown
that Mutten belongs to the Rheinwald group and does not
represent an extension of the Ursern-Obersaxen thrust
(Hotzenköcherle **MM** 486ff.). The time of settlement
seems to have been before 1338 (Kreis **DW** 84f.), but the
exact date cannot be determined.

Walser settled in Schall and Fidaz before the end
of the fourteenth century (Joos **WW** 307ff.), and are mentioned in Jux in 1472 (Kreis **DW** 94; Joos **WW** 329).

c) The Davos Settlements

Shortly after the colony in the Rheinwald was
founded about 1260, Walser appeared to the northeast
on the headwaters of the Landwasser River in Davos.
Tax records from 1170 and 1213 indicate that Davos,
like the Rheinwald area, once may have been lightly
settled by Romance speakers (Juvalt **NC** 27; Mohr **CD** I,
365). Although Romance field names appear in the
highest regions, they account for only about five percent of all field names in the area. This is likely
the lowest percentage of Romance field names among all

the Walser colonies of Graubünden (Kreis DW 88), and
we may assume that the Walser encountered little resistance from the native population there.[33]

It seems probable that the Walser came to Davos
about 1280. In a document from 1289 a German named
Wilhelm der ammen received land in fief from Graf Hugo
von Werdenberg (Branger RW 161), and as early as 1335
the Walser not only had extended their influence as far
east as the Flüela Pass and far to the southwest in the
Landwasser Valley, but also had constructed three churches in Frauenkirch, Davos-Platz, and Glaris (Kreis DW
89; Joos WW 338ff.).

Less than twenty years may have passed before the
desire for more land took the Walser west over the
Strela Pass into Schanfigg, the valley of the Plessur.
Fondei and Sapün were probably the first Walser settlements there, and Arosa followed at the source of the
river. In 1384 the Walser in Schanfigg decided to build
a church on the Romansh property called pratum longum,[34]
which soon became the center of the Walser community as
Langwies (Kessler MS 88; Joos WW 327f.). Praden,
Tschiertschen, Runcalier, Pradaschier, and the Churwald-
nerberg were later colonies of the Schanfigg Walser.

Another group of Walser from Davos entered Prättigau, the valley of the Landquart River, and descended
into Klosters about 1320. Here, the Germans settled

among Romance speakers; many, however, pressed on
north to uninhabited territory and founded Schlappin
and St. Antönien in the first half of the fourteenth
century. Walser are not documented in Tarnuz until
1389.

It is uncertain how Valzeina, Danusa, and the
areas behind them to the south were settled. Walser
may have climbed over the Hochwang from Schanfigg (Clavadetscher WD), crossed over the Duranna Pass from Fondei and headed northwest (Zimpel EW 127), or simply migrated northwest along the Landquart toward the Rhine
and ascended the Furnerberg (Zinsli WV 33). They were
probably there by 1350 (Kreis DW 92), a few years after
Stürvis was settled across the valley (Joos WW 335).
From Stürvis the Walser moved farther west to Maienfeld.

Outside of Graubünden are several other Walser
colonies. The Calfeisental, in the canton of St. Gallen,
was settled in the early fourteenth century, probably by
Germans from the Rheinwald or Safiental who entered the
valley by way of the Kunkels Pass.[35] The Weisstannental
was colonized from the Calfeisental over the Heidel Pass
(Kreis DW 96ff.).[36]

The settlements in Vorarlberg are the farthest removed from Wallis, and yet they were established relatively early. First mention of Walser in Vorarlberg
comes so soon after the Rheinwald and Davos were founded

that it is unlikely that the Vorarlberg group represented secondary settlement (Ilg <u>WV</u> 37). Here it will suffice to say that Walser may have come to Vorarlberg by way of the valley of the Vorderrhein (Kreis <u>DW</u> 101; Ilg <u>WV</u> 37), but again the unfortunate lack of historical documentation permits only guesses about the route of their immigration. Their dialect shows that they, like the Davos Walser, came from Lower Wallis below Brig.

This brief geographical survey shows that the Walser in Graubünden spread out from two central colonies: the Rheinwald and Davos. From the Rheinwald Walser migrated to the Safiental and Valsertal as well as to Avers and Mutten; from Davos they pushed west into Schanfigg and north into Prättigau.

d) The Geography of Walser Dialects in Graubünden

Franz Joseph Stalder, writing in the early 1800's, noticed that the geographic separation between southwest and northeast Walser groups has linguistic parallels, and his observations were refined in the early 1900's by Albert Bachmann. The chief differences between the Rheinwald and Davos dialects were clearly outlined by

Rudolf Hotzenköcherle in 1943 (BV 539-542).

Most important for this study are the linguistic correspondences between the German spoken in Wallis and the Walser dialects in Graubünden. The careful work of Bohnenberger (MW 65f., 95f., 104ff.) and especially Hotzenköcherle (BV 539ff.) has shown that the Rheinwald dialect closely resembles that of Upper Wallis, confirming the historical evidence presented above.[37] Similarly, the dialect of the Davos and Vorarlberg colonies corresponds to the German spoken in Lower Wallis (cf. also Zinsli MaWW 313, WV 176ff.). This supports the supposition that Davos was established as a primary settlement independent of the Rheinwald colony and perhaps with a substantial number of settlers directly from Lower Wallis.[38]

e) The Nature of Walser Colonizing Activity

The distribution of Walser settlements in Graubünden raises questions about the linguistic and cultural relationships which were the result of the Walser migrations. Why did the Walser come to Graubünden? Under what conditions were their settlements established? How did contact take place with Romance speakers and with the Germans who spoke the East Alemannic dialect of the Rhine Valley?

Much has been made of a mysterious gypsy wanderlust which is said to have driven the Walser from Wallis far to the north and east.[39] As widespread as
this folk belief may be, it has little relevance to
this discussion. Even before the turn of the thirteenth century the small amount of productive land at
the head of the Rhone valley had become overpopulated,
and it is reasonable to believe that the Walser were
forced more by circumstance than wanderlust to seek new
opportunities for expansion.[40] This situation was intensified by the social relationships of the time. The
residents of Wallis were bound to their local overlord
by a feudal agreement in which some farmers, the homines ligii, tilled his land, swore allegiance to him,
and payed him taxes in exchange for his protection. A
small number of farmers were freemen, but most, the
homines talliabiles, were virtually political captives
who could be sold along with the land they worked but
who could buy themselves into the class of homines
ligii (Kreis DW 28ff.). Thus the Walser were not simply free to migrate as they pleased.

Nor were they free to occupy land in the new territories. At this time virtually all property in Graubünden was held by several German-speaking ruling families and could not be colonized without their permission. The relocation of the Walser into Graubünden

was effected by these nobles, who saw in them a hardy
people able to settle unoccupied land and willing to
defend it for their masters.[41]

Among the most important members of the secular
aristocracy in Graubünden were the Freiherren von Sax-
Misox. This ruling family owned much land in northern
Italy as well and was responsible for settling the Walser in the Rheinwald in order to fortify their property
holdings against their political rivals, the Freiherren
von Vaz (Kreis DW 130f.). The house of Vaz owned
Schams, adjacent to the Rheinwald colony, and was able
to observe closely the political and military potential
of the Walser (Zinsli WV 313ff.). Soon thereafter Walter V. von Vaz allowed Walser to settle in Davos in
the Landwassertal, which his family had held as a private hunting ground (Kreis DW 14, 88f.).

Walser colonization in Graubünden was based on an
Erblehenbrief, a contract between settler and landowner.
Although the Walser did not own their own land, they
were guaranteed personal freedom as well as the right
of free inheritance and community self-government
(Branger RW 63ff.): remarkable concessions during the
feudal age, which indicate how vigorously their services were sought by the aristocracy. In return for
these benefits the Walser agreed to pay a yearly tax
and render military service to their overlords.[42]

The Walser seem to have been given rights in proportion to their ability to settle land and defend it
for their masters. Both the demand for Walser and
their favorable legal position, however, decreased as
their population increased[43] and they were forced to
find new lands.

As the residents of overpopulated Wallis were
granted permission to leave, and as the feudal structure in Graubünden began to crumble, the door to random
colonization in the east was opened. The Rheinwald and
Davos colonies must have drawn many of their number
from farmers in Wallis who were attracted by the advantages of settling in Graubünden; indeed, it would be
difficult to explain the rapid expansion from these
two centers in any other way.[44]

f) The Circumstances of Walser Colonization

The distribution of Walser settlements is a
good indication of the circumstances which these German
speakers faced. It will be remembered that most of the
productive land in Wallis was already occupied by Romance speakers when the Alemanni first penetrated from
the Upper Bernese area. This was again the case when
the Walser began moving into new territory. Because
the arable land along the rivers was already well settled, the German speakers were forced to remain at

higher altitudes, on the mountainsides and in the
alpine meadows. Most Walser colonies were established
at elevations close to 2000 meters and were far removed from the great trade routes which had already
attracted a large native Romance population. It will
be seen from map III, for example, that both the Vorderrhein and the Hinterrhein were relatively free of
Walser settlements, as they are today, whereas the
highest valleys of the Valsertal, the Safiental, the
Landwassertal, and Avers were colonized by German speakers from Wallis. Thus these settlements were extremely isolated, just as an independent existence with the
community seems to have been sought by each of the
Walser.

Each Walser family was in turn set apart within
the community. This is seen in the arrangement of the
houses, an immediately obvious characteristic of most
Walser towns. Whereas the Romance speakers in the
valleys clustered their homes together, the Germans on
the mountainsides spread their houses and barns over
a broad area, allowing some space for private grazing
within the physical limits of the town. The Romance
speakers farmed the soil and conserved as much arable
land as possible, but the intemperate climate and unproductive soil of the higher regions forced the Walser
to raise cattle. Each family normally farmed a small

pasture as well as a portion of the common grazing meadow high above the town,[45] and there was usually no acute need to preserve land for farming.

g) Initial Walser-Romance Contact

As tenuous an existence as many of the tiny villages were forced to lead, they received little sympathy from the Romance population in the valleys below. The Walser enjoyed a unique privilege in their freedom and were clearly favored by the overlords over their Romance neighbors, who were made to feel every disadvantage of the feudal system.

Land cleared and cultivated by natives was often turned over to the Walser immigrants (Zinsli WV 372f.). Because the lower valleys were already densely populated some Romance speakers were forced to the higher regions: the Romance town of Lohn in Schams is located at 1580m. Understandably, the native farmers were not eager to give up their land when it was so precious, and they turned away the Walser when they could do so without risking rebuke or punishment from the landowner. Disagreement over property rights often led to altercations and feuds, during which the Walser hid under the protective wing of their overlord because of their numerical minority (Kreis DW 281).

After the end of the Middle Ages had brought more political independence to the native Romance population,[46] the Walser were often the victims of legislation designed to contain their growing numbers. A law passed in Lugnez in 1457, for example, forbade the sale or rental of any land to strangers "die nit sind von vater stam Churwalhen dysenthalb den bergen oder gotzhuslüt" (Zinsli **WV** 374). Anyone who married a "foreigner" lost his right to inheritance of property in the valley. Because of this law Walser were frustrated from entering Lugnez, as may be seen from map III. Walser who settled in the Valsertal between Tersneus and Vals belonged politically to Lugnez; nevertheless, as late as the seventeenth century the Romance population there did not allow them to vote in public meetings unless they voted with the majority (Muoth **SPS** 220).

Little encouragement for unity was to be found in the clash between the two cultural groups. Walser youths married their own kind, searching neighboring colonies as well as their own and sometimes going as far as Wallis to find a bride.[47] The visits to market places in Italy brought together members of different settlements and strengthened the bonds which united Walser communities as a minority body in an understandably unsympathetic environment.

h) <u>The Progress of Germanization by Walser</u>

Romance speakers undoubtedly felt that their language was being assaulted along with other aspects of their culture. It has been seen above that the dialect of the Rhine Valley was beginning to be used in Graubünden in the thirteenth century: The area around Maienfeld was bilingual about 1300, and soon thereafter Germanization proceeded into Prättigau and Schanfigg. Now the native inhabitants found themselves attacked from the rear as well with the establishment of islands of German speakers in the Rheinwald in 1260 and Davos in 1280. The progress of Germanization in Schanfigg and Prättigau illustrates well the problem of linguistic survival which faced those who spoke a Romance idiom in Graubünden.

By 1300 Walser had undertaken secondary coloniza-tion in Fondei and Sapün, tributary valleys of the Ples-sur which were only lightly inhabited by Romance speakers. Soon Arosa was established, probably under similar conditions. This group of Walser built a church in Langwies and gradually made the town the center of the local Walser community. The Romance idiom of the valley was now faced with imminent suppression by either the Walser dialect to the east or that of the Rhine Valley to the west.

Langwies became the center of German influence in
Schanfigg during the 1300's, commanding the political
and economic attention of the entire valley. From here
Schanfigg was Germanized gradually, and it seems reasonable to assume the existence of a bilingual zone of
contact between Walser and Romance idioms which moved
slowly downstream toward Chur over a period of about
two hundred years (Zinsli **WV** 34).

Kessler (**MS** 177f.) makes it seem probable that
Maladers, at the mouth of Schanfigg, first adopted the
German dialect spoken in Chur. The two were politically
connected until the fourteenth century, and Maladers
remained loyal to the Catholic church in Chur as late
as the seventeenth century (the rest of Schanfigg became
Protestant by about 1550). By Campell's time, however,
even Maladers had succumbed as its Chur dialect was exposed to pressure from the valley interior. Now Maladers, Peist, St. Peter, and Molinis had all accepted
the West Alemannic dialect of the Walser; Lüen, Castiel,
and Calfreisen were still bilingual.[48] Today a sharp
boundary divides the Walser dialect in Maladers from the
German of the Rhine Valley (Kessler **MS** 173), and high
above the south bank of the Plessur the towns of Praden
and Tschiertschen, which could easily have adopted the
Chur dialect, speak the Walser idiom of their neighbors
across the valley.

The Germanization of Prättigau proceeded in
similar fashion. Walser crossed the Wolfgang Pass
from Davos in the early fourteenth century and settled
in the Romance community of St. Jacob, later renamed
Klosters.[49] Colonization soon took place to the north
in the Schlappintobel, where Schlappin was founded, perhaps as early as 1330 (Kreis DW 91). From Schlappin an
arm of German influence extended to St. Antönien, isolated from the Romance valley floor by the Schanielatobel.

In Prättigau, as in Schanfigg, Romance speakers
were surrounded by the advancing Germans. By 1350, when
Walser were solidly established at the east end of the
valley, the dialect of the Rhine Valley was making inroads from the west. The eastern edge of this dialect
area, the Schierser Becken, was the Buochner Tobel, a
natural geographic boundary which even today bisects
the town of Lunden. Today outer (western) Lunden is
religiously and politically affiliated with Schiers,
but inner (eastern) Lunden belongs to Jenaz and Luzein
in the valley interior (Hotzenköcherle BV 510). Similarly, the area east of inner Lunden maintains linguistic allegiance to the Walser idiom and shows little
trace of the Rhine Valley dialect. The Schierser Becken
was the last area in Prättigau to be Germanized, and
reflects both dialect traditions in its Walser phonology

and Rhine Valley morphology (<u>BV</u> 537).

Soon after St. Antönien was founded Walser appeared in Valzeina and Danusa, high above the south bank of the Landquart. Across the river Stürvis was established shortly before 1350 (Joos <u>WW</u> 331ff.), and Romance speakers now felt pressure from the north and south as well as from the east and west. Seewis was the last town in Prättigau to be Germanized, at a time when the Walser expansion in the valley had come to a standstill on its own or had been stopped by the intrusion of German from the Rhine Valley. The progress made by German in Prättigau was illustrated well by Campell, who reported that in about 1540 he had known several people in the valley who spoke the <u>Rhetica lingua</u> at home, but favored the German dialect of Davos in public. At the time only the residents of Seewis and Serneus had spoken Romansh, and their German was so poor that they had been ridiculed because of it. Now, in 1582, all had changed, and only rarely could a speaker of Romansh be found in Prättigau (<u>QSG</u> VII, 339).

The Germanization of Schanfigg and Prättigau was partially aided by external political affairs. Austria, eager to expand its land holdings in Vorarlberg toward the south, sought to control Davos as well as the colonies in Schanfigg and Prättigau. Although Austrian influence in these areas was limited, the presence of officials and administrators may have hastened the spread of German there. Reaction to Austrian presence in Graubünden also contributed to the Germanization: most members of the Zehngerichtenbund, a defensive alliance against Austria whose center was in Davos,[46] spoke Walser German and promoted its use among the Romance minority. With the formation of the Zehngerichtenbund German-speaking Langwies and Klosters greatly increased in importance because they controlled access to Davos over the Strela and Wolfgang passes.

R. Hotzenköcherle has shown that parallel morphological developments may point to similar conditions of settlement and Germanization in Schanfigg and Prättigau (BV 503). This is substantiated by the existence of three former lines of communication between the two valleys: the first known already in pre-Roman times (HBLS IV, 396) and extending from St. Peter in Schanfigg over the Arflinafurgga to Jenaz in Prättigau; the second reaching over the Hochwang to Hintervalzeina; and the third traversing the Duranna Pass from Fondei to Serneus. Hotzenköcherle also postulates the existence of a substratum "das wir vorläufig das Prätigauerisch-Schanfiggerische nennen wollen," (BV 511) which affected the German dialects of the two regions in the same way.

It has been seen that both Schanfigg and Prättigau were Germanized in similar fashion, from two directions

by two different dialects. In both cases the Germanization from the east proceeded from important secondary Walser settlements: Langwies and Klosters.
Today Langwies in Schanfigg and St. Antönien in Prättigau have retained characteristics of the Walser idiom
more faithfully than have those towns in the two
valleys which were Germanized later over a strong
Romance substratum (Hotzenköcherle BV 503; Escher
SA 13f.).

The present language relationships in Graubünden
were largely determined by the middle of the sixteenth
century. Writing in 1538, the historian Aegidius
Tschudi summarized the linguistic picture of the northeast in the following words:

> Diser Rhetijschen spraach gebrucht noch
> mehrteils die landschafft Rhetie / in
> sonnders was ob Chur gelegen / die wir
> Tütschen / Churwâlsch / vnd sy selbs
> Romanisch nemend . . . . Die gemelt
> Rhetijsch spraach ist iñert anderthalb-
> hundert jaren mercklich abgangen vñ die
> tütsch zůgenommen / als noch täglich
> beschicht / dañ wenig über menschē gedecht-
> nuss / die statt Chur vnd ferrer hinab /
> noch alles wâlscher spraach gewesen / yetz
> die Tütsch angenomēn . . . dañ all brieff
> vnd geschrifften in jrm lande / sind von
> alter har in Latin / vnd yetz mehrteils
> zů tütsch gestelt. (AR 5f.)

XI. Footnotes

[1]

Archeological and onomastic evidence shows that nearly all towns in present-day Graubünden (with the exception of colonies in the highest valleys) may be traced to pre-Roman settlements (RNB II, XL).

[2]

A concise summary of the various theories about the pre-Roman inhabitants of Raetia may be found in RNB II, XL. Most recently J.U. Hubschmied has convincingly argued that hundreds of place names in Raetia are of Etruscan origin and that Etruscan was the pre-Roman language of the area ("Etruskische Ortsnamen in Rätien" in Studia Onomastica Monacensia (Munich 1961), III, 403).

[3]

Initial Burgundian settlement was by no means restricted to the area south of Geneva, but extended far to the west and north as well. Sonderegger (VS 498, map 1) shows the distribution of Burgundian inscriptions north of Lake Geneva.

[4]

Sonderegger (VS 500, map 2) shows the distribution of Alemannic runic inscriptions of the sixth and seventh centuries north of Lake Constance: proof that a substantial number of Alemanni did not take part in the invasion south of the Rhine.

[5]

Cf. also J. Jud, "Die romanisch-deutsche Sprachgrenze der Schweiz" VR VIII (1945/46), 108, fig. 1.

[6]

Partly because of King Gundobad's preference for Latin, Romanization may have been realized within the first generations after Burgundian settlement. Procopius, in the middle of the sixth century, referred to the Franks, but not the Burgundians, as Germanoi (Zimmerli SW 114f.).

[7]

Stähelin SR 321 and Zimmerli SW 109ff.; "Von den 668 welschen Gemeinden der Kantone Genf, Waadt und Freiburg fallen nicht weniger als 111, d.h. 17%, in die Kategorie der Ingenorte" (Zimmerli SW 109). For maps of the distribution of Burgundo-Romance -ingōs names in the Freiburg and Jura areas see Sonderegger VS 504 and 506. The most complete collection of this evidence is found in Bruno Boesch, "Ortsnamen und Siedlungsgeschichte am Beispiel der -ingen-Orte der Schweiz" (Alemannisches Jahrbuch 1958, Lahr/Schwarzwald, 1959, 1-50), following Ernst Gamillscheg's

Romania Germanica, III (Berlin/Leipzig, 1936), esp.
map 1, pp. 16-17.

8   Hubschmied VR III, 48-155; Stähelin SR 326ff.,
497; Zinsli BO 334ff. and map 2.

9   All subsequent references are to Raetia Prima.

10   This was also of great significance for the
development of Romansh, which was now influenced
more by the Old French of the western Frankish empire than by the upper Italian dialects south of the
Raetian passes (Planta SU 85f.; Jud GK 12f.).

11   "German" and "Germany" are not to be understood
in the modern sense. Here "Germany" refers in general
to the eastern Frankish kingdom, including the former
Alemannic homeland bounded by the Rhine in the south
and west and the Main in the north. For purposes of
simplicity, "German" may thus refer to any subject of
the Frankish throne and to his language (a dialect of
Alemannic or Frankish) as well.

12   In 817, for instance, a German named Schultheiss
Folkwin bought property from Onorius and his wife
Valeria. The witnesses were Romance: Estradarius,
Laurencius, Valencio, Cervarius, Vigilius (2)--and
Unno, the only witness with a German name (Pult HU
179f.).

13   Cavigelli (GB 179f.) gives derivations of OHG
wald in present-day Romansh dialects ranging from
ueut (Medels) to gult (Innerferrera) to guát (Ra-
mosch/Engadin).

14   Planta counts 20 castles in an 11 kilometer
section of Domleschg and 40 in a 35 kilometer section
of the valley of the Vorderrhein. Understandably,
most of the castles had German names: Bärenburg,
Rietburg, Haldenstein, etc.

15   Contact between conquerors and conquered must
have produced varying degrees of language intermix-
ture. Because of the relative necessity for intercommunication in Curraetia, it is highly probable
that each language was "a source and a recipient of
interference" from the other. The precise degree of
interdependence, however, is difficult--if not impos-
sible--to estimate: ". . . in a given case of contact,
the prevalent type, direction, and extent of interference may change with time. Since the languages

themselves remain the same, it must be their relative
status with the agents of the contact and of inter-
ference--the bilingual individuals--that is under-
going the modification" (Weinreich LC 74).

Cultural and numerical superiority play key roles
in language contact. As we have already seen, a
relatively small number of Romans were able to influence significantly the language balance in Raetia
by virtue of their advanced culture. On the other
hand, the Burgundians in western Switzerland were
unable to survive as a separate people because they
offered the thoroughly Romanized population there no
substantial cultural improvements and because they
were not strong enough in number to affect a permanent
change even if they had represented a superior culture. The "conquering" Burgundians were culturally
overpowered by the "conquered" Gallo-Romans.

16   As is common in contact situations, the phono-
logical system of the one language--in this case
German--was not always adopted intact by the speakers
of the other. In the tenth century Ekkehard IV reported this anecdote about Enzelin, the abbot of Pfäfers:
When Enzelin was threatened at the court of Otto I by
Craloh, later an abbot in St. Gallen, he cried for
help: "Gotilf, erro!" respondit, id est: "Deus adjuvet,
domne!" Those present laughed because he, a Raetian,
had not mastered the Germanic initial h- in what
should have been "Gotthilf herro! (Pult HU 181).

17   Where the Alemanni had settled in the northern
regions of Raetia I, place names and personal names
are of Alemannic origin or show Alemannic influence.
To the south, however, all field names and almost all
personal names are Romance (Pult HU 178).

18   Using Romansh loan words in the German dialects
of Graubünden, Jakob Jud (GR) illustrates the gradual
de-Romanization (Entromanisierung) of the area between
the Walensee and Chur.

19   However, the present town of Walenstadt is mentioned in a Carolingian land register from about 850
in the form Vualahastad. OHG stad is a translation
of the Romance name for the town, Ripa 'shore.' Sonderegger reasons convincingly that the addition of
Vualaha (probably from the gen. pl. *walaho-stad
'shore of the Romance people') took place not only
because Romance speakers lived there, but also because
stad might have been confused with Staad, the present

name of a shore across the lake. No document refers
to the city by its German name again until two centuries later (Vualastade in 1045), and Romance forms
do not occur after that date (AS 51).

20   The Germanization of Chur was accelerated by the
influx of German speakers from Vorarlberg and Liechtenstein who helped to rebuild the city after it was
destroyed by fire in 1464 (Planta SC 115).

21   See the map "Die primären Berührungszonen Alt-
alemannisch-Galloromanisch im frühen Mittelalter" in
Sonderegger VS 512.

22   Cf. Sonderegger AS 33ff. and map 1 (Sonderegger's
discussion, from which much of the following evidence
of Alemannic progress southward is taken, is offered
again in VS 515-534); Zinsli BO 339ff. and map 3,
349ff.

23   Cf. the breakdown of this accent in the neighbor-
hood of Romance dialects in Moulton SG.

24   A place name (Ortsname) identifies a human settlement of any size. A field name (Flurname) refers
to a geographical landmark, such as a bridge, a
ravine, or a meadow. At some time during initial
colonization an area receives a place name; field
names are given later, when the environment becomes
more familiar and when more extensive colonization
necessitates the identification of natural or arti-
ficial boundaries.
      The suffixes -ingen and -wil (< OHG wilare <
Lat villare) combine with personal names to identify
towns settled by individuals during the Old High
German period, such as Ruadhereswilare, founded by
the father of Ruadheri (826 in the canton of St. Gallen). Most of the towns named in this fashion
(personal name with suffix -ingen, -inghofen, -wil,
-husen, -dorf, etc.) are primary settlements, founded
during the first centuries of Alemannic colonization.
Secondary settlements are usually named by a prominent field name in the area, such as Wasserwendi or
Grünenboden in the canton of Bern, and are generally
located in more remote regions not settled during
the first colonization period. (-ingen names also
occur in secondary settlements by analogy to older
-ingen formations. Here a field name, not a personal
name, is the first element: Selvaningen 'Waldhof'
(Müller WW 386).) A survey of place names in St.

Gallen from 700 to 920 shows 70% primary, 20% secondary, and 10% field names, corresponding to the very early Germanization of the area (Sonder-egger AS 45ff. and map 5).

25   The present canton of Valais includes the entire Rhone valley, from the Furka Pass in the east to Lake Geneva in the west. Today both French and German are spoken in the valley: French to the west of Siders/Sierre, and German to the east (Zimmerli SW 92ff.). The German-speaking area of the Rhone valley will be called by its German name, Wallis, consisting of Upper Wallis (east of Visp) and Lower Wallis (west of Visp); the French name Valais will refer here only to the French-speaking area of the valley (cf. Moulton SG 8 and 39).
        The Grimsel route was proposed as early as 1846 by J. Rudolf Burckhardt in "Untersuchungen über die erste Bevölkerung des Alpengebirgs" (ASG IV, 100ff.). Zimmerli (SW 87ff.), Stähelin (SR 113), Bachmann (GLS V, 61), Joos (WW 294) and Bohnenberger (MW 37) assume that this route was taken, probably in the ninth or tenth century.

26   Iso Müller (WW 356) believes that the Lötschen Pass may have been used, and Büttner (GG 203ff.) proposes a migration over the Gemmi Pass by way of the Kandertal. Hotzenköcherle (RS 216) and Zinsli (BO 333, note 6 and WV 20) argue for serious consideration of both routes.
        A heavy concentration of German place names in Upper Wallis (cf. Zimmerli SW) seems at first to point to the Grimsel route, but this is misleading. Because Valais was more arable and more accessible to the great centers of Roman trade and population in the west, Upper Wallis was never intensively colonized by Romance speakers. The German field names may appear there in such great numbers not only because Alemanni, having mounted the Grimsel Pass, settled the area at an early date, but also because there never was a stratum of Gallo-Roman field names there to interfere with later and more extensive name-giving by the German speakers, who may have come to the area from either direction.

27   Zimmerli (SW 75) shows that Steg and Hohtenn, located at the mouth of the Lötschental, were the westernmost of the initial German colonies. The oldest land register from the canton of Valais dates from the middle of the eleventh century and

mentions Raron, Visp, and Naters as the German colonies closest to the head of the Rhone valley. The
next register, from the middle of the thirteenth
century, includes Ernen, northeast of Naters and
closer to Goms (Büttner GG 205).

28   It is difficult to trace the Germanization of
the Rhone valley as carefully as that of Curraetia.
As has been said, a large Romance population inhabited Valais, and its influence extended far into
Wallis as well. Regardless of whether the Alemanni
came to the valley from the Haslital in the east or
the Kandertal in the west, it is certain that their
settlement brought them into contact with these
Romance speakers.

29   The Walser migration over the Oberalp Pass was
not accepted by scholars until Iso Müller offered
definite proof in 1936 (WW); cf. Peter Issler in
1935: "Dennoch wird immer noch von Pseudohistori-
kern mit Hartnäckigkeit in Zeitungsartikeln die alte
Theorie von der Einwanderung über Furka-Oberhalp
(sic) vertreten" (GR 29).

30   Brun MO 202f.; Zimpel EW 124; Iso Müller believes
that Walser from Ursern went as far into Graubünden
as Mutten (WW 358ff.). Planta (OS map 4) traces
Walser field names only as far east as Obersaxen.

31   Jakob and Hubert, sons of Peter von Riale. Riale
(today Kehrbächi) is located in the uppermost Val
Formazza (Zinsli WV 30).

32   Joos (WW 314f.) believes that Valendas belongs
to the Obersaxen group, but that Versam was established from Safien.

33   For evidence of clearing activity by the native
population in Graubünden see Zinsli WV 324ff.

34   "die Lang Wise": cf. document number four from
23 April 1384 in the Langwies community archive (GA
Langwies No. 4).

35   Zinsli, on the other hand, believes that these
Walser represented the first line of migration into
Graubünden, that from the Userntal to Obersaxen, and
did not come from the Rheinwald group (WV 29).

36   Mastrils, another Walser colony in Graubünden, is
located in the Rhine Valley above the confluence of

the Landquart and the Rhine. It was established
late, probably in the sixteenth century, and its
settlers may have come directly out of Prättigau
(as many family names show) or descended over the
Calanda Alp from the Calfeisental. Thus it may
ultimately be of either Davos (Prättigau) or Rheinwald (Calfeisental) origin. Cf. Meng BG.

37   This was noticed as early as 1582 by Campell,
who identified the German spoken in Davos with the
dialect of Upper Wallis (Pult HU 183). The linguistic correspondences are partially confirmed by
architectural comparisons in Simonett BG II, 242
and map 1. Cf. also H. Bandli, "Hausbau (Safier-
haus)" in Terra Grischuna, 1969, 300-304.

38   Cf. the Chur land register of 11 November 1300,
in which "illi de Wallis . . . in Tavaus" (Davos)
are mentioned (Hoppeler UW 26).

39   Walser penetrated as far north as Lake Constance,
where they established a colony below the mountain
Pfänder in the early fifteenth century (Zinsli WV
41 and note 94), and as far east as Walserschanze in
Vorarlberg.

40   Zimpel EW 130; Zinsli WV 44. The reason for
this overpopulation is explained in the folk tale
"Der Tod im Weinfass" by Karl Biffiger (Wir Walser
I (1964), 19-23).

41   The Walser were instrumental in preparing much
hitherto unproductive land for settlement. Many
German field names in Davos, for example, attest to
the extensive clearing activity which they undertook:
Rüti, Rütiwald, Rütlendji (< OHG riuten, NHG reuten,
roden 'make arable'; RNB I, 245f. and II, 477),
Schwendi, Gebrunst, Gsang (NHG sengen). See Kreis
DW 88; Zinsli WV 315ff., 323ff.; Schorta DR 222ff.

42   Liver notes the striking parallels between this
mode of colonization and that which characterized
the settlement of the eastern territories on the
Weser and Elbe (from the lower Rhine) and those in
Silesia, Bohemia, and the Siebenbürgen area (P. Liver,
Mittelalterliches Kolonistenrecht und freie Walser in
Graubünden. Kultur- und staatswissenschaftliche
Schriften der Eidgenössischen Technischen Hochschule,
vol. 36, Zürich, 1943; cited in Zinsli WV 45f.).

43   In spite of the high incidence of infant mor-
tality, families of a dozen children were the rule
rather than the exception. The Davos Ammann Hans
Ardüser had 23 children, three of whom were still
infants when he died at the age of 59 (Zinsli WV
42). Another Davos Ammann, Paul Buol, had 25 children and nearly 300 grandchildren and great-grand-
children when he died in 1567:

> Er ist 25 kinder vater gewessen, deren
> 14, mehren theils söhn, 9 söhn, 5 töchteren,
> lang und grosse leüth, bey seinem läben sind
> verheürath gewessen. Die kinder, enigkli,
> auch ur enigkli befunden sich ob 300 per-
> sohnen. Er starb seines alters ob 90 jahren,
> war noch ein hübscher, starckher man.
> (Sprecher DC 347)

Caspar Jun, Ammann in Safien, died at the age of 105,
having fathered 25 children. It was long the custom
in Davos that whoever was still single at age 30 or
had had no children after one year of marriage was
forced to pay a fine (Zinsli WV 42f.).

44   The first Walser colonies were quite small. In
1289 Davos had only 14 homesteads, and in the fourteenth century Tenna had but three. By 1450 Davos
had more than 70 homesteads, probably due to the influx of newcomers from Wallis (Zimpel EW 131f.).
    The migration from Wallis was certainly no mass
movement, but took place sporadically among small
groups of farmers:

> Die Annahme scheint berechtigt, dass das
> Wallis im 12. Jh. kaum 250, im 13. Jh. nur
> wenig mehr als 1000-1500 Menschen in eine
> neue Heimat entliess. (Zimpel EW 131)

45   Cf. Campell (p. 27): ". . . ut quisque utique
praedium suum habet, dispersis habitata" (cited by
Zinsli WV 437, note 157).

46   One of the most powerful feudal dynasties in
Curraetia died with Friedrich VII von Toggenburg.
After his death in 1436 his lands, including Maienfeld, Prättigau, Davos, Belfort, and Strassberg, were
divided among lesser overlords and some were subse-
quently sold to Austria. The Romance and German
residents of these areas immediately formed a defensive alliance against the threat of growing Austrian
hegemony south of Vorarlberg and called it the Zehngerichtenbund after the ten member communities

(Gillardon <u>GZ</u> 27ff.). Similar mutual defense alliances between landowners and farmers had already
been formed in Curraetia: the <u>Gotteshausbund</u> (1396)
in the Engadin and part of the Rhine Valley and the
<u>Oberer</u> (<u>Grauer</u>) <u>Bund</u> (1424) in the Oberland area of
the Hinterrhein and Vorderrhein. The substantial
political and social independence gained by the
peasant population was reflected in the formation
and structure of these alliances. By 1471 the three
<u>Bünde</u> had merged, and joined the Swiss Confederation
as a single political unit called Graubünden in 1803.
Cf. Müller <u>EGB</u> 139ff. and <u>HBLS</u> III, 645ff.

47   Clavadetscher <u>WD</u> 390. In the nineteenth century
it was the custom of residents of Agher, Pomat, An-
sone and Saley to choose marriage partners only from
their own numbers (Zinsli <u>WV</u> 205).

48   "Et (sermo) Germanicus tantum e contra vigeat,
praesertim Pesti, Molins, ad Sancti Petri et Mala-
derii, ad St. Georgii (Castiel) autem, Leonii (Lüen)
et Capresii (Calfreisen) non item, ubi utraque adhuc
hodie lingua pariter in vulgari usu custoditur" (<u>QSG</u>
VII, 316).

49   Zem Kloster (1478); for an explanation of the
hypercorrect -<u>s</u> see Planta <u>OS</u> 94.

CHAPTER TWO

NAME-GIVING IN MEDIEVAL RAETIA

During the later Iron Age and in the early centuries of the Christian era eastern Switzerland witnessed a nearly continuous change of cultures.
Raetians and Celts, Romans and Germanic peoples all
contributed in some way to the cultural unit which is
now Graubünden.

Much of what is now known about these early inhabitants has been interpreted from the several thousands of place names and field names found throughout
the canton. The rivers <u>Rhine</u>, <u>Plessur</u>, and <u>Inn</u> are
among the many natural objects named by the Celts;
Romance speakers named the valley <u>Tujetsch</u>, the meadow
<u>Danusa</u>, and the mountainside <u>Mastrils</u>; the field names
<u>Rüti</u>, <u>Brand</u>, and <u>Schwendi</u> recall the land-clearing
activities of the Walser. But is the <u>Mons Avium</u>, the
Medieval name of the St. Bernardino Pass, of Celtic or
Roman origin (<u>RNB</u> II, 620f.)? Did the Romans or the
Franks name the meadow <u>Palfrei</u> in Malix (<u>RNB</u> II, 775)?
A. Schorta identifies the Raeto-Illyrian suffix -<u>iste</u>
in the town <u>Peist</u>, but the stem is unclear (<u>RNB</u> II,
783). In no other canton of Switzerland has so much
onomastic research been conducted as in Graubünden,
and yet because of the intricate cultural

stratification there no other canton can claim so many unexplained name forms (Hubschmied BM (1948), 33; cf. also Schorta WO).

Fortunately, the evidence provided by personal names from early sources contributes significantly to our knowledge of Medieval Raetia. Nearly one-third of the pre-Roman, Romance, and Germanic place names and field names of Graubünden whose etymologies are fully understood are derived from personal names. More important, personal names can accurately reflect proportions of different nationalities in situations of cultural contact. The list of German and Romance witnesses to Bishop Tello's will--the earliest Raetian document--clearly shows the extent of Germanization in Raetia at the middle of the eighth century. In addition, the onomasticon of this and other documents from the period of Frankish rule shows that the existence of pre-Roman cultures in Raetia is reflected in personal names as well as in place names.

I. Pre-Roman Name-giving

Name-giving is one of the many aspects of pre-Roman civilization in Raetia which are not clearly discernible. Early inscriptions and signatures on pottery do show, however, that Raetian names could

consist of a single element (Cinges, Matto, Luppo)
or a compound (Udlu-gesus, Musi-ella) (Planta DaR
218). The structure of these names thus apparently
reflects the tradition which prevailed in the parent
Indo-European dialect group (Evans GPN 41; but Pulgram PN 197-206). More specific identification of
individuals was not required by the relatively uncom-
plicated Raetian culture, and family names did not
exist.[1]

The difference between Raetian and Roman name-
giving is especially evident in documents which mention the names of soldiers' wives. The non-Roman
origin of these names (Ispanilla, Sibulla, Bacadia)
attests to the many marriages which took place between
Roman soldiers and native women in transalpine Gaul
(Planta DaR 218).

As Roman influence extended into Raetia this
older stratum of names began to disappear. Yet because Raetia was not as intensively Romanized as the
rest of the transalpine provinces, some native elements
remained in the new era. In Bishop Tello's will of 765
several Raetian names (Crespio, Lidorius, Lobucio, etc.)
(Müller SB 115) are found next to Roman and German
names, showing that a substantial onomastic substratum
managed to survive the cultural upheaval of eight
centuries of foreign influence.

II.   Roman Names

Citizens of the Roman Empire normally bore three names, known as the tria nomina: praenomen, gentilicum, and cognomen. The praenomen, although literally a "first name," could be carried by several members of the same family and thus did not have the same function as the modern given name. The gentilicum designated the clan to which the person belonged. The cognomen was the most individualistic of the three names, telling the most about its bearer and setting him apart from others. Thus Marcus Tullius Cicero and Gaius Julius Caesar are best known by their cognomina, Cicero and Caesar.

With the fall of Rome this system broke down and was replaced by the less complex tradition which had flourished in pre-Roman western Europe. The man who had been merely a small unit of the vast social organization of Rome now became a member of a smaller, simpler, and less rigid society (Pulgram TN 160). One name, corresponding to the Roman cognomen, was now sufficient to identify the individual. In addition, the disappearance of the Roman tria nomina was hastened by the barbarian conquerors who knew only single proper names.

With the introduction of Christianity to the Roman provinces in the fourth and fifth centuries, specifically

"Christian" names became popular and are often equated
with Romance names. It will therefore be necessary
to assess the role which Christianity played in the
formation of the Raetian onomasticon.

III. Christianity and Christian Names
North of the Alps

It is uncertain how Christianity was introduced
to the transalpine provinces. The new religion may
have come from the East or directly from Rome, up the
Rhone Valley or over the Alps. Traces of Christianity
found in Lyon in 177 suggest that it was already established north of the Alps in the second century. The
first definite traces of Christianity in present-day
Swiss territory are found in Geneva and Avenches in
the late 300's. By the beginning of the fifth century
there were already bishops in Geneva, Avenches, Basel,
and Martigny (HBLS V, 673), following the establishment
of the early bishoprics of Trier and Cologne (314) and
Mainz (354) in the fourth century (Planta DaR 225).

If Christianity had become established north of
the Rhine by the fourth century, it was still a long
time before traces of Christian culture could be found
in personal names there. Monks and members of the
clergy of the Carolingian period were the first to
use Christian names, which were usually taken from

the Old Testament: <u>Aaron</u> 773 (Freising), <u>Abraham</u> 779 (Fulda), <u>Samuel</u> 789 (Murbach) and <u>David</u> 744 (Elsass) are some early examples (Bach <u>DN</u> I, 2, 12). A <u>Joseph</u> reigned as Bishop of Freising from 748 to 764, and a deacon <u>Solomon</u> appeared in Dachau in 805 (Scheidl <u>KV</u> 199).[2]

New Testament names were adopted as well. Among the most popular were <u>Johannes</u> 730 (Murbach), <u>Jacob</u> 749 (Strassburg), <u>Andreas</u> 780 (Freising), and <u>Petrus</u> 847 (Saargau) (Bach <u>DN</u> I, 2, 12). Paulus Diaconus' <u>Historia Langobardorum</u> (ca. 790) lists <u>Paul</u> and <u>Peter</u> among the Langobards as well as <u>Gregory</u>, one of King Liutprand's nephews (Woolf <u>GN</u> 234).

These Biblical names were isolated within the early German onomasticon and had no significant influence on Old High German name-giving. Biblical names were used in Germany almost solely within the confines of the church. Although some Old Testament names--<u>Adam</u>, <u>Daniel</u>, <u>Elias</u>, <u>Judith</u>, <u>Susanna</u>--survived the Old High German period, they were generally regarded as being specifically Jewish and were avoided even during this early period of Jewish persecution (Bach <u>DN</u> I, 2, 13; Socin <u>MN</u> 83f.).

There is some uncertainty about how Biblical names were brought to Germany. According to E. Nied (<u>HN</u> 15f.), the appearance of Biblical names in the Old

High German area is not so much the result of direct
contact with the Bible, but rather seems to have been
inspired by the naming tradition of Syria and Palestine,
the seat of Oriental Christianity, whose missionaries
brought a substantial part of Christian culture to the
West.

Socin notes that Old Testament names had nearly
vanished by the year 1000 and hypothesizes that their
disappearance might well be connected with the gradual
absorption of the native Gallo-Roman population into
the Frankish nation during the Merovingian and Carolingian epochs. If the dying out of Old Testament names
in Germany is to be attributed to the disappearance of
an autochthonous pre-German cultural group, then one
must suppose that (Eastern?) Biblical influence had
been powerful in the German area at a much earlier time,
even before the Germans themselves appeared.

IV. Christianity and Christian-Romance
Name-giving in Raetia

The earliest evidence of the existence of Christianity in Raetia is a reference to Bishop Asinio in
Chur in 451. Yet this does not mean that Asinio was
the first bishop there (Pieth __BG__ 18). Bishoprics were
founded only in cities where Christianity was already

well established, and considering that Chur is closer
to Rome than are the early German bishoprics on the
Rhine, it is probable that a bishop sat in Chur at
least as early as the middle of the fourth century
(Planta DaR 226). It is reasonable to believe that
some of the first Christians in Raetia may have been
native soldiers who returned home from service in the
Roman army (Jud GK 14). Planta (DaR 222) assumes that
by about 450 the urban population of both Raetian provinces was Christian, and that heathendom had been
largely subdued in rural areas as well.

*   *   *

The Christian church began early to reject the
Roman tria nomina and to recommend the adoption of
saints' names throughout the Christian world.[3] In
discussing the names of saints and church leaders it
is important to remember that the names of most Christian saints of Rome were present in the Romance onomasticon before the introduction of Christianity north
of the Alps. For example, Donatus (died 362) was
Bishop of Arezzo and Lidorius (fourth century) Bishop
of Tours (Müller AK 45f.). Both names are Romance, but
were promoted by the church because of the exalted
status of their bearers. A Romance name thus became a
"Christian" name because of its adoption into the

preferred onomasticon of the church. Virtually all
Romance names present in pre-Christian Raetia later
appeared in Christian inscriptions and texts, and for
this reason scholars speak of the Raetian "Christian-
Romance" onomasticon.

The church not only promoted the use of saints'
names, but also created new appellatives which were
intended to instill in their bearers the characteristics
of the ideal Christian: <u>Christianus</u>, <u>Dominicus</u> ('of the
Lord'), <u>Pius</u>, <u>Vitalis</u>, <u>Clemens</u>, <u>Benedictus</u>, <u>Gregorius</u>
(Gk. 'watchful') (Fleischer <u>DP</u> 46). These names joined
other neo-Latin adjectival formations such as <u>Pavaricius</u>
'of Bavarian origin,' <u>Montanarius</u> 'mountaineer,' and
<u>Sanatissimi</u> 'very healthy' (Planta <u>SU</u> 100; Müller <u>AK</u>
48), which were quickly absorbed into the Romance onomasticon.

The integration of neo-Latin Christian names within
the pre-Christian/Christian-Romance group is seen most
clearly in Tello's will, where they combine to form the
largest onomastic unit. Müller (<u>SB</u> 101f.) gives the
following complete list of names of saints and leading
church figures and of neo-Latin formations mentioned
in Tello's will. The will dates from 765 and reflects
a name inventory that had long been dominated by the
influence of the Christian church:

Amantius	Lobecenus
Augustus	Lupus
Aurelianus	Maiorinus
Aurelius	Martinus
Auster	Maurelius
Befanius	Maurentius
Claudius	Maurus
Columba	Paulus
Constantius	Praestantius
Desiderius	Projectus
Dominicus	Revocatus
Donatus	Rusticus
Exoberius	Salvia
Gaudentius	Saturninus
Gaudiosus	Silvanus
Jactatus	Silvio
Januarius	Ursacius
Johannes	Ursicinus
Julianus	Valerius
Justinianus	Victor
Juventius	Vigilius
Laurentius	Vincentius
Leo	Vitalianus
Leontius	Vitalinus
Lidorius	Vitalis
	Zacco (Jacob)

Tello's will gives a very accurate picture of the Raetian Christian-Romance onomasticon of the eighth century. Comparison of this document with sources from the monasteries of Pfäfers and Disentis shows that the most popular Christian-Romance names in post-Roman Raetia were Victor, Valerius, Vigilius, Silvanus, and Dominicus (Müller AK 59). Among other common Christian-Romance names were Honoratus, Ursicinus, and Lupicinus, the latter two probably reinforced by the popular German names Bero and Wolf.

Because of the far-reaching authority of the church, the large corpus of pre-Christian Romance

personal names was substantially reinforced and was
able to survive the pressure from the Germanic north
longer than it might have if the church had presented
and promoted an entirely foreign onomasticon.

V. German[4] Names

Most German names of the Middle Ages were composed of two elements (OHG Diot-rih). In addition,
there were shortened forms of these dithematic names
(Adalo < Adalbert, Adelmar) and names of only one element with no corresponding "full" form (Uffo, Atto).
Of these three types of names the most important were
those of two elements. Of 630 Old High German non-
Christian names in the St. Gallen Professbuch (8th-
12th century), for example, 480 are dithematic, 110
are shortened forms, and 40 are monothematic (Sonderegger AP 71).[5]

Dithematic names were normally composed of two
nouns (Sig-frid), noun and adjective (Diet-mar), or
two adjectives (Hart-lieb) (Bach DN I, 1, 75). The
total number of names possible in this system can
hardly be determined.[6] E. Förstemann's Altdeutsches
Namenbuch, which lists names to about 1200, includes
some 8000 attested single and compound names of German
origin.

The components of some early German names seem
to have been combined at random,[7] but normally the
name-giving traditions within each family were governed
by at least one of three principles, alliteration,
variation, or repetition, according to the pattern
established by the first prominent member. Alliteration prevailed in the names of the Burgundian kings
Gibica--Godomarus--Gislaharius. The Merovingians
Childerich--(son) Chlodwig--(grandsons) Chlodomir,
Childebert, Chlothar and the family Sigmund, Siglinde,
and Sigfrid from the heroic epic illustrate variation
of one suffix element in combination with the "dynastic" prefixes Child-, Chlod-, and Sig-.[8] Alliteration
was probably the original Germanic name-giving principle (Flom AV 11, Woolf GN 249ff.), but yielded to
pure repetition as the most common method of personal
nomenclature in the late Middle Ages.

The earliest evidence of name repetition in the
Germanic world is found about 470 A.D. in the Visi-
gothic family Alarich--(grandson) Eurich--(great-
grandson) Alarich (Flom AV 7). The popularity of this
naming principle grew in the following centuries. In
spite of the astounding number of elements from which
names could be formed, the total number of names used
by German speakers in the Upper German area began to
decline in the tenth century as "preferred" names

first became evident. By the twelfth century
Heinrich, Konrad, and Ulrich together made up over
one-fourth of all names recorded in Freising, and a
century later these names were borne by nearly two-
fifths of all men there (Scheidl KV 197f.). Heinrich,
Konrad, and Ulrich--and with them the principle of
repetition within as well as across family lines--
first achieved popularity among the nobility but were
quickly accepted by the lower classes. These three
names reached the apex of their popularity with the
nobility (40%) and peasants (45%) in the 1300's
(Scheidl KV 197f.).

The development of women's names seems to have
followed the same pattern, although less is known about
them due to their scarcity in early records.[9] Scheidl's
statistics from Freising again provide the most precise
information available. In the tenth century the most
popular name, Ellinpurch, appears only six times among
151 women. During the 1100's Adelheid was used by 20%
of the peasant women. In the following century Mathilde
(10%), Irmgard (9%), and Bertha (7.8%) made up 26.8%
of the entire female onomasticon of Freising (Scheidl
KV 198f.).

These figures show that the principle of repetition was most often used among males, and that women
were generally named on a more individual basis. This

may be explained by the necessity for males in prominent families to retain the names of their forebears
for social and legal reasons, especially during the
age of feudalism. Prime examples of dynastic repetition are the Ottonian kings of the tenth century
and the Austrian Habsburg family, which counted four
Rudolfs from 1218 to 1365 and five Albrechts from
1248 to 1439.

The appearance of double names should also be
mentioned here. These names are not attested before
the thirteenth century and seem to be a creation of
the late Middle Ages, perhaps as an attempt to reinforce the dying German naming tradition. The best-
known examples of double names appear in the heroic
epic, where Hugdietrich has a son Wolfdietrich.

Socin (MN 108) cites the Latinized name Walter-
bertoldus de Spilimbergo on the German-Italian language
border in 1208 and speculates that the strong Christian-
Romance tradition of compound names south of the Alps
fostered other examples within the German area to
the north.

VI. Initial German-Romance[10] Onomastic Contact

The Roman soldiers and settlers of the transalpine provinces in Spain, France, and Germany were
never entirely separated from the people whose lands

they occupied. Contact between Roman and barbarian cultures took place in both civilian and military affairs. When the Romans built the limes in the first century they intended to hold at bay the native armies to the north and thereby to hasten the peaceful Romanization of the provinces. Ironically, native help was used in the construction of the limes and natives were eventually called to service in the Roman army and made citizens of the Empire.

Men of exalted status in their native culture were given commissions in the Roman legions and often adopted Roman names as a proud sign of their elevation within the ranks of the conquerors. Their original names, however, were seldom abandoned. Some examples of bicultural nomenclature are rex Germanorum Septimius Aistomodius (ca. 200 A.D.), the Frankish consuls Flavius Merobaudes (377) and Flavius Bauto (385), and the Langobards Pertulu qui Baruccio (736) and Liutpert qui et Centolus archidiaconus (747) (Socin MN 226f.).[11]

Indicative of this Roman influence on German name-giving is the double name of the Ostrogothic king Theodoric, whom the Romans commissioned to expel King Odoaker from Italy in the fifth century. Probably because of his intimate connection with the Roman world, Theodoric adopted a second name. But it was German: Valamer. One may suppose that Roman tradition led him

to choose the second name as such, but that the importance of his own position within the German world
dictated that this name not be Roman.

The death of Theodoric in 526 was antedated by
the Alemannic breakthrough over the Rhine. Theodoric's
double German name symbolizes the beginning of German
rule in Roman territory and the weakening of Roman cultural influence there. Indeed, centuries before the
Goths or Alemanni ever occupied the Roman provinces,
Roman soldiers isolated in foreign territory had begun
to assume German names (Bach DN I, 2, 7), presaging a
trend which swept the Empire after the end of Roman rule.

*   *   *

At the beginning of the Old High German period
names of German speakers normally appeared in Latinized
form. With the growing strength and unity of German
rule, however, Latinized forms of German names decreased
in number (Sonderegger AP 72ff., AV 254-265) and Romance
speakers began to assume German names. Throughout the
period of German dominance in western Europe, pre-
viously Romanized peoples quickly accepted the naming
traditions of their conquerors.

In France, for example, the Frankish onomasticon
soon achieved widespread popularity even though the
Gallo-Romance dialects still prevailed. Dauzat estimates

the proportion of German to Romance names to have been about 1:3 in the fifth century and 1:1 in the sixth; one finds almost exclusively German names among the French Romance population of the ninth century (<u>EA</u> 35 and 114).

In eighth century Italy two-thirds to four-fifths of all names were of German origin; the Austrian monastery St. Peter shows strong German influence at the same time (Müller <u>AK</u> 57f.).

The oldest <u>Necrologium</u> and <u>Professbuch</u> from St. Gallen contain only German names, and Reichenau, founded in 724 by a Spanish monk, quickly became Germanized. Three name lists from ninth century Reichenau contain only 3% Romance names, and German names made up 99% of the onomasticon there in the following century (Baesecke <u>AR</u> 97-103). In the light of this Germanization throughout western Europe it is unlikely that the few Romance settlements which remained as far north as Salzburg and Regensburg managed to preserve their Romance names into the ninth century. German names had already effectively conquered the entire Romance area surrounding Raetia and now began to appear even in this traditionally isolated and conservative region.

VII. German-Romance Name-giving in Raetia

Just as the Romanization of the Raetian provinces
had been slow, so, too, was the penetration of German
civilization into Raetia during the age of migration
and the centuries that followed. Name lists from the
three monasteries of Raetia--Pfäfers, Disentis, and
Tuberis (Münster)--show that the area was still relatively free of German influence into the late eighth
century.[12] Bishop Tello's will (765) contains about
8% German names, thus fitting well into the eighth
century. The most popular names in Tello's will are
Romance, corresponding to those in the libri confrater-
nitates[13] of the three monasteries: Iactatus (mentioned
five times), Lidorius (5), Victor (4), Vigilius (4),
Evalens (3), Iulianus (3), Lobucio (3), Lopus (3),
Praestans (3), Proiectus (3) (Müller SB 104f.).

The most striking aspect of Tello's will is not,
however, the high concentration of Romance names.
This is expected in an eighth century document. Par-
ticularly indicative of the growing German influence
in Curraetia is the appearance of German names within
the family of the Bishop himself. Tello's father
Victor married a German, Theusinda; the intercultural
marriage shows that there must already have been a
number of Germans in the area and that they were not

regarded as enemies or inferiors. Nor did the German
name-giving tradition in the family end with Tello.
His nephew was <u>Victor</u>, named after the founder of the
Victoride dynasty of bishops, but his nieces bore the
German names <u>Teusinda</u> and <u>Odda</u>.

    After about 820 German names increased markedly
in popularity. The <u>Reichsgutsurbar</u> of 831 shows that
the ratio of German to Romance names had dramatically
changed from 1:10 in Tello's will to nearly 1:1.
During the sixty-six years between these two documents
there appears to have been a massive influx of Germans
into Raetia Prima. The <u>Urbar</u> of 831 shows that the
area was divided into nine <u>ministeria</u>, and that five
of the six district ministers mentioned bore German
names: <u>Siso</u>, <u>Otto</u>, <u>Mathrat</u>, <u>Adhalgis</u>, and <u>Richpert</u>
(Sprecher <u>AG</u> 73f.). German colonization in the <u>mini-
sterium Tuverasca</u>, the area around Ilanz in the Vorderrheintal, was especially heavy: Two-thirds of those
granted fiefs there had German names (Müller <u>AK</u> 50ff.).
The high concentration of German speakers in the Ilanz
basin permits the assumption that special political
circumstances in Curraetia favored the settlement of
well-to-do Swabians and Franks there: Tello, whose
mother was German, had held both secular and religious
authority in Raetia and could exercise control over
those foreigners who bought land in the large area

which was under his jurisdiction. Had a more national-
istic bishop and praeses overseen the settlement of
Curraetia, perhaps the degree of early Germanization
there would have been different.

When Charlemagne handed political authority in
Curraetia from the Bishop of Chur to the Frankish
province of Swabia 'in 806, the Bishop was forced to
surrender large amounts of land to wealthy Franks and
Swabians. The favoritism shown German nobles during
Tello's reign became more intense. The change of religious authority from Milan to Mainz in 843 further
strengthened the Frankish claim. Thus it is not surprising that the proportion of German names increased
dramatically from the time of Tello's will to that of
the Reichsgutsurbar in 831.

It must be emphasized that this German colonizing
activity was of a special nature: It was not carried
out by all classes of Germans, but only by those who
occupied the highest worldly offices. No documents
from this period mention that the native Romance
speakers were made to retreat before the Germans, and
the names of minor officials (mansionarii) in the Urbar
of 831 are mostly Romance. In addition, the language
of the Lugnez area and of Oberhalbstein/Obervaz--both
heavily represented by German landowners in 831--has
remained Romansh to the present time; in these areas

German field names, the best index of intensive settlement, are not known (Sprecher _AG_ 76). The German
ruling stratum in Raetia was thereby actually quite
thin.

In spite of Charlemagne's transfer of secular
authority in Curraetia to the duchy of Swabia in 806
and the change of religious supremacy in Chur from
Milan to Mainz in 843, the Bishop of Chur remained
the most important person in Curraetia. Although much
land was lost to the Swabian duke in 806, the Raetian
church retained property in all parts of the bishopric.
In speaking of the German ruling stratum in Curraetia,
therefore, one must think not only of the secular
leaders from north of the Rhine, but also of the head
of the church hierarchy in Chur.

In 1645 Bishop Flugi compiled a list of the
bishops of Chur, mentioning first Bishop Asinio in
451. During the next three centuries only three
bishops with German names appear: Eddo, Ruthardus, and
Adelbertus, a monk from Reichenau. All other names
are Romance, showing that even the highest office of
the land remained virtually untouched by Germans during
that period. In the eighth century the name of Bishop
Tello, of mixed German-Romance parentage, is the only-
hint of foreign blood in the succession of Romance
bishops. After Tello come Constantius, Remedius,

Victor, and Verendarius, the last bishop under the rule of Milan.

The transfer of authority over the bishopric of Chur to the archdiocese of Mainz in 843 is immediately evident from the German names of the new bishops: Hesso, Luitvvardus, Rotharius, and Diotolphus. This trend continued into the tenth century with Walso, Hartbertus, Hiltibaldus, and others (Mayer-Jecklin KF 5ff.).

Yet do names accurately reflect nationality? Can we be sure that the early bishops Eddo, Ruthardus, and Adelbertus were Germans and that Constantius, Remedius, Victor, and Verendarius were Romance speakers? The answers to these questions demand consideration of the extent of intercultural contact at the time these bishops reigned. In Italy, France, and Spain early contact with Germanic peoples was so intense that by the fifth century it was already impossible to find a German behind every German name. Müller (AK 53f.) and Pult (HU 79) rightly emphasize that names accurately reflect nationality at a time when there is little or no intercultural contact. But the greater the influence of one people on another, the greater the probability that the onomasticon of the "higher" culture will not be confined to that culture alone.

Because of the absence of German influence in Raetia Prima in the sixth and seventh centuries, there is no reason to doubt that Bishops Eddo, Ruthardus, and Adelbertus were Germans. Nor is it unlikely that Tello's immediate successors were indeed of Romance origin, as their names imply. But after the gates were opened for intensive German colonization in Curraetia in 806 it becomes more difficult to identify accurately the nationality of a person from his name alone. After the middle of the ninth century this is practically impossible.

It is natural to suspect that German names were popular among Romance speakers anxious to assume a part of the culture of the ruling stratum. Yet Germans may also have adopted Romance names, although in much smaller numbers. A German family living in Curraetia could have assumed many of the cultural trappings of its new home. Intercultural marriages were not unknown (cf. Tello's parents), and it is likely that one Priectus, mentioned in 802, had a German wife who dictated that one of their sons, Balfred and Onoratus, have a German name (Müller AK 53; cf. also Planta SU 97). Finally, it must be remembered that Romance names were generally equated with Christian names and that a German couple may have chosen Romance names for their children in an attempt to be pious.

Romance names in German families were still the exception rather than the rule. In 920 when Bishop

Waldo I of Chur argued with the church in St. Gallen
over ownership of the Pfäfers monastery, the court in
Bussnang was presided over by both Romance and German
judges. The Romance judges bore both Romance and
German names, but the names of the German judges were
exclusively German (Muoth BG 14f.).

By the tenth century very few Romance names appear
among the nobility of Raetia, which had maintained close
ties with southern Germany. German names were assumed
not only by the Romance nobility (cf. the Bishops
Dietmar and Ulrich II von Montfort), but by many peasants as well. According to a document from 1084 de-
claring the founding of the church in Lüen in Schanfigg
(Schorta NL 111), nearly half of the Lüen population
bore German names although the Romansh language survived there for another five hundred years. Some of the
Romance names still in use in Schanfigg in 1084 were
Acarios, Augustus, Cenzanius, Dominicus, Grillus,
Jovianus, Magirinus, Silvester, and Victor.

*   *   *

It has been seen that the Germanization of Curraetia produced a change in the native onomasticon.
German names were not only brought south and retained
within most German families; they were also adopted by
Romance speakers, with the result that after the

beginning of the ninth century it becomes increasingly
difficult to identify the nationality of a person from
his name alone. It is possible to talk of "German"
names and "Romance" names, for they are still separate
groups. If one speaks of "German" speakers and
"Romance" speakers in ninth-century Raetia, the line
drawn between the groups is in a sense intracultural,
between two separate language groups. The line between
"German" names and "Romance" names is then extracul-
tural, for although the names exist in separate groups,
they cut across cultural borders.

The so-called "Christian" names illustrate well
this cross-cultural phenomenon of naming. The Christians who bore these names were not a separate national
group, but were members of both German and Romance
communities. The Christian onomasticon includes Biblical, Romance, and German names and cuts clearly across
national borders. Thus from now on it will be wise to
speak only of name groups and not to associate them
categorically with the cultural or national units to
which they seem to belong.

VIII. German-Christian Name-giving

It will be well to summarize here the onomastic
relationships which prevailed in Raetia by the tenth

and eleventh centuries:

Romance names were in the minority, especially among the most favored members of the feudal secular and religious hierarchy. Old Testament names were practically nonexistent; New Testament names, included in the Romance inventory, had not yet begun to gain widespread popularity. German names, on the other hand, were by far the most popular, even during the strict religious reign of the Ottonian kings of the tenth century. Leading church figures in the north had borne German names early in the Christian era (Alcuin, Hraban) and continued the practice (Notker, Williram) in spite of the official support given Christian-Romance names by the church.

At this time the practice of repetition in German name-giving was increasing in popularity. The German onomasticon, having once included a rich array of name-forming elements, began to lose its flexibility as many elements were no longer understood and favored names developed both within and across family lines.

With the weakening of this most characteristic element in the German name system came the increasing popularity of saints' names. The composition of the Raetian onomasticon of the high Middle Ages was deter-mined by the relationship between the weakened German system and the growing body of Christian names.

*   *   *

Secular and religious leaders in both Germany
and Raetia held fast to German naming tradition until
the high Middle Ages. The first German king of this
period to have a Christian name was <u>Philipp</u> of Swabia
(died 1208); the first Bavarian duke with a non-German
name was <u>Stephan</u> I (died 1310) (Scheidl <u>KV</u> 201 note).
Among the archbishops of Cologne, Mainz, and Trier,
the bishops of Lüttich, Utrecht, and Münster, and the
abbots of Fulda, Werden, Hersfeld, and Corvey before
1500, only 10% have non-German names (Bach <u>DN</u> I, 2, 20).
The first Bishop of Basel to bear a Christian name
between 1100 and 1300 was <u>Peter</u> Reich in 1286 (Socin
<u>MN</u> 84).

In Germany the lasting popularity of German names
may also be seen among the peasant class. In twelfth
century Cologne, for example, the favorite male names
in order of frequency were <u>Heinrich</u>, <u>Hermann</u>, <u>Dietrich</u>,
<u>Gerhart</u>, <u>Gotfrid</u>, <u>Conrat</u>, <u>Johannes</u>, <u>Albert</u>, and <u>Rudolf</u>.[14]
Only the appearance of <u>Johannes</u> among the nine most
common names betrays any local familiarity with the
new Christian onomasticon.

Scheidl (<u>KV</u> 205) shows that the transition from
German to Christian name-giving in Freising took place
sometime between 1350 and 1450. In 1100 virtually no

foreign names are found there, but by 1517 German
names had receded to only 30% of the entire onomasticon. Scheidl (<u>KV</u> 204) gives examples of this change
from three peasant families:

In 1290 <u>Konrad</u> von Schönbrunn and his
wife <u>Richgard</u> have four children: <u>Gertrud</u>,
<u>Ulrich</u>, <u>Juta</u>, and <u>Berchta</u> (all names German).

In 1395 <u>Perchtold</u> der Engelprechtsmüller
and his wife <u>Chüngund</u> have seven children:
<u>Weindel</u>, <u>Hensel</u>, <u>Anna</u>, <u>Margred</u>, <u>Elzpett</u>, <u>Sophey</u>,
and <u>Agnes</u> (three German, six Christian names).

In 1465 <u>Andre</u> Schmid has four children:
<u>Georg</u>, <u>Anna</u>, <u>Lienhart</u>, and <u>Margret</u> (all names
Christian).

*   *   *

What are the reasons for the sudden popularity of
Christian names and the decline of German names at this
time? It would seem most reasonable to assume that the
increased use of Christian names accompanied the acceptance of Christianity, which had become established
north of the Alps by the fourth century. This, however,
was not the case. It was true in part for Romance-
speaking areas, where the Christian onomasticon was
built from the Romance name vocabulary and merely
served to support the names which already existed there.

Yet even in Romance territory the names under discussion here, those of New Testament saints, did not
enjoy immediate popularity. Peter appears in Tello's
will, but the most common names in that document were
Romance and did not share their popularity with those
saints' names which blossomed four centuries later.[15]
In German territory, where even the most prominent
members of the church hierarchy bore German names,
saints' names were not used frequently until the high
Middle Ages.

The answer to this question is probably to be
found in a Christian activity which became popular for
the first time in the high Middle Ages and which is
clearly associated with the adoration of saints. It
is possible that the reign of Pope Gregory VII (1073-85)
produced a new awareness of the importance of saints
as one aspect of his vast program of church reform,
and that the period of the Crusades (11th-13th centuries)
intensified the worship of saints as well as the practice of other Christian activities (Scheidl KV 207).
For example, crusaders and pilgrims brought back the
cults of St. Nicolaus, St. Georgius, and St. Antonius
from the East (Richard UG 145f.). More likely, however, the increase of Christian names is due to the
wave of saint worship spread by the wandering Franciscan and Dominican monks (Bettelmönche) and to the

change from the Roman to the Christian calendar in
the thirteenth century.

Until the end of the thirteenth century it was
common practice to date documents according to the
Roman calendar. Document 222 from volume I of Mohr's
Codex Diplomaticus of Raetian documents is dated

M.cc. xlviiii. viii Idus Junij vii. indict.,

or 6 June 1249. By the early 1300's the new church
calendar was in use, in which nearly every day carried
the name of a saint. The calendar varied from town to
town as saints of local importance were entered. This
produced a system of dating which was imprecise on an
international scale: Georgii was April 23 in Augsburg
and Prague but April 25 in Chur; Martini could be May
12 (Tours), July 4 (Tirol), November 15 (Trier), or
December 1 (Utrecht).[16] On the local level, however,
the new system was quite exact. Document 133 (CD II)
is dated 2 October 1309:

> dise brief wart geben ze Kur an dem
> nachsten donrestag nach sant Michels-
> tag in dem jare do von gotts geburt
> untz an den selben tag warent driuzehen
> hundert jar dar nach in dem nünde jare.

The new manner of dating documents, which was
largely the business of the nobility, was not the only
change brought about by the new system. The names of

saints now replaced dates (<u>Jacobi</u> instead of July 25)
and became well known as the times of seasonal festi-
vals; crops were planted and harvested, cattle driven
to and from the summer pastures, and taxes levied all
on days known only by the names of the appropriate
saints (Finsterwalder <u>FT</u> 10f.). Churches were consecrated in the name of one or more saints, who were
called upon to protect the community, and the name-days
of these saints were occasions for celebrations and for
gifts to the church.[17] People were encouraged to choose
patron saints according to their birthdays, and profes-
sions and trade unions all had favorite saints. <u>Nico-
laus</u> guarded sailors and merchants, <u>Georg</u> protected
knights, and so on.[18]

The adoption of the new calendar not only brought
a vast number of Christian names into the most remote
peasant settlements, but also made the most basic agri-
cultural and social affairs dependent on their use.
Thus with the new calendar Christian names became familiar to virtually all elements of society.

Finally, it must be said that fashion undoubtedly
played an important role in the adoption of the new
names. In German-speaking territory the Christian
names appeared first among the clergy in the twelfth
century, then among the nobility in the thirteenth.
At this time German nobles married women from the

fashionable Romance courts, where the Christian names
had been adopted a century before (Socin MN 83). These
intercultural marriages between Germans and members of
Romance courtly society reflected the strong ties which
existed with the style-setting courtly world. Barba-
rossa married Beatrix of Burgundy, and Friedrich II had
a succession of wives of foreign birth: Konstanze of
Aragon, Jolanthe of Jerusalem, Isabella of England,
and Bianca of Anglano. His daughters were named according to the new fashion: Agnes, Margarethe, Anna,
Katharina, Blanchefleur, Jolanthe, and Stemma (Bach
DN I, 2, 18).

It is clear that saints' names did not become
overly popular with the introduction of Christianity,
but only later with the upsurge of saint adoration.
The German onomasticon of the early Middle Ages was
not yet seriously threatened by the appearance of
Christian names and the support which they were later
given by wandering monks and the new calendar. The
absence of significant opposition, however, is not the
only reason that German names managed to survive so
long. Many names of German origin are still popular
today, but most of these names probably survived only
because they had been borne by saints and were thus
officially favored by the church and included in the
new calendar: Albert, Bernhard, Burkhard, Erhard,

Heinrich, Konrad, Lambert, Leonhard, Oswald, Wolfgang
(Nied HN 17). Other German names eventually came to
be used as family names (Armon < Hermann, Brunold <
Brun-walt, Remondino < Raginmund, Tibaldi < Theobald in
Graubünden (Muoth BG 16f.)), surviving the high Middle
Ages as evidence that a widespread German name-giving
tradition existed in Raetia up to the time when family
names became popular.

Finally, some German name elements survived as
suffixes in new compound names such as Christ-olf <
Christian.[19] These suffixes no longer carried a
meaning, but were used only to modify existing forms
(Finsterwalder FT 13).

It may be said that only those German names survived which were of some cultural or political importance. Just as saints with German names attained cultural significance, so did other German names retain
their popularity for political reasons: Cf. the German
kings named Heinrich, Konrad, or Otto. Just as alliteration had been used in the early Middle Ages to identify
families (Gernot--Gunther--Giselher), repetition of politically important names showed reverence for ancestral
tradition and helped to legitimize claims of family
identity and property inheritance.[20]

*   *   *

It has been seen that the German onomasticon
receded as the names of Christian saints became more
popular during the high Middle Ages. A brief comparison of naming customs in German areas at this time will
show which names of both groups were most popular and
which could be expected to determine the course of
name-giving toward the end of the feudal age.

The most popular male names in Cologne in the
twelfth century were Heinrich, Herman, Dietrich, Ger-
hart, Gotfrid, Conrat, Johannes, Albert, and Rudolf.
Gertrud was the most frequently used female name, followed by Mathilt, Adelheid, Elisabeth, and Hedwig
(Bach DN I, 2, 28f.). The appearance of Johannes and
Elisabeth, which later became the most popular names,
shows that the influence of Christian name-giving was
just beginning to be felt.

Metzger's study of female names in Freiburg/Br.
shows that Adelheid, Mechthild, Anna, and Gertrud were
favored in the early 1200's. At this time the female
onomasticon of Freiburg included 26 German and seven
Christian names. A century later the ratio had changed
to 48:42, and by the fifteenth century Christian names
outnumbered German names 40:18 (Bach DN I, 2, 28f.).

Peter and Johannes appear to have been among the
first of the Christian names to be adopted by German

speakers in general, both becoming relatively common
after about 1250 (Socin MN 83). The popularity of
Johannes was enormous: During the period from 1200
to 1500 in Baden Johannes occupied first place in front
of the German favorites, Heinrich and Conrat (Bach I,
2, 28f.). Twenty-three popes were named Johannes
before 1400, and fully 994 saints bear the name as
well (556 saints are named Peter) (Nied HN 39). Only
one Hans lived in thirteenth century Magdeburg, but
there were 302 in the following century (Bach DN I,
2, 32). The first farmer to bear the name in Freising
is mentioned in 1353; at this time the name is used by
9% of the nobility and $5\frac{1}{2}$% of the peasantry there. In
the fifteenth century Hans/Johannes was more popular
in Freising than were the three German favorites, Heinrich, Konrad, and Ulrich, and reached its zenith in
1532 with a popularity of 32% (Scheidl KV 201). Paulus
was not as common as Peter or Johannes, although 248
saints are so named (Nied HN 41). Other popular Christian men's names at the end of the Middle Ages were
Jacob, Nicolaus, Martin, Thomas, Andreas, Mathias, and
Philipp (Socin MN 83).

The popular Christian triumvirate of Hans, Georg,
and the Latin-German Lienhart accounted for 30% of all
males in Freising by 1450 and 52% by the Reformation.
By comparison, the most common German names, Heinrich,

Konrad, and Ulrich, reached a high point of 54% in the fourteenth century (Scheidl KV 202).

Among women in Freising the most common Christian names were Agnes, Anna (of both German and Christian origin), Margarete, Katharina, and Elisabeth (German Else or St. Elisabeth of Thüringen). Of these Elisabeth (25%) and Anna (21%) were the most popular at the end of the Middle Ages. Dorothea, Magdalena, and Ursula became well represented in the fourteenth century (Scheidl KV 202f.).

IX. German-Christian Name-giving in Raetia

It was shown above that geographic and political isolation played an important role in the formation of the onomasticon of Curraetia in the early Middle Ages. The Romance lands to the south and west readily accepted the German names introduced during the Merovingian period, and by the ninth century the Germanization of the native Romance onomasticon in these areas was virtually complete. Curraetia, however, was neither quickly nor thoroughly Germanized, and onomastic evidence shows that a Romance name-giving tradition was still apparent there long after it had ceased to exist in neighboring lands.

The distribution of late Medieval fortresses in Curraetia shows that Germanization there was confined

chiefly to the Rhine Valley (cf. Poeschel <u>BB</u> 54-78).
Yet although the German lords maintained constant contact with the north and promoted trade over the Raetian
passes to the south, the Germanization was most often
superficial and did not extend to all segments of the
native population even in this strategic and crucial
area.

It is characteristic of documents from the later
Middle Ages that the names of the nobility by far outnumber those of the peasantry. This is understandable:
Business transactions and inheritances involved only
those who controlled the wealth; to those who kept
records--the nobility--only the nobility itself was important. Thus it is fortunate that occasional documents
mention not only the lesser nobility and freemen, but
also the class of serfs, who far outnumbered those of
superior social position and whose names provide the
best measure of the true extent of Germanization.

For purposes of simplification, four groups of
names may be distinguished in Raetian documents of this
period: those of a) the upper nobility (<u>hoher Adel</u>),
b) the lesser nobility (<u>niederer Adel</u>, <u>Dienstadel</u>),
c) freemen (<u>Freie</u>), and d) serfs (<u>Hörige</u>, <u>Leibeigene</u>,
<u>Halbfreie</u>). The onomasticon of the first two groups is
briefly examined here for the period ca. 1200-1500 in
order to illustrate the degree of progress made among

the largely German nobility by the new corpus of
Christian names. The name-giving customs of the last
two groups, freemen and serfs, are reviewed only for
the thirteenth century in order to identify the immediate native tradition which the Walser encountered
when they immigrated at this time. Walser and native
Romance name-giving practices during the following
centuries are treated in Chapters III and IV.

a) The Upper Nobility[21]

Noble families who either granted land to the im-
migrating Walser or who later gained possession of lands
already settled by Walser included:

The Herren von Vaz, who appeared in the twelfth
century and owned land in Belfort and Obervaz as well
as in the Walser areas of Davos, Prättigau, and the
Rheinwald. The Vaz also held Schams, half of Domleschg,
Safien, Schanfigg, and other lands in fief from the
Bishop of Chur. When Donat von Vaz died in 1338, his
daughter Kunigunde married Friedrich V von Toggenburg
(Meinherz MBH 6; Thöny PG 31; Planta CH 334-343).

The Grafen von Toggenburg, who received half of
the Vaz inheritance in 1338, largely in Prättigau.
Ten years later Friedrich V bought the other half from
his brother-in-law, Rudolf von Werdenberg-Sargans.

When Friedrich VII von Toggenburg died in 1456 without
an heir, his land holdings included Maienfeld, Prättigau, Davos, Schanfigg, and Churwalden (HBLS III, 644;
Thöny PG 37ff.; Planta CH 378-416).

The Vögte von Matsch, who inherited part of Prättigau from Friedrich von Toggenburg. The Matsch owned
property in Vintschgau, the Münstertal, the Unterengadin,
and Puschlav as well as in the Albulatal, Domleschg, and
Malans (HBLS V, 49).

The Grafen von Werdenberg-Sargans, who received
from the Vaz inheritance (1338) Domleschg, Obervaz,
Schams, the Rheinwald, and later a part of Prättigau
which soon went over to the Toggenburger. Another
branch of the family, the Werdenberg-Heiligenberg,
owned property in the Bündner Oberland (Trins, Tamins,
Reichenau) and the Albulatal (Filisur, Bergün) (HBLS
III, 644).

The Herren von Rhäzüns, who inherited from the
Werdenberg-Sargans property in the Heinzenberg, Safien,
and Tenna; they held Obersaxen as well in fief from the
Bishop of Chur. Other holdings included Rhäzüns, Ems,
and Felsberg (Planta CH 417-432).

Among other important noble dynasties were the
Herren von Belmont, whose property in the Bündner Ober-
land (Flims, Ilanz, Lugnez, Ems) later went to the
Rhäzüns and to the Grafen von Sax-Misox. The latter

owned land in the Misox (Val Mesocco) south of the San
Bernardino Pass and in the Rheinwald as well, where
they granted land in fief to two of the first Walser
in 1274 (Planta CH 432-439 and 468ff.). The Edle von
Tarasp owned most of the present Unterengadin, which
went to the Matsch upon their demise in the thirteenth
century (BUB I, 504). The Freiherren von Aspermont
were among the most respected dynasties in Curraetia,
yet owned land (chiefly in the Rhine Valley) only in
fief from the Bishop of Chur. The Freiherren von
Brandis, a family from the present canton of Bern, did
not appear in Curraetia until the fifteenth century,
when Wolfhart V acquired the Herrschaft Maienfeld from
the inheritance of Friedrich VII von Toggenburg (HBLS
II, 342f.).

*   *   *

An investigation of the names used by these families
of the upper nobility shows that German names maintained
their popularity throughout the Middle Ages. No Christian names occurred until the thirteenth century, when
they made up only 15% of the onomasticon. But this
percentage doubled in the fourteenth century, and in
the 1400's German and Christian names shared equal popularity. Women were more apt to bear Christian names

than were men, who normally retained a German name
which had been well established as a dynastic trade-
mark.

Typical of the distribution of German and Christian names is the onomasticon of the Grafen von Werdenberg. In the 1200's all nine males in the family
bore German names. In the following century there appeared 26 German names and three Christian names.
During the 1400's the German:Christian ratio had
tightened to 23:12. Females, seldom mentioned in
Medieval documents, bore seven German and seven Christian names from 1200 to 1400; during the 1400's, however, there appeared 24 Christian names and only four
of German origin.

The names of abbots of the Pfävers monastery, who
belonged to the upper nobility, illustrate the lasting
popularity of the German tradition: All bore German
names until <u>Johann</u> von Mendelbüren (1361-1386), and he
was from Württemberg. The first abbot from Curraetia
with a Christian name was <u>Johannes</u> III Berger from
Ragaz late in the fifteenth century.[22]

Characteristic of the period before 1200 in Curraetia was not only the high percentage, but also the
great variety of German names in noble families. Yet
highly individualistic names such as <u>Folknand</u>, <u>Ludolf</u>,
<u>Wolchard</u>, and <u>Lutofrid</u> gradually disappeared as the

onomasticon became standardized and dynastic repetition
was extensive. A good illustration of repetition is
found in the Toggenburg family, where eleven Diethelms
appear from 1044 to 1385 and seven Friedrichs from 1226
to 1436; there were eleven Ulrichs von Aspermont before
1376 and eleven Ulrichs von Sax between 1220 and 1463.

The most popular names among the Curraetian upper
nobility from ca. 1200 to 1500 were:

MEN:	U(da)lrich	39	Eberhard	14
	Heinrich	36	Diethelm	12
	Rudolf	23	Hugo	12
	Johannes	18	Friedrich	9
	Albert	14	Walther	8

WOMEN:	Agnes/Nexia	11	Kunigunde	5
	Elisabeth	8	Adelheid	4
	Margaretha	8	Anna	3
	Clement(i)a	5	Barbara	3
	Katharina	5	Irmgard	3
			Verena	3

Of 283 men, 220 bore a total of 34 German names:
an average of nearly seven men for each name. The remaining 63 men bore 21 Christian names: only three men
for each name. These figures plainly reveal the extent
of standardization among the German onomasticon and the
comparative variety of Christian names made available
through the Christian calendar: 14 of the 21 Christian

names are mentioned only once or twice compared with only 16 of 34 German names.

Of 75 women, only 17 bore a total of seven German names; 58 women bore 18 Romance names.

b) The Lesser Nobility[23]

Source material from the thirteenth century shows that the lesser nobility in Curraetia was not inclined to supplement its onomasticon with Christian names. Of 191 men, fully 185 bore German names. The variety of German names was still great at this time, including the now-forgotten Wezelo, Reinger, Egilolf, and Ruodrih; yet Chuonrad, A(de)lbert, and O(da)lricus had already become so popular that these three names together made up nearly one-third of the onomasticon. Thirty-nine out of 53 names are mentioned only once or twice. Of the five non-German names which appear three (Victor, Wlpius, Initiolus) already existed in the native Romance onomasticon and two (Johannes and Jacobus) are of Christian origin.

The names most popular with the lesser nobility in the thirteenth century were:

Chuonrad	30	Svikerus	9
O(da)lricus	17	Burchardus	8
Heinricus	16	Fridericus	7
A(de)lbert	15	Sigifrid	7

The 1300's brought a sudden influx of Christian
names into the onomasticon of the lesser nobility.
Six German names are already outnumbered by fourteen
Christian names in the Salis family; the Tscharner
family bore exclusively Christian names. The German
names in the Planta family would be in a weak minority
were it not for the eleven Conrads from the 1100's to
the late 1400's; even so, Christian names outnumber
German in the Planta family in this period 29 to 19.

c) Freemen

The Lüener Stiftungsurkunde from 1084 (Schorta NL)
lists the names of 49 farmers in Schanfigg, the first
freemen to appear in Raetian documents.[24] Fortunately,
Schanfigg is one of the chief areas colonized by the
Walser in the early 1300's; the document thus provides
an important basis of comparison with later sources from
the Walser settlement of Langwies in the same valley.

Approximately one-half of the Lüen names are of
Romance origin and recall many of those mentioned in
Tello's will of 765 and the Reichsgutsurbar of 831:
Acarios, Augustus, Cenzo, Dominicus, Jovianus, and so
on. Five names--Daniel, Johannes, Jordanus, Petra, and
Petrus--betray Biblical origins, but must not neces-
sarily be associated with the spread of Christian names
in the high Middle Ages; such names were present in

Tello's will as well, and not surprisingly, for those whom the Bishop named in his will undoubtedly had something to do with church affairs.

Twelfth and thirteenth century documents from the Bündner Urkundenbuch mention a total of 226 freemen: 211 men and 15 women. Of the 83 men's names 65 are of German origin and are borne by 185 men. Twenty-six men have seventeen Christian-Romance names: Johannes (4), Bonellus (3), Alexius, Leo, Victor, Viventius (two each), Andrea, Dominicus, Heliseus, Iogi, Mapheus, Martinus, Mauricius, Militto, Silvester, Symon, and Vitalis (one each).

Eleven names account for 15 women, among them two with the Christian Elisabeth. All other women's names are German.

In spite of the relatively high percentage of men with Romance names (12%), the most popular names are all German:

Chuonradus	23	Herman	9
O(da)lricus	22	Fridericus	7
Heinrich	18	Walther	7
Albertus	9	Egino	6
Eberhard	9		

The comparison of sources from 1084 and 1100-1300 shows that among freemen German names had become very popular within two hundred years, decisively suppressing

the native Romance onomasticon. Moreover, it clearly
shows that freemen had not yet become receptive to the
concept of dynastic repetition.[25] Fully 75 of the 93
German and Romance names occur only once or twice, and
the forms of many German names (Raiker, Pruning, Al-
gisus, Gerung) show that the richness of the Old Germanic onomastic vocabulary had survived in the hands
of the Romance freemen more successfully than in those
of the German nobility which had originally popularized
its use in Curraetia centuries before.

The spread of saint worship had not yet begun to
affect the name inventory of freemen: Johannes appears
only four times among 211 men, and in view of its popularity already established by the time Tello's will
was written in 765, it is best not even to assume that
its presence here has something to do with the glorification of saints in the later Middle Ages.

d) Serfs

Members of the lowest social order are mentioned
only infrequently in Curraetian documents of the thirteenth century. Many freemen appeared as witnesses to
land transactions, but serfs were not accorded this legal
privilege; they were normally recorded only when they
and the land which they farmed were transferred from
one overlord to another. Thus only 35 men and seven

women are mentioned from 1200 to 1300: too small a
number for any degree of statistical precision. Yet
these few names are extremely valuable, for they reveal much about the naming traditions of those with
whom the Walser had the closest contact.

If a "favorite" name was present among serfs at
this time, it is unclear from the small amount of evidence available. Chunrat is mentioned four times, and
Bonus and Johannes each three; Marquardus, Hainricus,
and Benedictus each appear twice. Obviously, no clear
order of favoritism can be established from these
figures, for the appearance of three Victors in three
generations of one family would move this name from
"last" to "first" place in such a list.

Highly significant is the fact that 19 men share
14 German names, while 16 men have 11 Romance names.
This gives a German:Romance ratio of 54%:46%, placing
the percentage of Romance names among serfs far above
that present in the higher social orders.

Five women have German names (Bertha, Gerdrut,
Iudintha (2), Machthilda) and two have Romance names
(Sculla, Tilia).

Only Johannes and Joseph betray any familiarity
with Biblical figures, but both fit well within the
Christian-Romance onomastic framework visible in Tello's
will. Other Romance names are:

Benedictus	Veneris
Bonus (3)	Victor
Iaunit	Vigilius
Martinus	Viuencius
Mauricius	

Other documents from this period confirm the data presented above. The tax books of the Churwalden and St. Nicolai monasteries record only isolated Christian names in 1270 (Nicolaus Stude), 1279 (Ambrosius de Cristas), 1282 (Agnes Boso), 1292 (Johannes), and so on.

The fragmentary Raetian debt list of 1325 published by Wartmann[26] records 430 persons of mixed social standing. The list may be divided roughly into 171 witnesses (fideiussores) and 259 non-witnesses, although the distinction between the two groups is unclear; presumably, witnesses are of a more privileged background because of their power to sign legal documents. If this is so, the names of the two groups reveal something of the difference according to the findings presented above Sixty percent of the fideiussores have German names, and only 45% of the names of non-witnesses--tentatively assumed to be of lower social standing--are German. Romance names are borne by proportionately twice as many non-witnesses, among whom the new Christian names are slightly more popular.[27]

*   *   *

The material presented above may be summarized
as follows:

German names, which had been introduced into Raetia
by the nobility in the early Middle Ages, still accounted for the majority of names in noble families throughout the Medieval period. Yet the late 1200's and
especially the 1300's saw a dramatic increase in the
use of Christian names among members of the highest
social order. What German names were still in use were
chosen from a standardized group which served to identify successive generations of the various noble dynasties. Although the lesser nobility used an astoun-
dingly high percentage (97%) of German names in the
thirteenth century, the following centuries brought
Christian names into the majority there as well.

Among freemen and serfs German names never did
totally suppress the native Romance onomasticon. At
the peak of their popularity in the thirteenth century
German names accounted for 88% of freemen and only 54%
of serfs. The rest of the names were Romance. The
degrees of cultural interpenetration in these various
name groups recall a contact phenomenon which had occurred in Raetia several centuries before:

The Romanization of Raetia was never complete,
and when Germanic peoples first made contact with the
area they encountered elements of the pre-Roman Raetian

civilization which had never been totally assimilated into the Empire. Similarly, the superficial Germanization of Curraetia during the Middle Ages allowed Romance names to continue in use among the lower social orders. The serf class, bearing largely Romance names, was exposed to saint adoration and the Christian name vocabulary before the intermediate stage of German acculturization could be completed.

X. Footnotes

1   The dual name Cassitalos Versicnos 'Cassitalos,
the son of Versos' (Woolf GN 180) is probably the
result of contamination by the Roman culture, which
demanded greater precision.

2   Some Old Testament names were probably adopted
because they sounded like Old High German names.
Bach (DN I, 2, 14) notes similarities between Salomon
and Salman; Judith and Judita, Judinta, Jutta; Margarethe and Mergard; Philipp and Filibert; Michel and
MHG michel 'large.' For the -a in Old Testament and
OHG Anna (masc. OHG Anno) see note 11.

3   Not a single example of the tria nomina is to be
found in Christian inscriptions since the time of
Constantine (died 337) (Müller AK 42). Müller (AK
43) cites a letter from St. Chrysostomus (died 407)
promoting the change:

      Igitur nos neque quaevis nomina pueris indamus,
      neque avorum et abavorum et eorum, qui genere
      clari fuerunt, nomina tribuamus: sed sanctorum
      virorum, qui virtutibus fulserunt, plurimamque
      erga Deum habuerunt fudiciam.

      Cf. also Nied HN 21.

4   'German' here includes the peoples actively involved in the colonization of Raetia--Alemanni, Franks,
Langobards, and Ostrogoths. It is neither so specific
as its modern definition nor so general as to mean
'Germanic.' If this seems imprecise, it must be remembered that it is often extremely difficult to
separate the German from the Romance names in Raetian
documents; to assign accurately each German name to
its rightful nation would be impossible. First names
occasionally reflected contact between two tribes, as
Hungoz (Hun and Goth) and Suabalah (Swabian and
Romance (Walah)): Socin MN 215; cf. Chapter I,
note 11.

5   Pulgram (PN 189) shows that Indo-European names
of two elements belonged primarily to the upper
classes, and documents from St. Gallen show that
this was still true in the Old High German period.
Seventy percent of freemen in St. Gallen bore names
of two elements and thirty percent bore single names;
among bondsmen the proportion changed to 57%:43%
(Sonderegger AP 75). Official affairs, conducted by

the nobility, called for the more elegant double
names, which were too cumbersome for daily use by
peasants (Socin MN 191f.; cf. Bach DN I, 2, 191f.).

6   An indication is given by Bach (DN I, 1, 86),
who hypothesizes that the parents Hildebrant and
Gertrud could have the sons Gerbrant, Trudbrant,
Hildger, Brantger, and Trudger and the daughters
Hildtrud, Branttrud, Gerhild, Branthild, and
Trudhild.

7   Förstemann (Zeitschrift für vergleichende
Sprachforschung I, 103f.) and Socin (MN 200 and
216) believed that Germanic name-giving elements
were put together with no regard to meaning, but
most recently Benno Eide Siebs (Die Personennamen
der Germanen, Wiesbaden, 1969) sees meaningful ex-
pressions in most Germanic names. It is not unreason-
able to assume that very early names were formed with
an intended meaning, but that this characteristic
disappeared later when names were formed by the combination of two elements with opposite meanings:
Frid-hild 'peace and battle,' Gund-frid 'battle and
peace' (Bach DN I, 1, 85f.). Names with obvious
meanings such as Coufman, Divelspot, and Unrat are
of later origin (Socin MN 216ff.).

8   It is because of this tradition that old Hildebrand knows that if his son tells his own name he
reveals the identity of the entire family: ibu du
mi aenon (the suffix -brant) sages, ik mi de odre
wet (Socin MN 201).

9   Only 31 women's names are attested before 400
A.D. (Bach DN I, 1, 15).

10   The Christian-Romance onomasticon discussed
above is basically Romance and will be referred to
as such in the consideration of its contact with
German name-giving. This should avoid confusion
with the later problem of specific German-Christian
contact of the later Middle Ages, which is treated
below (77ff.).

11   Striking--but rare--examples of Christian-German
name formation are given by Socin (MN 201): Petri-
bert, Paul-hart, Petr-ualt, Pauli-bert, Christe-
hildis (West Franks and Langobards). Of definite
Christian origin are names in Heid- (Heidan, Heithan-
rih (8th century)) and Gotes- (Cotesdegan (824) in
St. Gallen, Gotesman (791) in the Elsass).

More common among Germans in contact with Romance
speakers was the custom of creating feminine names
from masculine ones. According to the Latin patterns
of Martinus/Martina, Clemens/Clementia, the masculine
forms Theudeberht and Berhtram could become feminized
as Theudeberhta and Berhtramma (Bach DN I, 2, 6;
Socin MN 213). This possibility already existed in
Old High German, where names such as Immo/Imma and
Hezelo/Hezela were not uncommon (Bach DN I, 1, 193);
yet the practice of adding -a to masculine names was
more in vogue in or near Romance-speaking areas.
Note, too, the more modern custom of adding the feminine -in to family names: die Gottschedin, die Neu-
berin, Schiller's Luise Müllerin.

12
    Müller AK 58; Buck LV 177; Planta SU 96. See
also the map "Streuungsbereich romanischer Personennamen in den lateinischen Urkunden der Nordostschweiz
und Vorarlbergs von 700-1100 (Donatoren und Zeugen an
den Ausstellungsorten) und den Verbrüderungsbüchern
von St. Gallen, Reichenau und Pfäfers" in Sonderegger
AS 53 and VS 507, map 6.

13
    'Verbrüderungsbücher': Lists containing the names
of monks were exchanged between monasteries, permit-
ting the members of one brotherhood to invoke the
names of their distant associates, praying for their
salvation in the afterlife.

14
    F. Wagner, Studien über die Namengebung in Köln
im zwölften Jahrhundert, diss. Göttingen, 1913, 41
and 57; cited by Bach DN I, 2, 28f.

15
    Names of saints were understandably common in and
around monasteries. Tello's will mentions a field
belonging to the Disentis monastery and named ager
Sancti Martini. Christian naming traditions already
played a role in church affairs at the time when the
practice of coining field names was just beginning
(Schorta EK 266).

16
    H. Grotefend, Taschenbuch der Zeitrechnung des
deutschen Mittelalters und der Neuzeit, Hannover,
1960, 60 and 78.

17
    Larger areas as well had their own saints: Ru-
precht in Bavaria, Florian in southern Austria, and
Kilian on the Main (Bach DN I, 2, 17). The patron
saint of Graubünden is Lucius, a Scottish king who
died as a missionary in Chur about 190 A.D. (HBLS
III, 690).

18   This inspired the following bitter comment from
the enthusiastic Protestant Biblical historian E.
Camenisch:

        Selbst Trunkenbolde und Schlemmer, ja
        sogar Räuber, die beim einsamen Bergwirts-
        haus auf den ahnungslosen Wanderer lauerten,
        hatten ihre Heiligen und Schutzpatrone. (BR 19)

19   A Iustefrit appears in a Curraetian document
from 1161 (BUB I, 345).

20   This practice was already well developed among
the Romans:

        In speaking of my tutor, Marcus Portius
        Cato, I must make it plain that he was neither
        Marcus Portius Cato, the Censor, instigator
        of the Third Punic War; nor his son of the
        same name, the well-known jurist; nor his
        grandson, the Consul of the same name, nor
        his great-grandson of the same name, Julius
        Caesar's enemy; nor his great-great-grandson
        of the same name, who fell at the Battle of
        Philippi; but an absolutely undistinguished
        great-great-great-grandson, still of the same
        name, who never bore any public dignity and
        who deserved none. (Robert Graves, I, Claudius,
        Suffolk, 1967, 14.)

21   The family trees of the upper nobility are con-
structed from information provided in the HBLS with
the following exceptions: Theodor von Liebenau, "Die
Herren von Sax zu Misox" JHGG XIX (1889), 1-48;
Geneologisches Handbuch zur Schweizer Geschichte,
Zürich, 1900-1908, 188f.; E. Meyer-Marthaler and F.
Perret, ed., Bündner Urkundenbuch I, 504; Matthias
Thöny, Prättigauer Geschichte, Schiers, 1948, 31.

22   Joseph Anton Hardegger, Beiträge zur spätmittel-
alterlichen Geschichte der Benediktinerabtei Pfävers,
Freiburg, 1969, 189f.

23   The principal sources consulted for onomastic
information about the lesser nobility are the family
trees of the families von Salis, von Planta, Buol, and
Tscharner, Mohr's Regesten der Landschaft Schanfigg,
and the Bündner Urkundenbuch. The latter two sources
are consulted for the period 1100-1300; the family
trees reveal something of the name-giving traditions
of the following two centuries.

24
    Anton v. Castelmur, "Eine rätische Kirchen-
stiftung vom Jahre 1084" <u>Zeitschrift für Kirchen-
geschichte</u> XXIII (1929), 298.

25
    Yet repetition was by no means unknown. A docu-
ment from Vintschgau in 1161 mentions (in genitive
form) "Ůdalrici, uxoris sue Ůte et filii Ůdalrici et
patris Ůdalrici et uxoris Irmgarde" (<u>BUB</u> I, 345).

26
    "Bruchstücke eines rätischen Schuldenverzeich-
nisses" in Wartmann <u>RU</u>.

27
    These figures are not intended to determine pre-
cise trends in name-giving, but only to indicate the
approximate composition of the onomastica of various
segments of the population. Obviously, Romance names
cannot always be separated from the later Christian
names (<u>Johannes</u>, <u>Jacobus</u>, and <u>Lucius</u> are found long
before the Christian onomasticon became popular in
the 1400's); nor can German names justifiably be distinguished from Christian in combinations such as
<u>Iuste-frit</u> (1161) or <u>Heinrich Martin</u> von Sax (1333).

CHAPTER THREE

PRE-REFORMATION NAME-GIVING IN GRAUBUENDEN[1]

The German and Christian-Romance name-giving
traditions established above for Medieval Curraetia
were treated separately by the three major population
groups: German speakers in Walser colonies, Romance
speakers in the Bündner Oberland and the Unterengadin,
and German speakers in the Rhine Valley north of Chur.
Distinctive onomastic traditions may be observed within each of these three cultural units and are discussed
here for the period from 1200 to the Reformation in
the sixteenth century. The results obtained from this
period provide a solid basis for the investigation of
post-Reformation name-giving in Graubünden in Chapter
IV.

I. Walser Names

a) Wallis

Paul Zinsli suggests in his comprehensive study
of Walser folk culture that the Walser brought their
onomastic traditions with them from Wallis when they
came to Graubünden in the thirteenth century:

> Zwar haben die Auswanderer aus dem Rhonetal
> eben noch keine festen Sippenbenennungen getra-
> gen; aber sie haben doch gleichsam schon einen
> grossen Teil des Rohmaterials zur künftigen
> Namenbildung in ihre neue Heimat mitgebracht,
> nämlich die damals im Wallis bevorzugten und
> üblichen Rufnamen und dazu wohl auch einen Be-
> stand von kennzeichnenden individuellen Zunamen.
> Diese Tauf- und Beinamentradition wird sich dann
> in den Aussenorten erhalten und bei der nun ein-
> setzenden Entfaltung der Familiennamen nachhal-
> tig ausgewirkt haben. (<u>WV</u> 74)

It is difficult to establish a specific name-giving tradition among the emigrants from Wallis at this early date. The chief source of information about the population of Wallis and Valais from the thirteenth century is Gremaud's <u>Documents relatifs à l'histoire du Vallais</u>, which includes 684 Latin documents from the period between 1200 and 1280.[2]

The 559 people mentioned in these Wallis documents are members of all social groups and do not all represent the class of farmers and herdsmen who were the first to move out of Wallis into the Italian Piedmont and shortly thereafter to migrate east to Graubünden. As was the case in Raetian documents, only freemen or members of noble families were likely to be mentioned in legal sources.

The identification of many of these 559 people is impossible; to assign each to a firm place in the social hierarchy would be folly. In some cases a person is well identified: "<u>Petrus</u> maior de Chamosum" (document no. 237) is probably a freeman and "Willer-mus comes de Morgio" (275) doubtless belongs to the upper nobility. But what of "Gotefredus comes de Blandrato maior de Vespia" (725)? This shows that "maior" was not a title given only to freemen. And who are Jordanes (249), Petrus Niger (457), or Nico-laus (528)? Not even Aymo de Turre (437) or Beatrix de Arennun (793) can be placed within a social order, because de was used by peasants and nobles alike at this time (Socin MN 233-262). In addition, the exi-stence of both secular and religious hierarchies prevents members of the church (capellanus, canonicus, curatus, rector, etc.) from being identified because church offices did not necessarily reflect the secular background of their holders.

Only when specific secular offices are mentioned, and this is not always the case, is identification possible: Comes, nobilis, ingenuus apply to the upper nobility (hoher Adel) and ministerialis and miles to the lesser nobility (Dienstadel).

In view of these difficulties it is best to exa-mine the Gremaud material under the assumption that it presents a rough cross-section of the Wallis population from freemen to the upper nobility. It will be remem-bered that the Raetian debt list of 1325 (Chapter II, p. 100) could be broken down into only two groups--

witnesses and non-witnesses--and presented similar
difficulties.

The Wallis sources reveal a mixture of German,
Romance, and Christian cultural groups similar to that
found in Raetia. The ten most popular names show that
Biblical names were more widespread in Wallis than in
Raetia at this time, but that German names were still
in the majority:

Willel/ermus	16%	Aymo	5%
Petrus[3]	15%	Rodulphus	5%
Johannes	11%	Waltherus	5%
Jacobus	6%	(H)Enricus	4%
Anselmus	5%	Ul(d)ricus	3%

Although 58% of the men in Wallis bore German
names, fully 32% shared the Biblical Petrus, Johannes,
and Jacobus. This leaves only 10% of the male population, most of whom bore other Christian names (Nicolaus,
Matheus, Michael, etc.). A few pre-Christian Romance
names (Maior, Gilio, Sequinus, Aldis, Romanus, Graci-
anus) show that some onomastic remnants of the native
culture managed to survive the Germanization of Wallis,
but these names account for less than two percent of
the entire name inventory.

Women's names in Wallis confirm the onomastic
tradition found in Raetian documents: Of 98 women
only 19 bore German names. Most popular were:

Agnes	13[18]	Margareta	9
Beatrix	10	Matelda	5
Salomea	9	Agatha	5

These women's names are at once standardized and
varied. Nearly one-fourth of the women are named
either Agnes or Beatrix, but for 98 persons there
exists an astounding total of 42 names, only ten of
which are German. Romance tradition is much more evident among women than among men: Salina, Odilia,
Alasia, Felisia, Antonia, and other Romance names account for 13% of the female onomasticon. It would
probably be incorrect to see in these Romance names
onomastic remains of the pre-German culture of Wallis;
most, if not all, doubtless reflect the widespread
fashion of choosing unusual forms for women, partly
from foreign sources (Ysabel, Bonjoi), and show that
the choice of women's names was generally not based on
the need for dynastic repetition.

Who are these people mentioned in the Gremaud
collection? It must be remembered that historical and
onomastic sources (field names) show that Wallis, which
had escaped intensive colonization by the Romans, eventually became so densely populated by German speakers
that in the early 1200's some were forced to find new
lands to the south and east. Because the names listed
above are taken from documents written in towns to the

east of the German-French language border, they should
include a minimum number of Romance speakers. It is
nevertheless impossible to determine the precise percentage of German speakers here.

A comparison of these names with those of Romance
speakers in Valais shows that definite differences
existed between the onomastica of the two cultural
groups. Zimmerli's study of the German-French language
border in Switzerland lists hundreds of personal names
from fourteenth century Sitten/Sion in Romance-speaking
Valais (SW 18ff.). An analysis of 592 names from
Valais shows that only 104, or 17%, are of German origin. The ten most popular men's names in Valais during
the 1300's were:

Johannes (Johannodus) 21%

Petrus (Perrodus,   19%
Perr(on)etus, Per-
rerius, Perrusodus)

Willermus (Willer-   10%
modus, Willelmus,
Guilliermodus, Guil-
liermus, Guillielmus)

Jacobus (Jacodus,   4%
Jaquetus, Jaquemetus)

Martinus   4%

Antonius   3%

Aymo(nodus)   2%

Franciscus   2%

Nicholaus   1%

Uldricus   1%

It is immediately apparent that Christian names were much more popular in Romance-speaking Valais than in the German area to the east. Fully 58% of men's names in Wallis are of German origin, compared with only 17% in Valais. Six out of the ten favorite names in Wallis and only three of ten in Valais are German. The Wallis sources show that <u>Petrus</u> and <u>Johannes</u> were as popular there as in the rest of Europe, and it is certainly no surprise that they occupy first and second place in Valais as well. The appearance of the other Christian names (<u>Martinus</u>, <u>Antonius</u>, <u>Franciscus</u>, <u>Jacobus</u>, <u>Nicholaus</u>) in Valais and their relative lack of popularity in Wallis (where only <u>Jacobus</u> is represented in significant numbers) indicate that the area of the lower Rhone valley, which had been thoroughly Romanized, was more receptive to the new Christian naming traditions than was German-speaking Wallis, which for the most part maintained allegiance to the German onomastico

Some of the difference may be accounted for by the discrepancy between the periods compared: 1200-1280 for Wallis and 1300-1400 for Valais. Yet a decade-by-decade examination of the Valais figures shows that the German names which appear there during the fourteenth century are as well represented in 1391-1400 as in 1301-1310. Similarly, the percentage of Christian names used in Wallis does not increase appreciably

from the early 1200's to the end of the 1270's. This
suggests that the comparison of the two periods is
indeed valid and that the results would not be significantly different if the Wallis names from 1200-
1280 were compared with Valais names from the same
century.[4]

A naming tradition has now tentatively been established for the original home of the Walser. The
descendants of the Alemanni who entered Wallis from
the east (Grimsel Pass) and west (Gemmi or Lötschen
Pass) brought with them a solid Germanic name vocabulary and seem to have retained their onomastic tradition in spite of their contact with the Romance
speakers who occupied the fertile floor of the Rhone
valley. Bearing largely German names, they settled
for a short time in the Italian Piedmont and within a
generation or two began pushing eastward toward the
two secondary settlements of Rheinwald and Davos in
Graubünden.

b) Pomat and Bosco-Gurin

The first step east toward present-day Graubünden
took the Walser into the upper Val Formazza (Pomat),
which they colonized thoroughly by the middle of the
thirteenth century (Meyer AW 208f.). From here many

moved on to Bosco-Gurin, which was settled in the
early 1240's (Tomamichel <u>BG</u> 19 and 86). No early
records are available from the Val Formazza, but a
document from 11 May 1253 proclaiming the consecration of the church in "Bosco Quarino" mentions "ser
<u>Honricus</u> filius condam ser <u>Petri</u> Bruchardi consul et
ante comunis et loci de Buscho (Bosco)" as well as
the following "infrascripti homines et vicini et habitatores de Buscho" (Meyer <u>AW</u> 287ff.):

> <u>Anricus</u> et <u>Petrus</u> fratres dicti Honrici
> <u>Gualterus</u> et <u>Guilielmus</u> fratres
> <u>Anselmus</u> et <u>Philipus</u> fratres filii condam ser
> Bruchardi
> <u>Giroldus</u> filius <u>Philipi</u>
> <u>Petrus</u> eius frater
> <u>Petrus</u> filius <u>Conradii</u>
> <u>Conradinus</u> filius condam <u>Anrici</u> di Tirono (Tirano)
> <u>Guido</u> de Casso (Gäschen in the lower Val Formazza)
> <u>Petrus</u> filius <u>Guidonis</u> de Faedo Plano (Foppiano)
> <u>Gualterus</u> de Faedo Plano
> <u>Homodeus</u> de Pichinzollo (Piganzollo near Foppiano)
> <u>Anricus</u> Brunca

Witnesses to the church consecration were:

> <u>Johannes</u> dominus presbiterus ecllesie (sic)
> sancti Johannis de Ceuio
> dominus <u>Massio</u> de Duno filius condam domini
> <u>Raynerii</u> de Duno de Scona (Ascona)
> <u>Petrus</u> filius condam <u>Martini</u> Pescatoris de Scona
> <u>Martinus</u> filius <u>Inghelfredus</u> de Scona

notarius <u>Guercius</u> de Lodino (Lodano)
<u>Bonfantus</u> notarius de Scona filius condam
<u>Marchexii</u> Zanelli

These short lists are obviously too incomplete to
justify a comparison of the Christian and German name
elements present. Nevertheless, important facts about
the population of Bosco-Gurin can be deduced from other
information.

The church in Bosco-Gurin was affiliated with that
of Ceuio (Cevio), the largest village in the Valle Maggia, and the witnesses to the consecration were all
Italians from the southern end of the valley (Ascona,
Lodano). But these were not the only Romance speakers
present: Five of the last six names included among the
"habitatores de Buscho" are not those of Walser, for
their bearers are identified as being from Tirono,
Casso, Faedo Plano, and Pichinzollo. It is uncertain
from this document where <u>Anricus</u> Brunca is from, but a
Rheinwald document from 1274 lists an <u>Anricus</u> Bruxe de
Formaza. The "de Formaza" suggests that he was a Walser,
although this is open to doubt.

The last six men, all but one of whom are clearly
Italians, seem to have been consciously grouped together by the Italian scribe, <u>Bonfantus</u> notarius de
Scona, perhaps as an indication that they formed a cultural unit apart from those first mentioned. It is

significant that no place of origin is given for the
first several men, all of whom were probably Walser.

The most important member of the community, ser
Petrus Bruchardi consul, is honored by the title _ser_
(< _senior_) as well as by the addition of the patro-
nymicum _Bruchardi_ 'son of Burchard.' It is doubtful
that he was known among his fellow citizens by his
surname, which was probably added by the scribe to
emphasize his social prominence. _Ser Petrus_ may be
a Walser or an Italian. The fact that no place of
origin (such as Faedo Plano or de Tirono) is given for
him speaks for the former; the latter is also plausible:
Meyer (_AW_ 213 note 24) shows that even at this early
date the alpine valleys of Italy were at least as
heavily populated, or overpopulated, as was Wallis,
and a small Italian population, with _ser Petrus_ as its
leader, may well have been settled in Bosco-Gurin
before the appearance of the Walser.

These considerations suggest that if all the men
listed were indeed "vicini et habitatores de Buscho,"
the Walser who came to Bosco-Gurin from the Val Formazza did not live together in an isolated community,
but came into close contact with Romance speakers. In
view of the overpopulation of even the most remote
alpine valleys of Italy, this was probably the case in
nearly every one of the Italian Walser settlements.

The precise degree of contact with Romance speakers here is, of course, impossible to determine. The Romance culture of Bosco-Gurin was eventually assimilated by the Walser; today the village is the only German-speaking settlement in the canton of Ticino. It is important to know how the brief contact with Romance speakers in Bosco-Gurin affected the naming traditions of those Walser who did not stay there for more than a generation or two, but pushed on to the Rheinwald soon after the church in Bosco-Gurin was consecrated in 1253. Because of the few sources available from this period, however, it will have to suffice to say that contact could well have taken place, but that the degree of influence of the one culture on the other for the short time involved is simply inestimable.

Contact with the Italian colonies was by no means severed with the founding of the Rheinwald settlement in the 1260's. The Walser in Graubünden flourished to such a degree that part of their later population must have been attracted eastward from the Val Formazza and Bosco-Gurin and even from Wallis itself. Elements of Romance culture were undoubtedly brought by later settlers from the alpine valleys of Italy, but again any concrete estimate of their nature would be hypothetical at this point in view of the source material available.

c) The Rheinwald

The oldest document mentioning Walser in Graubünden dates from 24 July 1274 and names "Jacobus et
Ubertus fratres filios (sic) condam Petri de Riale
de Formaza," who swear allegiance to Freiherr Albert
von Sax in the presence of, among others, "Redulfus
filius condam Anrici de Guldo de Formaza and Gualterius
filius Anrici Bruxe de Formaza, qui habitat in valle
Reni" (Meyer WR 39f.). This evidence of the connection of the inner Rheinwald settlement with the Italian colonies is supported by the Rheinwald Erblehensvertrag of 1286 (Meyer AW 289ff.), which also clearly
shows that some Walser came to the Rheinwald directly
from Wallis. In this document the church in Misox,
with the permission of Henricus de Sacho (Sax), gives
land in fief to the following men:

> ser Jacobus de Cresta tunc castaldus vallis
> Rheni filius quondam ser Petri de Rialle
>
> Petrus Bisarnus f.q. Hanrici de Sempiono
>
> Julius de Cardegio frater superscripti ser
> Jacobi de Cresta
>
> Magninus de Uallmadia f.q. Delaydi de Lanfrancho
> de Vallmadia
>
> Giroldus f.q. Henrici dell' Molino
>
> Giulius et generaliter fratres filii q.
> Gualter de Sempiono
>
> Laurentius f.q. Petri de Ponte de Cadansa
>
> Petrus f.q. Gualter de Cadansa
>
> Anricus f.q. Jorii della Casta

Nicolla et Jacominus fratres filii dicti Anrici

Giulius f.q. Broncardi de Briga

Johannes de Pretorogio f.q. Johannis Valix[5]

Anrigetus f.q. Petri de Cadansa

Ubertinus et Jacominus fratres f.q. Petri de Cadansa de Formaza

Guido f.q. Henrici de Cadansa

Lambertinus f.q. Martini de Morascho de Formaza

Johannes et Gualter fratres filii q. Gualter Longi

According to this document of 1286, the small Walser colony which is attested in 1274 grew suddenly by some twenty members,[6] fourteen of whom clearly came either from Wallis (Brig and Simpeln), the upper Val Formazza (Cadansa, Rialle, Morasco), or the Maggiatal. In a later document from 1301 (Mohr CD II, 310) Symon de Sacho, the son of Albert von Sax-Misox, gives land in fief to the Rheinwald colonists, who are represented by Gualterinus de Sempiono (Simpeln), Johannes de Piliana, and Rossinus de Formaza (Val Formaza).

*   *   *

It will be useful here to call to mind the conditions faced by the first settlers in the Rheinwald and to estimate the extent to which the valley had already been colonized by Romance speakers before the Walser came.

In 1538 Tschudi marvelled at the German speakers,

> Rhinwalder genannt / noch hüt by tag
> gůt heyter tütsch redend . ͤ . . sy sit-
> zend in obersten wildenen hȯhinen / zů
> grosser notdurfft die ban vnd strassen /
> steg vnd weg / so etwa durch schnee vnnd
> sunst verwůstend / zů erhalten. (AR 90)

The field names from the Rheinwald reveal that
the inner valley, now comprising the communities of
Hinterrhein and Nufenen, was at one time largely a
forested area (BUB I, 181ff.). Historical sources indicate that there was also pasture area there, which
was probably used by farmers from the outer valley
(today Medels, Splügen, and Sufers) as well as by
herdsmen from the Val Mesocco to the south of the
San Bernardino Pass. Lorez (BR 7) reckons that some
20% of the field names in Hinterrhein are of Romance
origin, showing that the inner valley was well known to
a Romance population which had grazing lands and perhaps even a small permanent settlement there (cf. also
Lorez WO 292).

Freiherr Albert von Sax intended for the Walser
whom he settled in the inner valley to clear much of
the forested land there and to secure it from the
Freiherren von Vaz, who controlled Schams and the outer
valley (Kreis DW 131). The inhabitants of the more
arable outer valley were Romance speakers, whose

allegiance to the Vaz family probably isolated them
politically from the inner valley for some time. Although the settlers in the inner valley controlled
access to the San Bernardino Pass, the Romance population could trade with northern Italy over the Splügen Pass and could thus further maintain their independence in the valley. Yet the outer valley eventually became Germanized by the expanding Walser.
Legal records and tax lists from the late 1500's show
almost exclusively German family names (Issler GR 42f.
note), but some names (e.g. Tuschgan and Zoya in the
1580's) either managed to retain their native form or
showed that the population of the valley was contin-
ually supplemented by the immigration of Romance speakers
from the south. The family Schorsch, for example, came
from Gravadonna on Lake Como in Italy (Issler GR 63
note) and became one of the most powerful and prolific
families in the valley. In considering the Walser
colonization of the inner Rheinwald one must therefore
keep in mind the distinct probability of contact with
Romance speakers there.

*   *   *

Contact with the Romance population began even as
the colony in the inner valley was being founded. Meyer,
Issler, and others point to the Erblehensvertrag of

1286 as evidence that the settlers came from Wallis
or from other Walser colonies; yet they make nothing
of the fact that no definite home can be found for six
of the 23 men:

> Giroldus filius quondam Henrici dell' Molino
> Anricus f.q. Jorii della Casta
> Nicolla et Jacominus fratres filii dicti Anrici
> Johannes et Gualter fratres filii q. Gualter
> Longi

The possibility that these men might be Italian
seems never to have been considered. The probability
that they were indeed Italian is suggested by the appearance of so many names from the Italian Piedmont,
where the Walser had settled for a time among Romance
speakers (cf. above, p. 118f.). Even Meyer (AW 207
note 14) concedes that Magninus de Uallmadia is not a
Walser, but a Lombard from the Valle Maggia.

The Rheinwald document from 1301 presents similar
important evidence which seems to have been overlooked.
Three men are mentioned: Gualterinus de Sempiono,
Rossinus de Formaza, and Johannes de Piliana. The
first is clearly from Simpeln in Wallis. The second
may or may not be a Walser; he does come from the secondary Walser colony in the Val Formazza, but his first
name--Rossinus--does not appear once among the 559
Gremaud names from thirteenth century Wallis.[7] The

home of the third, Johannes de Piliana, is "nicht
bestimmbar" according to Meyer. The field or place
name Piliana is known neither in Wallis nor in the
well-researched Walser settlements in Italy. Because
it is not to be found in "Walser" territory, it seems
most sensible to locate it near one of the Italian
Walser colonies. Wherever Piliana is or was, it can
reasonably be assumed that Johannes was not a Walser.

The three documents in question here are the
first records of one of the oldest Walser settlements
in Graubünden and date from 1274, 1286, and 1301. Of
the 26 men mentioned, five come from Wallis and thirteen are from the Val Formazza; seven are uncertain
(Johannes de Piliana, etc.) and one is Italian (Magninus de Uallmadia).

This group of five Walser, thirteen men from the
Val Formazza (where contact with the Italian population
was practically inevitable), one Italian, and seven men
of undetermined origin (also the Val Formazza?) formed
in the inner valley what Issler calls "rein deutsche
Dörfer" (GR 21). An indication that they were not as
"pure" as scholars have assumed is found in the group
of three men whom the entire community chose as representatives (sindici: CD II, 239) in the negotiations
with Albert von Sax-Misox in 1301: one man from Wallis
(Gualterinus de Sempione) and two whose cultural

backgrounds are unclear (Rossinus de Formaza and Johannes de Piliana).

The colony in the Rheinwald was composed almost entirely of German speakers. If one assumes that every colonist from the Val Formazza was a German speaker, there were then few men in the Rheinwald who could not be called "Walser." But an undetermined degree of contact with Romance speakers must be assumed, not only among those who settled in the Val Formazza, but also among the men whose immediate origins are unclear. At least one Romance speaker settled in the Rheinwald (Magninus de Uallmadia), and there may well have been others (Johannes de Pretorogio, Johannes de Piliana, Rossinus de Formaza?).

The distressing lack of further documents from the Rheinwald makes a study of early name-giving there impossible: Only seven other pre-Reformation documents exist from the entire valley, and the oldest of these is from 1472 (Gemeindearchiv Splügen no. 1).[8] One may suppose that the weak Romance minority among the Rheinwald settlers was soon assimilated by the Walser, but that any distinct Romance onomastic tradition which survived the cultural mixture was supported by later contact with the Romance population of the outer valley. It is, however, equally plausible that no distinct aspect of the minority culture in the inner valley

survived the rapid Walser expansion, and that even
the name-giving traditions of the Romance speakers in
Medels, Splügen, and Sufers became Germanized with
the language change in these undocumented early centuries.

Soon after the inner Rheinwald was settled,
daughter colonies were established in the Valsertal
and the Safiental immediately to the north. No name
lists or other useful documentary material have been
preserved from Vals or Safien from the pre-Reformation
period with the exception of the two land registers of
the cloister Cazis (1495 and 1502). Because field
names in Safien indicate that a sizeable Romance population existed there before the Walser immigrated in
the fourteenth century (BUB I, 101-105), these registers
are treated below in conjunction with other documents
from culturally mixed areas.

The only impression of Walser name-giving which
can be gained from pre-Reformation documents in Graubünden is provided by material from the other chief
Walser settlement of Davos, from its daughter colony
in Langwies, and from Tavetsch, the oldest Walser town
in the Oberland.

d) <u>Davos</u>

Walser are first mentioned in Davos in 1289,
when Graf Hugo von Werdenberg and his nephews Johannes,
Donat, and Walther von Vaz give to "<u>Wilhelm</u> dem ammen
und sinen gesellen und iren rechten erben . . . daz
gůt ze Tavaus ze rechtem lehen" (Branger <u>RW</u> 161). It
is generally assumed that there were thirteen <u>gesellen</u>
with Wilhelm because a document written soon afterward
states that "Des gůtes in Tafaus sint 14 tail" (Wartmann <u>RU</u> 469; Branger <u>RW</u> 27). The home of the early
Davos Walser is clearly stated in a document from the
cloister St. Luzi in Chur from 1300: "illi de Wallis
. . . in Tafaus" (<u>CD</u> II, 165). From the first document it is evident that Walther V von Vaz (died 1284),
the father of Johannes, Donat, and Walther, had caused
the Walser to settle in Davos. It is possible that
some of the first men in Davos had fought under Walther
V in northern Italy and were now being rewarded for
their services. The Vaz family stood to gain from this
settlement, for the Walser in Davos paid taxes,[9] protected their new homeland, and were in a position to
transport goods across the Strela, Flüela, and Scaletta
passes.

Walther V von Vaz may well have recruited his
colonists directly from lower Wallis, where the Vaz

were related to the Freiherren von Raron (Schmid-
Gartmann ED 3; Gadmer DW 8). The route of their
journey to Graubünden is unknown. No evidence has
been found to date to suggest that they paused for a
short time in intermediate colonies, as did the Rheinwald settlers in the Val Formazza and Bosco-Gurin. If
they were indeed recruited from Wallis, one could assume that they came directly to Davos with no significant contact with Romance speakers underway.[10]

The document of 1289 is not the first mention of
Davos, nor were the Walser the first to colonize the
area. Juvalt's Necrologium Curiense (27) lists a
pratum Tauaus between 1160 and 1180, perhaps a pasture
used by Romance speakers from another area. Tauauns
ualle is mentioned in 1213 as property belonging to
the cloister in Churwalden (CD I, 365).

Whether the existence of these two early records
of Davos proves that the valley was once lightly settled by Romance speakers (Liver WG 264) remains open
to question. It is true that Romance field names there
are found even at the highest elevations (Strela, Par-
senn), showing that the valley was well known to the
native population; but it is likely that this population lived in one of the lower valleys nearby, perhaps
near present-day Klosters, Filisur, or even in the
Unterengadin. Schorta (DR 222ff.) shows that most
field names in Davos merely describe the topography

and that only a few point to the existence of a former
settlement there (Pravigau < pratum vicanum 'village
meadow'). Clavadel (< *clavadiegl 'hay barn') shows
that hay was harvested in the valley, and it may be
that Romance speakers from nearby used the lower
regions as Maiensässe[11] and the higher elevations as
summer pastureland (Senn GH 276).

Davos and its daughter colony Langwies were among
the most sparsely settled areas in Graubünden: Only
four to five percent of the field names of Davos have
Romance derivations, for most of the land-clearing and
colonizing was carried out by the Walser. An investigation of names from Davos should thus tell much about
the degree to which the naming traditions observed in
Wallis were preserved after the Walser settled in
Graubünden.

Unfortunately, early records containing names
from Davos are scarce. Sprecher's Davoser Chronik of
1573 (322, 336) mentions tax lists from as early as
1293, but these have been lost, perhaps in the fire
which destroyed the town archives in 1559. The Erblehensvertrag of 1289 which mentions Wilhelm de(r)
ammen is followed by a document from 1300 (CD II, 165),
in which the cloister St. Luci in Chur gives land in
Schanfigg in fief to "Walthero de Wallis dicto Röttiner
et Johanne de Wallis dicto Aier et ipsorum uxoribus

seu infantibus." Among the witnesses to the document
are <u>Citerli</u> de Tafaus and <u>Petrus</u> Anderwise, undoubtedly
two of the <u>gesellen</u> mentioned in 1289. Only occasional
mention is made of the Walser in Davos for the next
century and a half. Perhaps merely by coincidence,
records become more numerous after the founding of the
<u>Zehngerichtenbund</u> in 1436 (cf. Chapter I, note 46).
Some 21 documents now in the Davos archives yield information about name-giving there between this time and
the Reformation, which was accepted in Davos in the
late 1520's. In addition, the names of all Davos <u>Land-
ammänner</u> from 1289 to 1643 are listed in Sprecher's
<u>Davoser Chronik</u>, and six Davos names are mentioned in
the tax records of the cloister St. Nicolai in Chur in
1515. Most important, however, is the Davos <u>Spendbuch</u>
of 1562, which contains the names of some 350 landowners from the mountain community (Jecklin <u>DS</u>).

The pre-Reformation documents in the Davos archives and the St. Nicolai records list 95 men, only
eight of whom have German names. The nineteen women
bear eleven names, all of which are Christian. All of
the most popular names are Christian:

<u>Hans</u> (Hansy,	28[18]	<u>Jakob</u>	7
Cleinhans,		<u>Paul</u>	5
Grosshans,			
Hannsmann)		<u>Caspar</u>	4
<u>Marti</u>	8	<u>Jörg</u>	4
<u>Cristan</u>	7	<u>Peter</u>	4

Sprecher's list of Davos Landammänner shows similar results. Of the 32 men named after Wilhelm de(r)
ammen and before the Reformation, only four have German
names: Ulrich Beeli (1426), Heinz Niggen (1451), Wilhelm Beeli (1487), and Ulrich Beeli (1524). Family
names of other Landammänner show that German names
once may have been more popular in Davos: Jakob Hug
(1472), Hans Heintz, genambt Jung Schuoler (1498),
Hans Rüedi (1517).

The most accurate accounting of pre-Reformation
name-giving can be made from the Davos Spendbuch of
1562. This list was written 34 years after the Reformation was accepted in Davos and contains the names of
all men and women who owned land at the time. Among
these people are few who were not named before 1528:
Since men normally did not become landowners until
they took over their fathers' farms, it can be expected that nearly everyone mentioned is more than 34
years old and was therefore named before the Reformation came to Davos in 1528.[12] Among 351 men the
most popular names are:

Hans[13] (Hännsly, Häni, Kleinhannsy, Junghans, Johann, Geross Hans, Knabenhans)	20%
Cristen/-an	8%
Peter	6%

Jöri/-ig	5%
Marti	5%
Claus	3%
Casper	3%
Jacob	3%
Üli/-rich	3%
Thöny	3%

German names account for only 28 of the 351 men (8%), and not one of the women. Only the German Üli/ Ülrich can claim any popularity, but still accounts for less than 3% of the population. By contrast, one-third of the men are named either Hans (20%), Cristen/ Cristan (8%), or Peter (6%). It is apparent from family names that the German onomasticon was once more popular in Davos. Of approximately 150 family names, fully 68 are derived from first names, and 18 of these (Cüntz, Hug, Rüdi, etc.) are German.

All of the 71 non-German names in Davos are Christian, including Old Testament (Aberham, Michel), New Testament (Bertschy < Bartholomeus, Enderly < Andreas), neo-Latin (Thicht < Benedictus, Cristen, Hitz < Christianus), and other holy names (Joder < Theodor, Ambrys < Ambrosius). Among the ten most popular names listed above, three (all saints) come from the New Testament (Hans, Peter, Jacob), and five are those of other saints (Jöri < Georg, Marti, Claus < Nicolaus, Ulrich,[14] Thöny < Antonius). Casper is one of the three kings from the Orient in Biblical legend. <u>Christian</u> was already popular in Raetia in the early Middle Ages (cf. Chapter II, p. 61).

The addition of names from Langwies provides a broader statistical base for comparing these Walser names with the onomasticon of communities in Romance-speaking areas and in the German-speaking Rhine Valley.

e) <u>Langwies</u>

High above the Plessur River at the head of the Schanfigg valley lies Langwies, attested already in 998 as <u>in prato longo</u> (Zinsli <u>WV</u> 326). A small number of Romance field names shows that Langwies, like the nearby valleys Sapün and Fondei, was known to Romance speakers, who may once have transported goods over the Strela Pass to the Davos valley, a three hour walk to the east. Although outer Schanfigg was densely popu-lated even in 1084,[15] the small number of Romance field names in Langwies shows that there was probably no permanent Romance colony there until the Walser from Davos colonized the area about 1300.

The inner valley, including present-day Arosa, Fondei, and Sapün as well as Langwies, offered the Walser the same prospects for colonization as they had enjoyed in Davos: The Freiherren von Vaz owned "daz

tal daz man nempt Schanuigge" as well as Davos (GA
St. Peter no. 1; CD III, 77) and were undoubtedly
pleased to see the formerly unsettled land colonized
by Walser who paid taxes, defended their new property,
and maintained active communication and trade relations with the mother colony in Davos.[16]

Walser are first mentioned in Langwies in the
document cited above (p. 130) in which the cloister
St. Luzi gives land in Schanfigg in fief to "Walthero
de Wallis dicto Röttiner et Johanne de Wallis dicto
Aier et ipsorum uxoribus seu infantibus" (CD II, 165).
The presence of a witness named Petrus Anderwise indicates that at least one Walser already lived in
Langwies when the document was written in 1300. Thus
it is safe to assume that initial Walser colonization
in Schanfigg had already begun before the turn of the
fourteenth century.

A document from 23 April 1384 proclaiming the
founding of a church in Langwies shows that Arosa and
the side valleys Sapün and Fondei had been more extensively settled than Langwies, where apparently only one
man owned property:

> Ich Hannss mattlis säligen sun an der
> Langen wisen genant pregenzer Kund mit disem
> brief allen dien, die in sehent oder hörent
> lesen und veriich offenlichen. Als wir die
> undertaun und die erberen lüt in Sapünne in

> vendên und in Arâsen gemainlich ain
> capelle got ze lob vnd siner hailigen
> mu̇ter ünser frowen sant marien ze eren
> styften und buwen wellent . . . .
> (GA Langwies no. 4)

The apparent absence of a permanent Walser community in Langwies and the presence of settlements in
the side valleys and Arosa at this time have led some
scholars to believe that Langwies was originally a
Romance colony and that the Walser were discouraged
from settling there (Kreis DW 90f.). The small percentage of Romance field names and the purity of the
Walser dialect in Langwies (Hotzenköcherle BV 503),
however, indicate that this is highly unlikely
(Poeschel KG II, 186).

Only four men--the two settlers "de Wàllis,"
Petrus Anderwise, and Hannss mattlis sàligen sun"--
are mentioned in the Langwies archives prior to 1400.
In 1454 an argument arises between "Hans Niggen sun"
and Haintz Bregentzer "von der langen wisen,"[17] and
the following judges are called upon to hear the case:
Ꝋlrich Belin von Tavaus (Davos) ain obmann, . . . Jos
Grestan von pretegew (Prättigau), haintz flurẏ von
closter (Klosters), Martin niggen sun uff Tafaus und
hans martin von den Schmitten." A Martin Maisser is
also named, but his home is not indicated (GA Langwies
no. 16). Other persons mentioned in the Langwies

archives before 1500 are:

(1475) <u>Christoff</u> Aggtha ab thafass (no. 21)

(1481) <u>Syman</u> (,) <u>Jössl</u>ÿ brunoltz salliger
elliicher sun (no. 34)

(1490) <u>Elsa</u> (,) <u>Hansen</u> maissers selgen von
sappün genant <u>hesthy</u> eliche husfrow;
(her son) <u>petter</u>; (and) <u>petter</u> schmid
der amman an der langen wiss (no. 36).

Other sources yield names of additional Walser
in inner Schanfigg. The tax book of the St. Nicolai
cloister mentions "des schniders gůt, den man nempt
'Hansenson'" in Langwies in 1427 (p. 65), and records
of the Churwalden cloister list the following men from
Arosa in 1515:

<u>Peter</u> Held	<u>Schnider</u> Russ
<u>Peter</u> Schmid	<u>Cristan</u> Held
<u>Uolrich</u> Held	<u>Peterli</u> Metgär
<u>Gaudentz</u> Nitt	<u>Cristan</u> Goldschmid
<u>Hans</u> Schüchter	<u>Töntz</u> Schmid
<u>Schmid</u> Brügger	<u>Thöni</u> Metgär
<u>Töntz</u> Hannsen	

Fortunately, a complete accounting of the Langwies
population in the late pre-Reformation period may be
found in the <u>Jahrzeitbuch</u> from Langwies (Jecklin <u>JK</u>),
which dates from about 1488-1500. Forty-four, or 22%,
of the men bear German names; as in Davos, no women
have German names. Most popular among 203 men in
Langwies are:

Hans (Henni, Hensli, Henno, Hans Jacob, Johannes, Clein Hans)	24%
Heini (Heintz (man), Heinrich)	9%
Jos/Jösli/Jost	7%
Marti(n)	6%
Peter	6%
Jacob (Jägli)	4%
Ulrich	4%
Casper	4%
Symon	4%
Christen	4%

and among 86 women:

Elsa/Elsi	23%
(Mar)Gretta	21%
Anna	17%
Urschla	8%
Cristina	6%
(Ce)Cilia	5%

f) Conclusion

Is there such a thing as a "Walser name?" In order to answer this question the evidence presented above is condensed in the following lists, which include the most popular names found in Wallis (1200-1280), Davos (1289-ca. 1530), and Langwies (1300-1500):

Wallis (461 men)		Davos (480 men)	
Willermus	16%	Hans	20%
Petrus	15%	Cristen	7%
Johannes	11%	Marti	7%
Jacobus	6%	Peter	5%
Anselmus	5%	Jörig	5%
Aymo	5%	Jakob	4%
Rodulphus	5%	Caspar	3%
Waltherus	5%	Ulrich	3%
Henricus	4%	Paul	3%
Uldricus	3%	Claus	2%
Nicholaus	2%	Thöny	2%
Conrad	2%	Symon	2%

Langwies (235 men)	
Hans	24%
Heini	9%
Jos	8%
Peter	8%
Martin	6%
Christen	4%
Symon	4%
Ulrich	4%
Töntz	4%
Casper	3%
Jacob	3%
Claus	3%

Wallis (98 women)		Davos (65 women)	
Agnes	13[18]	Anna	16
Beatrix	10	Urschla	8
Margareta	9	Elsi/-a	6
Salomea	9	Barbla	5
Agatha	5	Doritte	5
Matelda	5	Fida	5
		Margaretta	5

Langwies (89 women)	
Elsa	22
Gretta	18
Anna	15
Urschla	7
Cristina	6
Cilia	5

The most striking feature of these lists is the fundamental difference between the onomasticon of Wallis and that of Davos and Langwies. Fifty-eight percent of the men in Wallis bore German names, compared with eight percent in Davos and twenty percent in Langwies. Willermus, the second most popular name in Wallis, appears only four times--as Wilhel(le)m and Willi-- among 715 men in the Graubünden colonies. Aymo has disappeared entirely in Davos-Langwies, as have Anselm and Rudolf. Walther appears 21 times in Wallis and only twice in Langwies.

Hans is by far the most popular name in Davos (20%) and Langwies (24%), but enjoys only modest popularity

(as <u>Johannes</u>) in Wallis (11%). <u>Cristen</u>, <u>Martin</u>,
<u>Georg</u>, <u>Caspar</u>, <u>Claus</u>, and <u>Thŏny</u> are virtually unknown
in Wallis. In spite of the standardization of name-
giving in Davos (Langwies), where one man in five
(four) is named <u>Hans</u>, the principle of general repetition seems to enjoy uniform popularity in all three
areas: The first three names in Wallis are borne by
39%, in Davos 37%, and in Langwies 39% of the male
population.

Most indicative of the difference between the
Graubünden colonies and Wallis are the women's names.
<u>Margareta</u> is the only popular Wallis name which is
also popular in Davos and Langwies. <u>Beatrix</u> and <u>Matelda</u>
do not appear in Davos-Langwies, and the Wallis <u>Salome</u>,
<u>Agatha</u>, and <u>Nesa</u> (< <u>Agnes</u>) are found only seven times
among the women there.

If the Davos and Langwies names are to be compared
with an onomasticon from western Switzerland, they are
closer to that of French-speaking Valais than to that
of German-speaking Wallis (cf. above, p. 114):

<u>Valais</u> (1300-1400) (592 men)		<u>Davos-Langwies</u> (1289-1530) (715 men)	
<u>Johannes</u>	22%	<u>Hans</u>	22%
<u>Petrus</u>	19%	<u>Peter</u>	6%
<u>Willermus</u>	10%	<u>Cristen</u>	6%
<u>Jacobus</u>	4%	<u>Marti</u>	6%
<u>Martinus</u>	4%	<u>Jakob</u>	4%

Antonius	3%	Jörig	3%
Aymo	2%	Caspar	3%
Uldricus	2%	Heintz	3%
Franciscus	2%	Ulrich	3%
Nicholaus	1%	Jos	3%
Rodulphus	1%	Symon	3%
Cristinus	1%	Thöny	3%

Seven of the favorite names of Valais appear in Graubünden as well, with Johannes/Hans in first place in both cases. Willermus, Aymo, and Franciscus (total 14%) in Valais are replaced by Cristen, Jörig, Caspar, and Heintz (15%) in Davos and Langwies.

Is there such a thing as a "Walser name?" If so, it seems to exist at different times in different places. The Walser who came to Davos and later to Langwies may have brought with them what amounted to a Wallis onomasticon; unfortunately, early records are too scarce to confirm this. Neither first names nor family names in the available early documents suggest that there was a majority of German names--the most striking onomastic feature of thirteenth-century Wallis-- among the first few generations of Davos and Langwies Walser. If the early Davos tax lists mentioned by Sprecher's Davoser Chronik had not been lost, Professor Zinsli's supposition that "Walser names" existed (above, p. 109) might be proven correct for the Davos Walser.

The comparisons between names from Wallis and from the Graubünden colonies are inherently inaccurate to some degree because of the time difference involved. Thirteenth century Wallis is not fifteenth or sixteenth century Graubünden. It should be remembered, however, that the Wallis sources were investigated to see whether a tradition could be established which might have been brought to Graubünden; for this reason a comparison of later Wallis sources would not have been fruitful.

The comparisons made above between names from Wallis and Valais, Wallis and Graubünden, and Valais and Graubünden show that the presence or absence of German and Christian names was one fundamental criterion by which these onomastica could be judged. The material from Davos and Langwies clearly shows that these Walser settlements readily accepted the Christian name vocabulary and suggests that other criteria might be used to judge differences in name-giving between Walser and Romance communities in Graubünden.

For purposes of later comparison the pre-Reformation Davos-Langwies names are listed here in the order of their popularity:

g) List One: Davos-Langwies Names

MEN (718):

1. Hans (Hansy, Hännsly, Häni,   158 (22%)
   Henno, Junghans, Knabenhans,
   Clainhanns(y), Hannsmann,
   Gross Hans, Hans Jakob)

2. Peter   45 (6%)

3. Cristen/-an   44 (6%)

    Marti   44 (6%)

5. Jacob (Jagg, Jägli)   28 (4%)

6. Jöry/-ig (Georyus, Georg)   26 (3%)

7. Casper   25 (3%)

    Heini/Heintz (Heinrich,   25 (3%)
   Heintzman)

9. Üli (Ulrich, Ütz)   24 (3%)

10. Jos (Jost, Jösch, Jössly)   22 (3%)

11. Symon   20 (3%)

    Thöny/Töntz   20 (3%)

13. Claus   19 (3%)

14. Mattli (Mathig, Matgen,   16 (2%)
    Mattyo) / Thewus (Diss,
    Thisly)

15. Paul (Pauli)   15 (2%)

16. Nigg (Niggli)   11 (2%)

17. Conrat (Conradin)   10 (1%)

18. Bertschy (Bartholome,   9 (1%)
    Bartly, Bärtly)

    Steffen   9 (1%)

20. Michel   8 (1%)

    Thomen/-an   8 (1%)

22. Andris (Enderli)   7 (1%)

    Bernet/Berenhart (Bern,   7 (1%)
   Bernli)

    Lorentz   7 (1%)

25.	Berchtold	6
	Flury/-in	6
	Vallentin	6
28.	Luci	5
	Os(ch)walt	5
	Stoffel	5
	Thichtus (Benedicht, Dicht)	5
32.	Gallus	4
	Janett (Jan, Johanett)	4
	Wilhel(le)m (Willi)	4
35.	Bastian	3
	Blesly	3
	Erhart (Ernen)	3
	Fydt (Vitt)	3
	Gaudentz	3
	Jochim	3
	Lienhart	3
	Marck/Merckli/Merigeli	3
43.	Aberham	2
	Balthisar/Baulluser	2
	Dauit	2
	Fridly	2
	Gilius/Kilian	2
	Jeronimus/Jorimyus	2
	Johannes	2
	Melckert	2
	Walther	2

52. (one each) Aderyan, Ambrys, Denys, Gilg,
Gorius, Hitz, Joder, Kindschi, Köly, Liepert,
Lius, Loni, Lucas, Niklaus, Rysch, Schmid,
Schnider, Urban, Vestly.

WOMEN (156):

1.	Anna	31 (20%)
2.	Elsa/Elsi	28 (18%)

3. Gretta/Margaretta   23 (14%)
4. Urs(ch)la/-y   15 (10%)
5. Cristina   8 (5%)
6. Barbla/Barbara   7 (4%)
   Cilia   7 (4%)
   Doritte/Dorle/Dorothe   7 (4%)
9. Ag(a)tha   4 (3%)
   Meretta/Emerita   4 (3%)
11. Frena/Fröna   3 (2%)
12. Brida   2 (1%)
    Clara   2 (1%)
    Dena/Denno   2 (1%)
    Drina   2 (1%)
    Fida   2 (1%)
    Nesa   2 (1%)
18. (one each) Ida, Lena, Luna, Madlena,
    Rosyna, Sallame, Velicita.

II. Romance Names

Name-giving in Romance communities not influenced
by the Walser colonization can be observed in seven
sources dating from 1358 to 1560. Because the Walser
were by then well established in Graubünden, Romance
areas were selected in the Bündner Oberland and the
Engadin in which the Walser did not settle and which
are still Romance today:[19]

In the Oberland:

Ruschein: Jahrzeitbuch from 1358; fragment of
          a 15th century tax list;

<u>Disentis</u>: List of <u>Landammänner</u> from 1377
        to 1560;

<u>Pleif</u> (Lugnez): <u>Jahrzeitbuch</u> from 1443ff.;

<u>Tamins</u>: <u>Jahrzeitbuch</u> from ca. 1475-1500;

<u>Luvis</u>: Luviser <u>Anniversar</u> from 1548;

In the Unterengadin:

<u>Tschlin</u>, <u>Ramosch</u>, <u>Sins</u>, <u>Scuol</u>, <u>Ftan</u>: List of
farmers in the fourteenth century;

<u>Marienberg</u>: List of farmers in 1353 and 1392.

In addition, the tax registers of the Churwalden
and St. Nicolai cloisters (1513 and 1515) yield information from Domleschg and the Oberland. A list of the
<u>Ammänner</u> and <u>Schreiber</u> from Bravuogn as well as some
material from the cloister tax registers gives an impression of Romance name-giving in the Albula Valley.

a) <u>The Bündner Oberland</u>

The only significant Walser settlements in the
Romance Bündner Oberland are Obersaxen, Versam, and
Valendas. The Vals and Safien valleys, colonies of
the Rheinwald group, are geographically cut off from
the Romance Oberland; the Walser there never became
so populous that their presence threatened the Romance
stronghold which extended from Domat/Ems west to the
Oberalp Pass. Field names in Tavetsch and Medels, at
the head of the Vorderrheintal, show that Walser once

settled there on their way east from Wallis over the
Furka and Oberalp passes to Obersaxen and beyond.
Yet Tavetsch and Medels, like the isolated settle-
ment of Fidaz above Flims, became Romanized.[20]

   The Jahrzeitbuch of Ruschein from 1358 (Castelmur JR) contains the names of 67 men and 32 women;
these names are supplemented by a fragment of a fifteenth century tax list containing nineteen names.
The names of 1358 are given in both "official" Latin
and popular forms: Johannes, Jacobus, and Martinus,
but Magelda (< Magdalena), Haintz, and Jöri (< Georg).
Cůnradus de Vig is represented twice as Chůntzo/-un
de Vig. The later list is similarly constructed, but
gives important variants of the popular names Johannes
(Jon, Janet) and Petrus (Padrut). The 85 men and 33
women included in the two lists are represented by 33
and 20 names respectively, showing that the onomasticon had not yet become highly standardized. The most
popular name, Johannes, is borne by only 14% of the
male population. Although this lack of standardization prevents a truly valid ordering, an indication
of the most popular names is given in this list:

Johannes (Jon, Janet)	12^{18}
Martinus	7
Menisch/-ig	7

Rudolfus	6
Albert	5
Jöri	5
Jacobus	5
Petrus/Padrut	4
Ůlricus	3
Lucius	3
Simon	3

As in Davos and Langwies, the majority of names
are Christian. Menisch/-ig (< Dominicus), which may
show the influence of the Dominican monks in the Oberland, is the only one of the most popular names not
found in the Walser colonies to the east. Other names
found for the first time in Ruschein are: Lieta, Fumia,
Cultrida, Vigilius, Lunarin (< Laurentius?), Guigs
(< *wig-?), Fleize, Nugair, Folrina, Pia, Judentaus,
Galduncz (< Gaudenz), and Matzina (< Magdalena?).

Johannes had not yet become the overwhelming
favorite in the 1300's: The Jahrzeitbuch of 1358 includes only five Johannes out of 67 men. Jon and
Janet, however, account for six of nineteen men in
the fragment from the following century. Jöri also
increases in popularity, occurring only once in 1358
but four times out of nineteen in the 1400's.

German names are borne by 26 of the men (30%) and
by only two of the women. Included among them beside
the more popular Rudolfus, Albert, and Ůlricus are

such rarities as <u>Richenza</u>, <u>Lut</u> (< <u>Liutold</u>?), and
<u>Giselo</u>.

Most instructive are the family names in Ruschein, many of which are derived from place names
(<u>de Vico</u> < <u>vicus</u> 'village'; <u>Debutz</u> < <u>de puteo</u> 'from the
well'). Of those family names derived from first names,
only two of German origin are found: <u>de Lut</u> and <u>de Ca
Rigenzaus</u> 'of the house of Richencza.' Each of these
names appears only once. The paucity of German names
among family names suggests that German names, now relatively popular (<u>Rudolf</u>, <u>Albert</u>, <u>Ulrich</u>), had not been
in frequent use when family names were beginning to be
formed during the preceding century. The German onomasticon, although strong in 1358 (30%), seems to have
experienced a sudden growth of influence in Ruschein
within the preceding four of five generations.

*   *   *

The most common names among the 31 <u>Landammänner</u>
of Disentis (1377-1560) (Pradella <u>LD</u>) are <u>Johannes</u> (6),
<u>Ulrich</u>/<u>Durig</u> (5), <u>Martin</u> (4), <u>Jacob</u> (4), and <u>Badrutt</u>/
<u>Peter</u> (3).

There are indications that these Disentis names
do not represent the Romance peasants of the type encountered in Ruschein. These men are <u>Landammänner</u>,
chosen from the community elite; because the community

is Disentis, the location of the important Medieval
cloister, it is the home of numerous noble families.
The first Landammann (1377-87) is Junker Heinrich von
Pontaninga, "Vogt zu Dissentis gewesen"; he is related to Peter Pultinger, the abbot of Disentis who
played an important role in the formation of the
Grauer (Oberer) Bund in 1424 (GLS IV, 9; cf. Chapter
I, note 46), and to the later Landammann Wilhelm von
Pontaninga, "des alten Waibels von Salva plauna Sohn"
(1450). The family von Vontana, already prominent in
the Oberland in 1261 (HBLS III, 192), is also represented among the Landammänner.

For the first time double names appear: Johann
Rudolf de Vontana (1487) and Hanz Ulrich Berther (1497).
The appearance of these names recalls combinations en-
countered among the noble families investigated in
Chapter II: Heinrich Martin von Sax (1333), Ulrich
Walther von Belmont (1371), and so on. Yet even among
families of high social standing the "official" name
forms were not always used in practice. Hanz Ulrich
Berther, probably named the popular Johann Ulrich at
birth, also appears as Schuwan Ulrich in 1503. Johann
Rudolf de Vontana is simply Rudolf de Vontana in 1465.

*   *   *

The other three chief sources of names from the Oberland come from Pleif (1443ff.) and Luvis (1548), both in Lugnez, and from Tamins (1475-1500).[21]

Johannes is the most popular name here in the fifteenth and early sixteenth centuries, appearing 28 times as Jan (9), Hans (9), Gion (8, in Pleif only), and twice as Johannes. Martin (7), Heinrich (4, once as Raget), Peter (4), and Conrad (twice as Cüntz, once each as Curau and Cünraw) are also popular; Loring (< Laurentius), Cryst, Moretzy (< Mauritius), and Jacob/Giacon each appear three times. Forty names for only 106 men show the rich variation in the onomasticon, which includes the uncommon Gyll (< Aegidius or Julius), Duff (< Theophil or David), Medart (< Metardus), and Tschegn (< Egino or Vincentius).

Twenty-one out of 106 men--and no women--bear names of German origin. This figure includes the Romanized forms Durisch (< Ulrich), Reget (< Heinrich), Thiefel (< Diebold?), Gugliam (< Wilhelm), and Curau (< Conrad). Some family names preserve German forms which no longer exist as first names: Humbart, Fryschen (Friedrich), Oschwald, Waltier, Kieni (< Conrad).

*   *   *

The most popular names among the 199 men included in these five sources in the Oberland are:

Johannes (Jan, Jon, Gion, Janet, Jenny, Hans)	23%
Martinus	9%
Jacobus (Giacon)	6%
Ulricus (Durig, Durisch, Uöli)	6%
Petrus	6%
Cunradus (Cuntz, Curau, Cunraw)	4%
Menisch (Domenig)	4%
Heinrich (Haincz, Reget)	4%
Albert	3%
Jöri	3%

Not surprisingly, the Johannes complex includes the most common names during the 14th-16th centuries. Hans appears as such only ten times, and Jan, Janet, Jon, Jenny, and Gion a total of 25. Johannes, listed eleven times, could be counted in either group.

In the Romansh-speaking Oberland Romansh name forms are consistently in the minority. Giacon, the Romansh form of Jacobus, is given only one time in twelve; Durig/-isch appears three times, but Ulrich seven and Uöli once; Petrus outnumbers Padrut seven to four; Cunradus and Cuntz appear five times and Curau and Cunraw only once each; six men are named Heinrich or Haincz and only two Reget/Rigiet; Simon appears three times and Schamun and Schimunett once each.

This is not because the Romansh forms were simply
not used, but most likely because they were too often
felt to be inferior to the "official" names in public
records throughout the canton and were thus not recorded in their vulgar form. By contrast, Menisch appears six times and Domenig only once; Loring is
attested three times and Laurencius once. These two
names were popular only in Romance-speaking areas;
since their "official" form was thus not determined
by the form in use in German-speaking parts of the canton, they could appear as Menisch and Loring. These
popular forms could not be considered inferior to
their German counterparts if the names were practically
nonexistent in German-speaking areas. Jöri is never
recorded as Georgius, perhaps because it was felt that
it had reached such popularity among German and Romance populations alike that this alone gave it a
certain validity and elevated it above other popular
Romansh nicknames.

b)   The Unterengadin

The most complete collection of pre-Reformation
names from Romance communities in Graubünden comes
from the Unterengadin, to the south and east of the
Davos Walser colonies (Jecklin LL; Valèr ST). Here

there were no Walser settlements.[22] The only contact
which may have existed with the German-speaking Walser
was made possible by the Flüela Pass, the only bar-
rier to trade between the Unterengadin and--by way of
Davos and Prättigau or the Strela Pass--the Rhine
Valley to the west (cf. Senn GH 267; Poeschel KG II,
143). The Unterengadin is on approximately the same
latitude as the Bündner Oberland. The two areas are
equidistant from Italian territory: the Oberland by
way of the Lukmanier Pass south of Disentis, and the
Unterengadin by way of the Oberengadin and the Bernina
Pass. They are also equidistant from the Walser colonies in Schanfigg and Prättigau.[23]

The sources from the Unterengadin and the Albula
Valley include 512 men and 212 women. The most popular
names are:

Johannes (Hans, Hensl, Jan, Jannut, Genätt, Nütt)	25%
(Ni)Klaw(s)	14%
Jakob (Jäkl)	9%
(Do)Minig	7%
Hainrich (Heins)	6%
Egen (Egno, Egnallus)	2%
Peder (Pedrut)	2%
Matheus (Thysch, Dyslin)	2%
Kunrad (Chuoni, Conrau, Chunallus)	2%

Ulrich (Rysch)   2%

Simon   2%

German names account for 20% of the men and 3% of the women. Kunrad appears in the Romansh forms Conrau and Chunallus as well as the German Chuoni. There seems to be no specific Unterengadin Romansh equivalent for Heinrich, which is often spelled Heinreich by a Romance scribe unsure of the correct form; Heins(l) appears only twice. Ulrich, often subjected to the hypercorrection to Ulreich, is listed only once in one of its shortened forms, Rysch; Duri(g) does not appear in the Unterengadin.

*   *   *

A comparison of the names collected from Unterengadin and Oberland sources should now be made to determine the approximate composition of the native Romance onomasticon of Graubünden for the pre-Reformation period:

Oberland (199 men)		Unterengadin (512 men)	
Jan/Jon (Gion, Janet, Jenny)	13%	(Ni)Klaw(s) (Klawot)	14%
Martinus	9%	Hans (Hensl)	13%
Jacobus (Giacon, Jecklin)	7%	Jan (Genätt, Jannut, Nutt, Nott)	11%
Ulricus (Durig, Durisch, Uoli)	6%	Jakob (Jekl, Jachian)	9%

Johannes	6%	(Do)Minig	7%
Petrus (Padrut)	6%	Haínrich (Heins)	6%
Hans	5%	Egen (Egno, Egnal-	2%
Cŭnradus (Cŭntz, Cŭnraw, Curau)	4%	lus)	
		Peder (Pedrut)	2%
Menisch (Domenig)	4%	Matheus (Thysch,	2%
Heinrich (Haincz, Henricus, Reget, Rigiet)	4%	Dyslin)	
		Kunrad (Chuoni, Conrau, Chunallus)	2%
Albert	3%	Ulrích (Rysch)	2%
Jöri	3%	Simon	2%
Luci (Lucius)	3%	Michel	2%
Simon (Schamun, Schimunett)	3%	Florian	2%
		Johannes	2%
Loring (Laurencius)	2%	Caspar	1%
Cryst	2%	Luci(us)	1%
Gyll (Gielly)	2%	Jörg (Jöry)	1%
Moretzy	2%		
Wilhelmus	2%		

Perhaps most characteristic of the Romance name
vocabulary is the frequent appearance of the diminutive suffixes -allus/-ellus and -at/-et/-ot/-ut (cf.
Muoth BG 45f.): Egnallus, Chunallus (Oberland), Petronella (Unterengadin); Paudett (< Paul), Klawot
(< Claus), Thomaschutt (< Thomas) (Unterengadin),
Jannut, Pedrut (both). The latter suffix is most prevalent in variations of Johannes in the Unterengadin,
where it appears in 29 names. It became so standardized
in Janutt/Genätt that a new name, Nŭtt, was formed as
a nickname, twice removing it from the parent form

Johannes. In other areas Nutt is then treated as an independent name and is again assuffixed to Nuttin and the feminine Nuta/Nutina. By this time the original association with Johannes has been lost and two nomemes have grown from the original.

The problem with Johannes in both the Oberland and the Unterengadin is similar to that found in Davos,[13] where an entire name complex accomodates both Jan and Hensli. In the Oberland the Johannes names have been broken down into two groups: Hans and the Jan/Jon complex. Johannes could justifiably be assigned to either group, or both, and is treated separately. It is disregarded in discussion of the Hans/Jan dichotomy, but is included where the entire name group is concerned. In the Unterengadin it is wise to treat Hans and Hensl as one nomeme and Jan, Jannut, Genātt, and Nūtt as another. Hensl(i) is treated throughout the sources as a diminutive to Hans, especially where father and son are both named Hans and must be distinguished.

The two areas show distinctly different treatments of Johannes. Most apparent in the Unterengadin are the 29 names in -at/-ot/-ut: Jannut (2), Genātt (20), and Nūtt (7). Only one Janet is recorded in the Oberland. Hans/Hensl appears more frequently in the Unterengadin (13%) than in the Oberland (5%). Jan represents 5%

of the men in the Unterengadin and Jan/Jon/Gion 12%
of the Oberländer. The two groups formed are:

Oberland		Unterengadin	
Hans	10	Hans	49
Jan	9	Hensl	18
Jon	6	Jan	26
Gion	8	Nutt	7
Janet	1	Genatt	20
Jenny	1	Jannut	2
Johannes	11	Johannes	7
	46 (23%)		129 (25%)

Martinus occurs 18 times among 199 men in the
Oberland and only once among 512 in the Unterengadin
and provides a good example of church influence on
name-giving. The cult of St. Martin was brought to
Graubünden from the west over the Lukmanier Pass and
through the Oberland to Chur, where the St. Martin's
church is mentioned at the end of the eighth century
(Farner KG 63ff.).[24] The total absence of St. Martin
churches in the Unterengadin accounts for the lack of
popularity of Martinus there.

Florian is mentioned seven times in the Unterengadin, but does not appear in the Oberland. This,
too, is a case of church influence on name-giving:
Florian is the patron saint of upper Austria (LV 82)

and shows that the Unterengadin, while virtually un-
exposed to the Walser, may have been partially influenced by the naming traditions of Tirol to the
east. This might explain the popularity of Hans and
the Bavarian Hensl over the Jan/Genatt group in the
Unterengadin.

Nicolaus, attested most often as Klaws, is the
most popular name in the Unterengadin (14%), yet occurs only twice in the Oberland. This situation is
exactly the reverse of that seen in Martinus, yet the
contrast of Nicolaus' popularity in the Unterengadin
and its nearly total absence in the Oberland cannot
readily be explained by the distribution of churches
consecrated to St. Nicholaus. It is true that no St.
Nicholaus church exists in the six communities investigated in the Oberland; yet only one such church was
once found among the five towns investigated in the
Unterengadin, and it was only a small chapel in Sins
mentioned in 1341 and is no longer standing (Poeschel
KG III, 490). A St. Nicolaus monastery once existed
in the Oberengadin, but may not have been consecrated
to Nicolaus by the time the names under discussion were
recorded in the fourteenth century (Farner KG 151f.).
It would be presumptuous to believe that the presence
of three Nicolaus altars in the Marienberg cloister in
the distant Puschlav (Farner KG 153) had any effect on

name-giving in the Unterengadin, even though they were
consecrated as early as 1160. Thus the appearance of
<u>Nicolaus</u> as the most popular name in the Unterengadin
remains unexplained.

Names of German origin account for 20% of the
men in the Unterengadin and 24% of those in the Oberland. This may be a reflection of the slightly greater
degree of German influence in the Oberland, especially
in the former <u>ministerium Tuverasca</u> in the Ilanz basin
(cf. Chapter II, p. 71). <u>Ulrich</u>, <u>Heinrich</u>, and <u>Konrad</u>
are slightly more popular in the Oberland (13%) than
in the Unterengadin (10%). <u>Albert</u>, represented six
times in the Oberland, occurs only once in the Unterengadin. <u>Egen</u>, appearing twice in the Oberland and
eleven times in the Unterengadin, presents a special
problem: It and its secondary forms <u>Egno</u> (2) and
<u>Egnallus</u> (3) can be derived from either German <u>Egino</u>
or <u>Eugen</u>, which is of Greek origin. The appearance of
<u>Egin(o)</u> in several other parts of Graubünden and the
absence of <u>Eugen</u> elsewhere (<u>Tschegn</u> ⟨ <u>Vincentius</u>: cf.
Muoth <u>BG</u> 40), however, make it most advisable to de-
rive <u>Egen</u> and its secondary forms from the German
<u>Egino</u>.[25]

Family names of German origin are conspicuously
rare in both Romance-speaking areas.[26] As noted above
for Ruschein (p. 150), family names are most commonly

derived from place or field names: <u>Vig</u>, <u>Muntàtsch</u>, <u>Ramoschka</u>. Of those formed from first names, only a small minority come from German first names. This may cautiously be interpreted to mean that the German names, which now accounted for 22% of the onomasticon, had not been so well known when family names were beginning to be formed during the preceding century. This is negative evidence, however; if German names were indeed rare among these families, what names stood in their place?

<u>Bartota</u> (< <u>Bartholome</u>), <u>Galitz</u> (< <u>Gallicius</u>), and <u>Frantz</u> (< <u>Franciscus</u>) appear in early sources from the Oberland. Family names in <u>Ca</u> or <u>de Ca</u> '(from) the house of' are especially popular there: <u>Katieschin</u> (< <u>Ca Mathias</u>/<u>Theodosius</u>), <u>de Ca Bertolomei</u>, <u>de Ca Fluri</u>, <u>de Ca Margaretas</u>, <u>de Ca Simon</u>, <u>de Ca Cristoffoli</u>, <u>de Ca Ambriesch</u> (< <u>Ambrosius</u>). In the Unterengadin <u>Copoldi</u> (< <u>Ca Paul</u>) is the only family name of this type. Other family names of non-German origin are <u>Pederus</u>, <u>Monigun</u> (< <u>Monica</u> < <u>Dominica</u>), <u>Matheo</u>/<u>Mathesen</u>/<u>Mathie</u>, <u>Ann</u>, <u>Nesa</u> (< <u>Agnes</u>), <u>Michel</u>, <u>Luci</u>, and <u>Mertan</u> (< <u>Emerita</u>).

Family names were just beginning to be formed at this time. A substantial proportion of those in use were of non-German origin and suggest that at the time of their formation German names--such as the popular

Heinrich, Ulrich, and Konrad--had not achieved widespread popularity among the peasantry. Instead, the
names of Christian saints swiftly suppressed whatever
native Romance names had been in use[27] and were already popular by the time family names began to be
formed in the late thirteenth century.

Such widespread use of Christian names as family
names supports the conclusion reached in Chapter II
(p. 101f.): that the German onomasticon, which was used
chiefly by the nobility, did not become popular with
the peasantry before the introduction of Christian
names by the new Christian calendar and the Dominican
and Franciscan holy orders. The popularity of Menisch/
Minig (< Dominicus) in both the Oberland and the Unterengadin attests to the widespread influence of the
Dominican monks who brought the new Christian onomasticon to Romance speakers in Graubünden.[28]

*   *   *

It will now be useful to present a single list
of names from the Oberland and the Unterengadin with
which the names from Davos and Langwies and from the
towns in the Rhine Valley can be compared:

c) List Two: Romance Names

MEN (711):

1. Jan/Jon (Gion, Janet, Jenny, 80 (11%)
   Genätt, Jannut, Nutt, Nott)

2. Hans (Hensl) 77 (11%)

3. (Ni)Klau(s) (Klawot) 74 (10%)

4. Jakob (Jᵃekl, Jachian) 58 (8%)

5. Minig (Menisch, Domenig) 42 (6%)

6. Heinrich (Henricus, Heintz, 38 (5%)
   Heinsl, Reget, Rigiet)

7. Petrus (Peder, Pedrut, 22 (3%)
   Padrut)

8. Uolricus (Uᵉoli, Durig, 20 (3%)
   Durisch, Rysch)

9. Martinus 19 (3%)

10. Johannes 18 (3%)

11. Cᵒunrad (Cᵒuntz, Chᵒuni, 16 (2%)
    Curau, Conrau, Chunallus)

12. Simon (Schamun, Schimunett) 14 (2%)

13. Egen (Egno, Egino, 12 (2%)
    Egnallus)

    Matheus (Matthiu, Thysch, 12 (2%)
    Dyslin)

    Jöri (Jörg) 12 (2%)

16. Luci (Lucius) 11 (2%)

17. Michel (Misch) 9 (1%)

18. Caspar 8 (1%)

19. Kristan (Cryst) 7 (1%)

    Albert 7 (1%)

    Florian 7 (1%)

    Kristofel/-er 7 (1%)

23. Loring (Laurencius) 5

    Benedictus (Benedeg, 5
    Beneuemott)

    Moretzy (Marici) 5

    Wilhelm (Gugliam) 5

	Andrea (Andreas)	5
	Purkhart	5
	Schkor/Sker (Schkir)	5
	Bartholome	5
31.	Rudolph	4
	Stephel/-an	4
	Thomas (ch)(utt)	4
	Vallentin	4
	Linhart (Liem, Lunarin)	4
36.	Gyll (Gielly)	3
	Paul (Paudett)	3
	Judocus (Jos, Josch)	3
	Albrecht	3
	Balthasar	3
	Walfin	3
	Pernhart (Bernard)	3
43.	Duff	2
	Friedrich	2
	Oswalt/Schwald	2
	Orttwein	2
	Parcziual	2
	Philipp	2
	Theny/Thöni	2

50. (one each) Adam, Arnold, Augustin, Baldaweg,
Bonadeus, Clement, Dalrigallen, Daniel, Diet-
egen, Eger, Elias, Ezzelo, Fidéll, Flander,
Fleize, Fort, Gerold, Giargieli, Giselo, Gott,
Gregor, Guigs, Hartwin, Hercli, Herman, Joder,
Judentaus, Lut, Marcolf, Medart, Mes, Nugair,
Otto, Raphael, Rig, Schkein, Selm, Thiefel,
Tschegn, Vigilius, Vincentius, Walch, Waltier,
Wellukg, Wûdencz.

WOMEN (254):

1.	Anna	34 (13%)
2.	Mingia (Menga, Dominiga)	28 (11%)
	Nesa (Agnes)	28 (11%)
4.	Leta (Lieta)	24 (9%)
5.	Gretha (Margarita)	23 (9%)
6.	Nuta	16 (6%)
7.	Els(a) (Beta, Elisabetha)	14 (6%)
	Katheri(na)	14 (6%)
9.	Barbara	11 (4%)
10.	Nega	4 (2%)
	Burga	4 (2%)
12.	Ursl(a)	3 (1%)
	Magdalen/Matzina/Magelda	3 (1%)
14.	Antiocha	2 (1%)
	Christina	2 (1%)
	Fumia/Famea	2 (1%)
	Gwẽrd	2 (1%)
	Lucia	2 (1%)
	Otilia/Otili	2 (1%)
	Riga	2 (1%)
	Tascha	2 (1%)

22. (one each) Agatha, Angel, Anna Leta, Balonia, Berta, Breida, Columba, Conforta, Cultrida, Domina, Folrina, Frena, Frideresa, Genola, Gesa, Gisla, Iudenta, Jeconina, Jolda, Karrin, Laria, Merta, Pedrascha, Petronella, Pia, Rebotscha, Richencza, Ritscha, Santta, Schera, Sinnella, Solame.

III. Rhine Valley Names

The third major group of names to be investigated in Graubünden is taken from sources in the Rhine
Valley extending from Chur north to Buchs in the present canton of St. Gallen. The towns included between
Chur and Buchs are Haldenstein, Trimmis, Zizers, Untervaz, Igis, and Maienfeld.

The higher regions above Trimmis, Haldenstein,
and Maienfeld as well as Mastrils were tertiary Walser
colonies, settled by Walser from Prättigau. Says,
above Trimmis, was colonized from Danusa and Hintervalzeina during the 1400's (Meng TH 60) and still belongs
to the Walser dialect group of Valzeina--Furna--inner
Prättigau (Hotzenköcherle BV 490f.). Batänien, above
Haldenstein on the west bank of the Rhine, seems to
have been settled by three Walser brothers from Maienfeld in 1424 (Dalbert BM (1950), 226). Walser are
first mentioned in Mastrils in 1515 and soon are the
"Walsern ab dem Bastrilserberg" (GA Mastrils no. 5).
A sizeable number of Walser left Stürvis in Prättigau
and settled in the Bündner Herrschaft (Maienfeld,
Fläsch, Jenins, and Malans) during the 1400's.

The linguistic influence of Walser in the communities of the Rhine Valley is negligible. Trimmis shows
some traces of Walser dialect as the result of its

close ties with Says and Hintervalzeina; but the
Bündner Herrschaft and the other towns in the valley
maintained contact with Chur and had already been
heavily influenced by the Swabian dialect of German
nobles and by the east Alemannic dialect brought to
the Raetian capital from the St. Gallen valley and
from north central Switzerland.

It will be instructive at this point to recall
briefly the progress of Germanization in the Rhine
Valley (cf. Chapter I, p. 12ff.). Contact with a thin
stratum of German speakers began in the ninth century
and quickly intensified as Germans assumed control of
the secular and religious leadership of Raetia. The
towns in the Rhine Valley were closely associated with
the political center of Chur and maintained contact
with other nearby Romance-speaking areas as well.
Germanization thus took place over a strong Romance
base and proceeded in similar fashion in all the
Rhine Valley communities. The German superstratum
imposed on the Romance population resulted in a unique
sort of bilingualism by the 1300's: German names and
documents show that the use of German was widespread
among the nobility, but place names clearly indicate
that Romansh was the popular language (Meinherz MBH
221f.).

Within the next two hundred years the Germanization of the Rhine Valley was nearly completed. Romansh was the mother tongue of a large minority in
Chur until a fire in 1464 nearly destroyed the entire
city. After the fire a large number of German speakers
from the upper Rhine Valley helped to rebuild Chur, and
their heavy influx hastened the Germanization.[29]
Romansh was used by only a weak minority in Chur and
the Rhine Valley after the Reformation.[30]

An impression of pre-Reformation name-giving in
the Rhine Valley may be gained from sources from the
following communities:

> Chur: 1292-1515
> Buchs: 1484
> Maienfeld: 1346-1524
> Zizers, Trimmis, Igis, Untervaz: 1448-1515
> Haldenstein: 1503

a) Chur

Tax records from the St. Nicolai cloister show
that Christian names came into the majority in Chur
during the 1300's. Not surprisingly, Johannes is the
first Christian name listed and belongs to a chaplain
of the cloister in 1292. Other early names are Symon
and Gaudentius (1292-1293). A Paratin Hartung appears
in 1293, suggesting that some native Romance tradition

survived at this time, but the German <u>Hartung</u> throws
some doubt on his nationality. The German names which
appear after the mid-1300's occasionally belong to the
nobility (<u>Burkard</u> von Schauwenstain (1399), <u>Eglolf</u> de
la Porta (1446)), but are borne by peasants as well:
<u>Bürkelin</u> Snider (1350), <u>Kůntz</u> ze Scheid (1399), <u>Berch-
told</u> Keller (1406).

Pre-Reformation sources from Chur[31] show the following distribution of first names among 614 men from
all segments of the population:

<u>Hans</u> (Hensly, Johannes, Langhans, Jung Hans, Klainhans, Frischhanns, Schwartz Hanns, Yttel- hans, Hans Jakob)	28%
<u>Uolrich</u> (Uoliman)	7%
<u>Jörg/Jőry</u>	5%
<u>Hainrich</u> (Hainy)	4%
<u>Claus</u> (Niclas)	4%
<u>Peter</u>	4%
<u>Caspar</u>	3%
<u>Jos</u>	3%
<u>Crista(n)</u>	3%
<u>Cůnrat</u>	3%

German names account for 26% of the 614 men listed
in Chur from ca. 1360 to 1515. This proportion is more
than offset by the appearance of <u>Hans</u> and its variations among 28% of the men. <u>Uolrich</u>, <u>Hainrich</u>, and
<u>Cůnrat</u>, once the most popular names, together make up

only 13% of the onomasticon. Most striking is the
small number of the typical "Romance" names: <u>Jann(li)</u>
appears only twice and <u>(Do)Menig</u>/<u>Mang</u> only six times
among 614 men.

b) <u>Buchs and Maienfeld</u>

A list of church members in Buchs from 1484
(Senn <u>UB</u>) shows that fully 44% of the population bore
German names. Most popular were <u>Heinrich</u>/<u>Heintz</u>, <u>Vol-
rich</u>, <u>Burckhart</u>, <u>Oswalt</u>, and <u>Ludwig</u>; <u>Conrat</u> does not
appear. If the eighty names from Buchs are indeed
representative of the onomasticon of the Rhine Valley
north of Maienfeld, a substantial difference in name-
giving seems to have existed between the two areas.
The Bündner Herrschaft, as Meinherz notes (<u>MBH</u> 9),
forms a geographic and linguistic unit separate from
the Rhine Valley to the north or the south. Yet it
has always maintained close relations with the Chur
valley in the south and today forms the northernmost
boundary of the canton of Graubünden. The names from
Buchs are valuable in that they confirm a distinct
tradition for the towns in the Rhine Valley of Graubünden. Because the names are so different from those
of the Bündner Herrschaft, however, they are not included among those gathered from the Maienfeld sources.

One of the oldest documents in the Maienfeld
archives (1364) mentions <u>Eberhart</u> ab der Röben, <u>Eber-
hart</u>, <u>Dyethelm</u> Zwenmans sel. Sohn ab der Röben, and
<u>Johans</u> and <u>Claus</u> genannt die Kobler (GA Maienfeld
no. 2) and indicates the approximate ratio of German
to Christian names there in the fourteenth century.
The ratio soon changed drastically: German names
lost popularity and accounted for 37% of the men listed between 1346 and 1474. <u>Hans</u> alone more than
outnumbered the German names, appearing among 43% of
the men.

Other sources[32] show that the most popular names
in Maienfeld among 640 men from 1346 to 1524 were:

<u>Hans</u> (Hens(l)i, Henni, Klein Hans, Gross Hans)	25%
<u>Hainrich</u>/<u>Haintz</u> (Haintzman)	6%
<u>Uolrich</u>	6%
<u>Peter</u>	5%
<u>Jörg</u> (Jöry)	4%
<u>(Ni)ch(o)laus</u>	4%
<u>Johannes</u>	4%
<u>Jacob</u>	3%
<u>Wernher</u>/<u>Werli</u> (Warnier)	2%
<u>Friedrich</u> (Frick)	2%
<u>Jos</u> (Joseph)	2%
<u>Cristen</u>	2%
<u>Andres</u> (Andli, Enderli)	2%
<u>Rüedi</u> (Rudolf, Ruetschi)	2%

Jann	2%
C^{o}unrat (Cuni, C^{o}untz(lin), Curat	2%
Lienhart	2%

As in Chur, the three German names <u>Uolrich</u>, <u>Hainrich</u>, and <u>C^{o}unrat</u> are borne by only 13% of the men; yet the presence of many other German names-- <u>Werner</u>, <u>Friedrich</u>, <u>Ru^{e}edi</u>, <u>Lienhart</u>--among the most popular betrays the greater proportion of German names in the Herrschaft, which account for 34% of the male onomasticon.

The entire <u>Johannes</u> complex (including both <u>Hans</u> and <u>Jann</u>) accounts for 30% of the men. <u>Jann</u> appears only eleven times and <u>Hans</u> 160.

The name <u>Mann</u> appears seven times in Maienfeld and seems to have its origin in <u>Amandus</u>, to whom one of the local churches is consecrated. The derivation from <u>Amandus</u> is supported by the appearance of the more complete form <u>Mannas</u> twice and of <u>Amandus</u> once in 1524. The St. Amandus church in Maienfeld is the only one of that name in Graubünden (Farner <u>KG</u> 97f.), and it is tempting to suppose that other attestations of <u>Mann(as)</u> in the canton might be assigned somehow to an origin in the Bündner Herrschaft.[33]

The <u>Jahrzeitbuch</u> from Maienfeld names fifteen Walser who came from Stürvis in Prättigau and settled

in the Herrschaft: <u>Jono</u> usser Stürvis, <u>Hensi</u> Midegger
. . . Walser (. . . die Walser uss Stürffis), <u>Lienhart</u>
Walser (later <u>Hans</u> Egers sáligen sun), <u>Egen</u> von Stür-
fiss, <u>Gerdrut</u> (his wife), <u>Wilhelm</u> (father), <u>Nesa</u>
(mother), <u>Fluri</u> (brother), <u>Hans</u> Lutzi ab Stürfis,
<u>Jäckli</u> Walser, <u>Else</u> (his wife), <u>Ursel</u> and <u>Anna</u> (his
daughters), <u>Henni</u> Jún von Stürfis, and <u>Wilhelm</u> von
Stürfis. These names are counted among those from
Prättigau below.

c) The Fünf Dörfer

In 1803 Haldenstein joined the association of the
<u>Vier Dörfer</u>, which included Zizers, Trimmis, Igis, and
Untervaz (<u>HBLS</u> III, 354). The five villages at that
time formed a judicial district including the territory between the Bündner Herrschaft and Chur/Masans.
Sources from these five Rhine Valley towns[34] reveal as
the most popular names among 156 men:

<u>Hans</u> (Hensly, Henni, Jung Hans, Hanseman)	29%
<u>Uolrich</u>	8%
<u>Jann</u> (Ganett, Nutt, Nutkli)	5%
<u>Claus</u>	5%
<u>Andres</u>	4%
<u>Gerion</u>	3%
<u>Haincz</u> (Hainrich)	3%
<u>Jacob</u> (Jacklin)	3%

Lucy	3%
Jörig	3%
Jos(eph)	3%
Peter	3%
Burkart	2%

The appearance of Gerion is another example of church influence on name-giving. The cult of St. Gereon found its way to Raetia from Germany, where it was especially popular in Cologne (Farner KG 59). The Gereon church in Haldenstein is the only one of that name in Graubünden, and the name Gerion appears only in Haldenstein and Trimmis in pre-Reformation sources. This is fortunate for an investigation of name-giving, because the shortened popular form could easily be confused with nicknames for Georg, Julius, Aegidius (cf. above, p. 152) and Hieronymus, which appears in Haldenstein as Geronimus.

Jann and its variations appear eight times among the 156 men in Haldenstein; it is much more popular here than in Chur, where only two out of 614 men are named Jann(li), or in the Herrschaft, where Jann appears eleven times among 640 men. Most interesting is the form Nutkli, probably written by a Romance speaker who contaminated the diminutive of Nutt (< Jan-utt) with the Romansh shift of -tl- to -cl- as in Hercules, Hartwig > Hertli or Hercli (cf. note 25). Ganett and

<u>Nutt</u>, which appear in the Fünf Dörfer, are not attested
in the Herrschaft or in Chur.

d) Conclusion

The Rhine Valley names show that Germanization in
and around Chur was somewhat more complete than in the
Oberland and the Unterengadin. The proportion of German names in the Fünf Dörfer (25%) is essentially
equal to that in Chur (26%). This proportion increases
to 34% in the Bündner Herrschaft and to 44% in Buchs.
Family names yield similar results. The <u>Jahrzeitbuch</u>
from Maienfeld lists 66 people with German family
names (<u>Cŭntz</u>, <u>Sifrid</u>, <u>Fricken</u>, etc.) and only 35 with
names of Christian origin (<u>Michel</u>, <u>Fluri</u>, <u>Verena</u>, etc.).
In Chur and the Fünf Dörfer German names were still in
the majority, but by only 56 to 40.

The Germanization of the valley from Maienfeld to
Buchs antedated that of the area immediately around
Chur by one to two hundred years. To the north the
German onomasticon could come into general use before
the Christian names attained their full popularity; as
a result a substantial proportion of German names survived the change to names of Christian origin. Because
the Christian onomasticon is to a large degree indebted
to the native Romance name vocabulary (cf. Tello's will)

and because German names did not become popular as quickly in Chur as to the north, the proportion of German names in the Raetian capital is relatively small.

The following compilation of Rhine Valley names may now be compared with those of the Walser and Romance areas investigated to determine what names are typical of each region. This comparison is then followed by an accounting of the contact zones throughout Graubünden.

e) List Three: Rhine Valley Names

MEN (1438):

1. Hans (Hennsly, Henni, Klein   400 (28%)
   Hans, Jung Hans, Yttelhans,
   Frisch Hans, Lang Hans,
   Schwartz Hanns, Gross Hans,
   Hanseman, Hans Jacob)
2. Uolrich (Uoliman)   91 (6%)
3. Hainrich/Haintz (Hainy,   69 (5%)
   Haintzman)
4. Peter   56 (4%)
5. Jörg/Jöry   55 (4%)
6. Claus (Nicholaus)   53 (4%)
7. Jacob (Jäcklin)   38 (3%)
8. Jos (Joseph)   32 (2%)
9. Crista(n)   31 (2%)
10. Cůnrat (Concz, Cůni,   30 (2%)
    Cůntzlin, Curat)
11. Andres (Andli, Enderli)   29 (2%)
12. Luci   27 (2%)

13. <u>Caspar</u>/-<u>er</u>   25 (2%)
14. <u>Johannes</u>   23 (2%)
    <u>Lienhart</u>   23 (2%)
16. <u>Jann</u> (Jannli, Ganett,   21 (1%)
    Nutt, Nuttkli)
    <u>Marti(n)</u>   21 (1%)
    <u>Rudolf</u>/<u>Rüedi</u> (Rüetschi)   21 (1%)
19. <u>Friedrich</u> (Frytsch, Fridli)   19 (1%)
20. <u>Wernher</u>/<u>Wer(n)li</u>   17 (1%)
    <u>Wilhelm</u>   17 (1%)
22. <u>Burkhart</u> (Burk, Bürkli)   16
23. <u>Stoffel</u>   15
24. <u>Steffan</u>   14
25. <u>Thöni</u>   13
    <u>Matheus</u> (This(ch),   13
    Diss, Mattli)
    <u>Bernhart</u>   13
    <u>Bartlome</u> (Bartle, Batt)   13
29. <u>Simon</u> (Schymun)   12
30. <u>Gaudentz</u> (Dens)   11
    <u>Michel</u>   11
    <u>Os(ch)walt</u>   11
33. <u>Mann</u> (Mannas, Amandus)   10
    <u>Sebastian</u> (Bastion, Baschon) 10
35. <u>Aeberli(n)</u> (Eberhard)   8
36. <u>Laurentz</u> (Lentz)   7
    <u>Philipp</u>   7
    <u>Sifrid</u>   7
    <u>Walther</u>/<u>Wälti</u>   7
40. <u>Hartwig</u>/<u>Hertli</u>   6
    (Do)<u>Menig</u> (Mang)   6
42. <u>Fluri</u>/<u>Florin</u>   5
    <u>Gallus</u>   5
    <u>Gerion</u>   5

	Hug(o)	5
	Sigmund	5
	Thoma(s)	5
48.	Albert (-ütsch)	4
	Berchtolt	4
	Dietrich	4
	Gebhart	4
	Herman	4
53.	Balthasar	3
	Eglolf/Egli	3
	Joachim	3
	Ott(o)	3
	Valentin	3
	Wolf (-gang)	3

59. (two each) Adam, Albrecht, Alexius, Anselm, Blasius, Felix, Fölcki/-n, Fridolin, Gabriel, Gregorius/Gorius, Juualt, Ludwig, Marcus, Markwart, Mauritzius/Morici, Melchior, Mentz, Othmar, Risch, Victor

79. (one each) Auberly, Biett, Brasart, Diethelm, Diettägen, Egen, Franciscus, Geronimus, Hemmi, Hilary, Hiltprant, Jarde, Karli, Meruly, Pauli, Ruprecht, Samuel, Schnider, Schuler, Symprecht, Urbaly, Walchaman, Zypertus.

WOMEN (307):

1.	Anna(ly)	77 (25%)
2.	Marg(a)reth(a)/Greta	52 (17%)
3.	Else (Elsbetha, Elly, Eliza)	51 (17%)
4.	Ursula	30 (10%)
5.	Nesa (Agnes)	16 (5%)
6.	Barbara (Barbelly)	7 (2%)
	Frena/Verena	7 (2%)

8.	Adelhait (Adla)	6 (2%)
9.	Catherina	5 (2%)
	Clara	5 (2%)
11.	Dorothea	4 (1%)
	Walpurgen/-a	4 (1%)
13.	Ag(a)tha	3 (1%)
	Lucya/Zya/Ciga	3 (1%)
	Magdalena	3 (1%)
16.	Anastasia	2
	Ceda	2
	Emerite/Emera	2
	Engla	2
	Fida	2
	Gerdrut	2
	Lucina	2
	Menga	2

24. (one each) Andly, Bina, Cecilia, Cordula, Cristina, Gúta, Hedi, Jocenta, Juliana, Kungund, Malya, Mechthild, Metzina, Otilia, Perpetua, Salome, Via, Wirat.

IV. Onomastic Contact in Graubünden

On the basis of the name lists from the Romance communities in the Oberland and the Unterengadin, from the Walser settlements in Davos and Langwies, and from the towns in the Rhine Valley it would now be possible to compile a rough pre-Reformation onomasticon for Graubünden. As has been seen, the names which make up this onomasticon differ markedly in popularity within the boundaries of each area as well as from one area

to another. Those used most often in the Unterengadin
do not always correspond to the favorites in the Oberland; Chur and Maienfeld show somewhat separate traditions; Davos and Langwies, in spite of their similar
cultural histories, also show onomastic differences.
Yet historically each of these three groups forms a
separate cultural unit.

If every pre-Reformation document from Graubünden
could be examined for first names, a detailed onomastic
map of the canton could be drawn from which the most
popular names in each cultural region could clearly
be read. Martin in the Oberland would contrast with
Claus in the Unterengadin, Gerion would appear in a
small area around Haldenstein, and so on.[35] Of special
interest for this study would be the zones of contact
between the name regions: If a Romance naming tradition and a Walser naming tradition can be established,
what are the onomastic consequences of cultural contact
between the two groups? Is it possible to establish a
meeting of two cultures by examining their name-giving
traditions before and after the contact? The preceding
chapter indicates that this is indeed possible in the
case of the contact between German and Christian name
vocabularies. The meeting of Romance and Walser--and
Rhine Valley--cultures will be more difficult to establish, however, since all three show similar Christian

onomastica. The distinctive features of all name
groups must now be examined to determine just how they
differ one from another. When these differences have
been established the question of onomastic contact
can be more fully investigated in the naming traditions
of Prättigau and Tavetsch.

a) Comparison of Walser, Romance,
and Rhine Valley Names

Here the question "What is a Walser name?" can be
taken up again and answered more satisfactorily, for a
basis of comparison with other names in Graubünden is
now available.

The most puzzling characteristic of the Davos-
Langwies onomasticon is the dearth of names of German
origin. Only 13% of the men from Davos and Langwies
bear German names, proportionately only half as many
as in Romance communities (22%) or the Rhine Valley
(29%). This is exactly the opposite of what one
might expect, for the Walser in Graubünden have their
onomastic roots in Wallis, where 58% of the men between
1200 and 1280 bore German names. Romance speakers, on
the other hand, bore Romance names far into the Middle
Ages (cf. the Lüen names from 1084) and acquired their
German names relatively late. In fact, the German

influence came so late in some Romance areas that
Christian names seem to have directly encountered and
suppressed the native name vocabulary before German
names could gain a foothold.

The differences within the Davos-Langwies group
are also confusing. Why do only 9% of the Davos Walser bear German names when 20% of those in Langwies
and 58% of those in Wallis have them? An answer to
this question is offered below following an investigation of other Walser colonies in Graubünden. If
both Langwies and Davos are treated as one cultural
unit, the small percentage of German names is certainly one of the chief characteristics of its onomasticon. The proportions of individual names,
compared with those of the Romance areas and the
Rhine Valley, show other "Walser" peculiarities.

Nigg(o) and Bertsch(y), nicknames for Nicolaus
and Bartholome or Berthold, appear only in Davos and
Langwies. Marti, which was extremely popular in the
Oberland (9%) but attested only once in the Unterengadin, is borne by 6% of the Davos men. Only 1% of the
men in the Rhine Valley is named Martin. Cristan
accounts for 6% of the Walser names and is far more
popular in Davos and Langwies than in the Romance (1%)
or Rhine Valley (2%) areas. Thöny and Paul enjoy
moderate popularity in Davos-Langwies, but are rare

in non-Walser areas.

The women's onomasticon in Davos and Langwies
does not include a single name of German origin, confirming the relative lack of German forms among men's
names there. German names account for 4% of the Romance and 5% of the Rhine Valley women. Cristina (5%)
and (E)Meretta (3%) are popular in Walser areas, but
appear only occasionally elsewhere. Dorothe (4%) and
Fida (3%) are not attested in the Oberland or the
Unterengadin.

The Rhine Valley onomasticon is characterized by
a high percentage of German names (29%), ranging from
25% in the Fünf Dörfer to 34% in Maienfeld. Of the
non-German names, the Johannes complex appears here
more often (31%) than in Romance (25%) or Walser (23%)
areas. Ulrich is attested twice as frequently in the
Rhine Valley (6%) as in the other areas (3%). Benedictus does not appear in the Rhine Valley, but is
represented by several variations elsewhere: Benedeg,
Beneuemott, Thichtus, Dicht.

Barbara (2%) does not appear as often in the Rhine
Valley as in the Walser or Romance regions (4% each);
Adelhait (Adla) is not attested in either of the latter
areas.

The Johannes names are divided equally between the
two nomemes Jan and Hans (11% each) in Romance areas.

Jan accounts for only 1% of the names elsewhere, where
Hans is the common nickname.[36]   Clau is the second
most popular name among Romance speakers (after the
Johannes names), but appears less frequently in Davos-
Langwies (3%) and the Rhine Valley (4%), where it is
always written Claus.   Jacob is twice as popular in
the Oberland and the Unterengadin (8%) as elsewhere
(Rhine Valley 3%, Davos-Langwies 4%).   Minig, appearing
in fifth place and accounting for 6% of the Romance
men, is not attested in Walser areas in any form and
is borne by only six ($\frac{1}{2}$%) in the Rhine Valley in the
form Menig/Mang.   The German Egen appears among 2% of
the Romance men, but is attested only once in the
Rhine Valley and not at all in Davos-Langwies.
Schkor/Sker (< Sigisher) is used only in the Oberland
and in the Unterengadin.   Jos (< Joseph, Jodocus) enjoys medium popularity in Davos-Langwies (tenth place)
and the Rhine Valley (eighth place), but appears only
three times among 711 Romance men.   The suffix -mann
is absent in Romance areas.

Most characteristic of the Romance names is the
diminutive suffix -att/-ett/-ott/-utt, which produced
five different diminutives of Jan (but never of Hans)
as well as Beneuemott, Klawot, Pedrut, Paudett, Reget/
Rigiet, and Thomaschutt from Benedictus, Claus, Peder,
Paul, Heinrich, and Thomas.   The suffix appears only

rarely in the Rhine Valley and in Davos, and there
only as a diminutive of <u>Jan</u>. Other characteristic
Romance formations are <u>Cla</u>/<u>Clau</u>, <u>Jachian</u> (< <u>Jacob</u>),
c^ounrau, <u>Schamun</u> (also attested once as <u>Schymun</u> in the
Fünf Dörfer), <u>Loring</u> (< <u>Laurentius</u>), <u>Andrea</u>, and
<u>Gugliam</u>.[37]

Women's names in the Romance areas differ markedly from those elsewhere. Many of the most popular
names in the Unterengadin and the Oberland appear either
seldom (<u>Mingia</u>, <u>Katherina</u>) or not at all (<u>Leta</u>, <u>Nuta</u>)
in Davos-Langwies and the Rhine Valley. Other names
which are popular in the latter areas enjoy no special
favor among Romance speakers:

	Rhine Valley	Davos-Langwies	Romance
<u>Anna</u>	25%	20%	13%
<u>Gretha</u>/<u>Margarita</u>	17%	14%	9%
<u>Elsa</u>/<u>Elisabetha</u>	17%	18%	6%
<u>Ursula</u>	10%	10%	1%

The distribution of Romance women's names is also
somewhat unusual. The three most popular names in the
Rhine Valley account for 59% of the onomasticon, and
in Davos-Langwies for 52%; only 35% of the Romance
women answer to one of the three most popular names.

b) Church Influence on Name-giving

What is the reason for these different naming
traditions? Do they exist as truly Walser, Rhine
Valley and Romance cultural phenomena, or does the
popularity of a name depend merely on the name of the
saint(s) to whom the local church is consecrated? If
the latter is true, the distribution of Christian names,
although they are largely of Romance stock, is in a
sense a supracultural matter which involves the suppression of some locally popular names by more or less
randomly chosen elements of the Christian name vocabulary.[38]

In three cases the influence of the church on name-
giving has already been made clear: The popularity of
Martin in the Oberland, Amandus in Maienfeld, and Gerion
in Haldenstein corresponds to the appearance of churches
dedicated to the three saints in those areas. Yet the
St. Martin's church does not appear to stand in the same
relationship to Marti (2%) in Chur, where twelve names
are more popular; and five of these twelve names--
Caspar, Cristan, Cunrat, Hainrich, Jos--are not represented by any church in Chur. Martin is popular in
Davos and Langwies, yet has no church there.

The popularity of Clau(s) in the Unterengadin cannot be explained by the presence of any such churches

there (cf. above, p. 160f.); nor is there a Nicolaus church in the Bündner Herrschaft, where the name is quite popular. Whether the popularity of Jacob in the Unterengadin and the Oberland is to be attributed to a total of two churches in these areas is a matter of some doubt. Minig, the fifth most popular name in the Romance areas, was cautiously assumed (above, p. 149) to owe its popularity to the activity of Dominican monks there in the fourteenth and fifteenth centuries. Yet if this is so, one wonders why the presence of the Dominican St. Nicolai monastery in Chur failed to inspire greater popularity for the name in the capital of Graubünden, where it appears only six times among 614 men.

If the scarcity of Katharina in the Rhine Valley and Davos-Langwies is to be attributed to the absence of St. Katharina churches there, its popularity in Romance areas can hardly be explained by the small Katharina chapel in Zuoz in the Oberengadin (first attested in 1484) or by the chapels in Funs and Campliun/Truns in the Oberland (Farner KG 147).

Thus the presence of a given name does not necessarily presuppose that of a religious figure who may have inspired its use. The converse is also often true.[39] For example, for the one case in the Fünf Dörfer in which a holy cult seems to have directly

influenced name-giving (St. Gereon in Haldenstein),
there are at least three in which no one appears to
have been named after the patron saint of the central
church in the community: St. Thomas in Igis, St. Car-
pophorus in Trimmis, and St. Laurentius in Untervaz.
Often it is simply impossible to tell how strongly a
local patron saint may have influenced name-giving:
Johannes accounts for 22% of the men in Davos, where
there is a Johannes church (CD II, 318), but for 34%
of the men in Maienfeld, where there is not. In 1477
three altars and a new cemetery in Langwies were dedicated to no fewer than eighteen saints, among them--by
coincidence or design--the most popular names in use
at the time.[40]

It may be concluded that, with a few exceptions,
local saints did not play an important role in name-
giving, but rather that names were chosen from a supracultural group which A. Bach calls "abendländisches
Gemeingut" (DN I, 2, 18).[41] In addition to the New
Testament names (Johannes, Jacob (the apostle), Peter,
Paul, etc.) there appeared names of saints of regional
popularity: Ruprecht in Bavaria, Florian in upper
Austria, and so on.

Of special importance in Graubünden are St. Lucius
and St. Theodor. Lucius was a Scottish king who died
as a Christian missionary in Chur about 190. Yet,

although he was revered as the apostle of Raetia (HBLS III, 690), it can be seen from the name lists of the Oberland-Unterengadin, Davos-Langwies, and the Rhine Valley that his name enjoyed only limited popularity.[42]

Theodor was the first Bishop of Wallis (349-391). Although his name appears in Raetia as early as the ninth century (cf. Muoth BG 20), it seems to have gained popularity only after the Walser came to Grau-bünden. Because of the large number of Theodor/Theo-dul/Joder churches in Walser settlements (Davos (1466 sant Teiodellos; 1500 sand joder)--Langwies--Avers--Safien--Tschappina--Obersaxen), the Wallis bishop is often referred to as "der Walser-Heilige."[43] Stoffel reports, presumably without exaggeration, that the most popular men's name in Avers "was" (when?) Tetli, an unmistakable abbreviation of Theodor (DA 167).[44] Yet the three occurrences of Joder as a family name and its single attestation as a first name in the Davos Spendbuch, and its absence among 150 men in Safien in 1502, show that it is not a universally popular element of the Walser onomasticon.

Of the several other saints mentioned by Muoth (BG 21) as being popular in Raetia, only Gaudentius and Florinus seem to have had any effect on name-giving.

Thus with few exceptions all three cultures--Romance, Walser, Rhine Valley--used the same onomasticon

varying it slightly, but in characteristic ways, to
their individual tastes. If on the one hand the relics
of pre-Christian Romance (Augustus, Sylvester, Victor),
West Alemannic Walser (Willel/ermus, Aymo, Anselmus),
and East Alemannic/Swabian Rhine Valley (Otto, Bruning,
Landulf[45]) naming traditions can no longer be discerned
in the sources examined, characterizing choices have
been made on the other hand which at least preserve
the principle of local onomastic autonomy.

c)   Walser-Romance Contact in Prättigau

When the Davos Walser came to Prättigau in the
early 1300's, they encountered a Romance population
which had colonized the long valley to its uppermost
habitable elevations. Just as the Lüen document from
1084 shows that Schanfigg was once more densely settled
than it is now, so do field names indicate that the
Romance population in Prättigau was well acquainted
with even the most remote parts of its valley. The
rugged Schlappin canyon had been penetrated to the high
pastures northeast of Klosters; the few residents of
Furna and Valzeina, some 2000 feet above the valley
floor, knew and named the meadows and cliffs 1000 feet
above them; and St. Antönien boasted not only a summer
settlement (Partnun), but a church as well (Schorta PZH;

Poeschel <u>KG</u> II, 110). The valley floor, extending from Klosters to Seewis, was densely settled by Romance farmers.

Perhaps the first Romance speakers whom the Walser encountered in Prättigau were the residents of Klosters, a settlement founded by the Churwalden monastery and attested in 1222 as <u>Sancti Jacobi</u> (<u>HBLS</u> IV, 509). Denied room to settle in the valley, the Walser finally became established in a tributary canyon above Klosters in Schlappin. Farther west the Walser founded a permanent colony in St. Antönien, where the Schanielatobel cut them off from the Romance speakers in Küblis and Luzein.[46] At about the same time Walser[47] became established in Valzeina and Danusa, where they are mentioned as "die Walser ab Danusen" in 1394 (GA Jenaz no. 1). Across the valley behind Seewis they had settled on "das gut daz man nempt Stürfis da die Walliser uff sesshaft sint und by Sewis gelegen ist" (<u>CD</u> III, 75) by 1352.

It is probable that the Walser came to Prättigau at about the same time they were settling in Sapün, Fondei, and Arosa. When the Schanfigg Walser built their church in Langwies in 1384 the colonies in Schlappin, St. Antönien, Valzeina, Danusa, and Stürvis were already prospering.

The Romance population of Prättigau, although numerically superior, was now surrounded. Soon the Walser from Schlappin formed a small colony in Klosters and within four or five generations became so populous there that they managed to have one of their own number declared __Ammann__ in 1489. Walser descended from Danusa to Furna and so thoroughly Germanized it that this small community today forms one of the last strongholds of Walser dialect in Prättigau (Hotzenköcherle __BV__ 507).

The pressure of the expanding Walser became felt throughout the valley.[48] The first wave of the Black Death in 1348-50 doubtless made room for some Walser among the valley population: If the fertile land along the river was not simply surrendered by default by the decimated Romance speakers, it was gradually acquired both by marriage and by purchase.[49] By the late fifteenth century the legal privileges which the Walser had once been granted (Chapter I, p. 33) were no longer unique: If they moved into the valley they were not forced to surrender their legal advantages, as had been the case in earlier centuries. Now they only stood to gain by their move.

Unfortunately, the presence of the first Walser on the valley floor is not documented; nor are the exact details of Walser-Romance contact known. If

these matters were ever recorded, their traces probably
disappeared when the Austrians laid waste to Prättigau
in 1621. It seems probable that the eastern end of
the valley around Klosters was subjected to more intensive Germanization than was the valley interior
(Saas--Jenaz). Communication among the members of the
Zehngerichtenbund seems to have played an important
role in the Germanization: Campell reported in 1582
that the only Romansh-speaking community in inner
Prättigau was Serneus, which is removed from the main
east-west trade route in the valley (QSG VII, 339).
Dialect studies show that as Germanization by the
Walser proceeded west from Klosters, the influence
of the German-speaking Rhine Valley began to be felt
in outer Prättigau. The two German dialects met and
combined in the Schierser Becken between Schiers and
Jenaz (Hotzenköcherle BV 501).

Historians agree that the final language change
in Prättigau took place during the sixteenth century.[50]
Sererhard wrote in 1742 that in the late 1400's Romansh was the standard language:

> vom ganzen Prettigeu in genere zu bemerken:
> dass vor noch nicht gar dreihundert Jahren die
> welsche oder romanische Sprach dieser Enden
> üblich gewesen, welche aber propter vicinita-
> tem cum Germanis und besserer Commoditaet zur
> Handlung mit den Teutschen nach und nach in
> grob Deutsch verwandelt worden. (ED 200)

By Campell's time hardly a Romansh speaker could
be found in Prättigau. The Romansh historian reported
in 1582 that many people had once used Walser German
in public and Romansh in private. In Seewis and Serneus, the last villages to be Germanized, Romansh
speakers were ridiculed in the 1580's for their im-
perfect command of German--the Rhine Valley dialect in
Seewis and the Walser dialect in Serneus (QSG VII, 339).
Romansh probably died out in Prättigau by the end of
the sixteenth century.

A. Schorta (PZH) points out that German influence
in Prättigau antedated the arrival of the Walser, just
as there existed a pre-Walser ruling class of German
overlords in Schanfigg. The St. Jakob monastery in
Klosters and the Chorherrengericht in Schiers both
maintained contact with the Rhine Valley, and the Germanizing influence of both institutions was undoubtedly
supported by the presence of German-speaking noble
families (Matsch, Aspermont, Vaz, and Toggenburg; cf.
Chapter II, pp. 90ff.) in the castles which once stood
in the valley.[51]

Yet the presence of these Germanizing elements
seems to have had a negligible linguistic influence on
the Romance population. Hotzenköcherle's dialect
studies clearly show the meeting of Walser (inner Valley) and Rhine Valley (outer valley) idioms in Lunden;

no Rhine Valley influence seems to have extended from the monastery in Klosters or from the <u>Chorherrengericht</u> in Schiers. The German dialect of the inner valley (east of Lunden) shows that if the feudal nobility ever influenced the Romansh language there, the Walser dialect erased all linguistic traces of their presence.[52]

d) <u>Name-giving in Prättigau</u>

The Reformation period seems to have represented a decisive stage in the Germanization of Prättigau. At this time the valley experienced a series of dramatic cultural changes: the total acceptance of the Reformation by 1590, the assimilation of a strong wave of Walser on the valley floor, and the change of language from Romansh to German. The cultural symbiosis which was the result of the Walser-Romance and Rhine Valley-Romance contact took place on many levels.

The degree to which the Reformation influenced name-giving in Prättigau is discussed below in Chapter IV. At this point it will be appropriate to examine the pre-Reformation names of the valley for evidence of contact between the Romance population and the German speakers who surrounded it.

The earliest collection of names from Prättigau
comes from the fourteenth century.[53] Unfortunately,
it mentions only 47 men and 23 women and thus precludes a meaningful statistical curvey. Most popular
among the men are:

<u>Hans</u>/<u>Hensly</u> (Henny)	9^{18}
<u>Jan</u> (Jänny, Nutt)	6
<u>Cristan</u>	6
<u>Uollrysch</u>/<u>Risch</u>	4
<u>Petter</u>	4

The most popular women's names are <u>Ursula</u> (5), <u>Chri</u>-
<u>stina</u> (4), <u>Gretta</u> (3), <u>Anna</u> (3), and <u>Elsi</u> (2). The
appearance of <u>Cristan</u>, <u>Ursula</u>, and <u>Christina</u> among the
preferred names seems unusual for Romance Prättigau
during the 1300's (cf. the list of Romance names above,
p. 164ff.), yet the total number of names in this tax
list is too small to permit more than this superficial
comparison with other onomastica.

Later sources from Prättigau are more plentiful,
and have been divided into two groups: Klosters-Serneus[54] and Conters-Seewis.[55] Documents from the three
outermost villages in Prättigau (Seewis, Fanas, and
Schiers[56]) were at first considered separately to see
whether the onomasticon of the Rhine Valley influenced
name-giving on the periphery of the area of Walser influence. No name evidence was found in outer Prättigau

which might point to a special onomastic relationship
between this area and the Rhine Valley. The names used
in Seewis, Fanas, and Schiers were found to correspond
closely to those popular in the middle of the valley
(Conters-Jenaz), and are therefore included in the
latter group. When the Klosters-Serneus and Conters-
Seewis names have been compared they, too, will be combined to give a picture of the pre-Reformation name
vocabulary of Prättigau.

The onomastica of the inner (Klosters-Serneus) and
outer (Conters-Seewis) valley are quite similar. The
most popular names are:

Inner valley (320 men)		Outer valley (512 men)	
Hans	17%	Hans	17%
Cristan	12%	Jan	12%
Jan	11%	Jacob	8%
Jacob	5%	Cristen	6%
Petter	5%	Peter	5%
Rysch	4%	Andrea(s)	4%
Marti(n)	4%	Simon	3%
Jos(eph)	3%	Claus	3%
Jöry	3%	Jos	3%
Barth(o)lome	3%	Toni	3%
Uolrich	3%		

The most noteworthy differences between the two
groups is the relatively frequent appearance of Cristan,
Rysch, Marti(n), and Barth(o)lome in the inner valley

and <u>Andrea(s)</u> and <u>Claus</u> in the outer valley. A part
of this difference might be explained by the presence
or absence of Walser in the two basically Romance populations. The relative popularity of <u>Cristan</u> (12%) in
Klosters-Serneus, for example, may reflect a substantial concentration of Davos Walser in the inner valley.
<u>Cristen</u> is the second most popular name in Davos, yet
ranks nineteenth in Romance areas. Its position in
second place in Klosters-Serneus suggests that in this
one case the name-giving tradition of the Walser was
influential enough in the inner valley to cause a minor
restructuring of the native onomasticon.[57] (It will be
remembered that the Walser were so well represented in
Klosters by 1489 that they managed to have one of their
number appointed <u>Ammann</u> by the Austrian archduke.)

Yet for this one case in which the popularity of
one name suggests the presence of Walser in the inner
valley, there are several names whose appearances justify no such hypothesis. <u>Jacob</u> is attested among 8% of
Romance men and 4% of the Davos Walser. This seems to
have a parallel in the popularity of <u>Jacob</u> in the (more
heavily Romance?) outer valley (8%) and the inner valley, but is hardly convincing by itself. <u>Claus</u> is the
most popular name in the Unterengadin (14%), yet appears in tenth place in Davos (3%). Does its relative
popularity in outer Prättigau (3%; inner Prättigau = 1%)

indicate a similar relationship, or must it be assumed
that in this case the most popular Romance names in
Prättigau simply did not include Claus? What accounts
for the popularity of Andrea(s) in the outer valley if
it is frequently used in neither Walser (1%) nor Romance (1%) areas? Why is Risch borne by 4% of the men
in Klosters-Serneus and only 1% of those in Seewis-
Conters if there is no substantial difference in the
use of Risch or Ulrich between Romance and Walser
areas? Does the more frequent use of Marti(n) in the
inner valley point to Walser influence? (This may be
the case, since the cult of St. Martin seems to have
been confined chiefly to the area between Chur and
Disentis in the Oberland and may not have influenced
the pre-Walser onomasticon in Prättigau. Yet this, too,
is purely hypothetical.)

The comparison of inner and outer valley names
raises more questions than it answers. This may be
attributed simply to the lack of sufficient documentation of the pre-Reformation period: Only a fraction
of the material once available has survived the inter-
vening four to six hundred years, yet it must be assumed that the material available records a true cross-
section of the names which were in use during this time
of Walser-Romance contact in Prättigau. Another difficulty is presented by the size of the valley population:

In all only 1129 men and women were counted in the
available documents over a span of some two hundred
years. An effective evaluation of the names gathered
from these sources is possible only if the inner and
outer valley names are considered together and compared
with the onomastica of other parts of Graubünden. Because the population of Prättigau presents a Romance
base with the addition of Davos Walser elements, the
1129 names from Prättigau (listed below) are viewed in
connection with the 965 Romance names and 548 Davos
names investigated above.

According to the onomastic criteria already established for Davos and for Romance Graubünden, the names
in use in Prättigau confirm the cultural dichotomy which
existed in the valley between the fourteenth and sixteenth centuries. In some cases the Prättigau naming
tradition shows similarities with that of Davos; in
others the existence of a strong Romance tradition is
unmistakable.

The intermediate onomastic position of Prättigau
is best represented by the popularity of names of German
origin there. In Davos only 9% of the men bore German
names; in Romance areas this figure rose to 22%. The
Prättigau figure, 15%, stands halfway between these two
values and shows the influence of both Davos and Romance
traditions. The popularity of Heinrich (5%), Egen (2%),

and Cunrad (2%) among Romance speakers contrasts with
their relative insignificance in Davos and Prättigau.

The treatment of Johannes is also characteristic
of this double cultural allegiance. For purposes of
comparison the name was broken down above into the two
nomemes Jan and Hans. Jan was found to be especially
popular in Romance areas and to be practically nonexistent among Walser; Hans shared first place with
Jan among Romance speakers, but was by far the most
popular name in Davos-Langwies. Jan is as popular in
Prättigau (12%) as in Romance areas (11%); its absence
among Walser seems to have had no influence on its
popularity among the mixed population. On the other
hand Hans, which was already in use in Prättigau before
the Walser came (Romance = 11%), became more popular
among the Walser-Romance population (17%) because of
its use by more than one-fifth (22%) of the Davos Walser.

Other names show similar treatment in Davos and
Prättigau (Cristan, Toni, Claus, Minig) and in Prättigau
and Romance areas (Jacob, Jöri, Paul). Cristan, used
by 8% of the men in Prättigau, is also popular in Davos
(7%) but ranks nineteenth (1%) among Romance speakers.
Toni, which enjoys medium popularity in Davos and Prättigau (2%), appears only twice in Romance areas. Claus
is borne by 10% of the Romance men, but far less frequently in Davos (3%) or Prättigau (2%). Minig is

solely a Romance name (6%); it is not represented in
Davos and appears only twice in Prättigau as <u>Mynsch</u>.
Prättigau resembles Romance areas in the use of <u>Jacob</u>
(7% and 8% respectively), which is in sixth place (4%)
in Davos. J^e<u>öry</u> is more popular in Davos (5%) than in
Prättigau or among Romance speakers (2% each). <u>Paul</u>,
used by 3% of the Davos men, appears only once in
Prättigau and three times among 711 Romance men.

Isolated forms betray the presence of a Romance
onomasticon: Andre<u>a</u>, Risch<u>ott</u>, <u>Cu</u>redin, Gudien<u>tg</u> in
addition to the rich variations of <u>Jan</u> (<u>Janutt</u>, <u>Genutt</u>,
<u>Nutt</u>, <u>Nutschi</u>, <u>Nett</u>, <u>Jenni</u>). In <u>Nutschi</u> the charac-
teristic Walser genitive -<u>schi</u> has been affixed to the
Romance <u>Nutt</u>, much as B^e<u>ärtsch</u> and <u>Fritsch</u> developed in
Prättigau as popular nicknames for <u>Bartolome</u> and <u>Fried-</u>
<u>rich</u>.

Women's names yield different results.[58] <u>Anna</u>,
<u>Greta</u>, <u>Elsa</u>, <u>Cristina</u>, and <u>Ursula</u> are the most popular
names in both Davos and Prättigau. <u>Cristina</u> is more
often used in Prättigau (12%) than in Davos (5%), but
the other four are essentially equally popular in both
areas. In most respects the Davos-Prättigau onomasticon
does not correspond to that of the Oberland and the
Unterengadin. Most indicative of this difference is
the popularity of <u>Urs(ch)ula</u> among Davos-Langwies (10%)
and Prättigau women (12%), but its relative unpopularity

among Romance speakers (1%). The following list
clearly shows the chief differences between the favorite Walser-Prättigau and Romance women's names:

Walser-Prättigau		Romance	
Anna	21%	Anna	13%
Greta	15%	Mingia	11%
Elsa	15%	Nesa	11%
Urschla	11%	Leta	9%
Cristina	9%	Gretha	9%
Barbla	4%	Nuta	6%

What accounts for the great similarity between the
women's names in Davos-Langwies and Prättigau? Why do
the expected "Romance" names virtually fail to appear?

The answer to these questions may lie in the very
practices of naming women. In each group of names investigated in this study, it has been the women's onomasticon which has been especially innovative. When
Christian names threatened to suppress German names in
the high Middle Ages it was the women who first showed
traces of the new tradition. A cross-section of the
Curraetian upper nobility showed above (Chapter II,
p. 94) that among Christian names only Johannes had
gained popularity with men. For the same period (1200-
1500) only Kunigunde, Adelheid, and Irmgard remained of
the most popular German women's names; all others were
Christian. In thirteenth century Wallis only 19% of

the women still bore German names. By the sixteenth
century women throughout Graubünden only rarely bore
names of German origin: The proportion of German names
consistently remained five percent or less in Walser,
Rhine Valley, and Romance communities.

The reason for an unstable naming tradition among
women has already been mentioned: There was simply no
cause for names to be perpetuated through generations
of women. Men, who inherited social position as well
as property, were normally identified by a "dynastic"
name which by itself expressed their relationship to
their forebears. This was true of peasant families as
well as of the nobility. For this reason the composition of the female name vocabulary is a better index of
cultural contact than is that of the male name group:
A new tradition is more visible in women's names. And
it is probably for this reason that the female onomasticon of the Landquart valley is so similar to that of
Davos, the immediate origin of the Walser who came into
contact with the Romance speakers in Prättigau.[59]

The pre-Reformation onomasticon of Prättigau is
now presented in its entirety for purposes of comparison with the Walser and Romance names given above (pp.
144ff. and 164ff.).

e) List Four: Prättigau Names

MEN (879):

1. Hans (Henni, Hensli, Wyss   152 (17%)
   Hensli, Hansmann, Schwartz
   Hans)

2. Jan(li) (Janutt, Genutt,   103 (12%)
   Nutt, Nutschi, Nett, Jenni)

3. Cristan/-en   73 (8%)

4. Jacob (Jäcklin)   58 (7%)

5. Peter   46 (5%)

6. Andrea(s) (Enderli)   25 (3%)

7. Marti(n)   24 (3%)

8. Jos (Josep(h), Jösli)   23 (3%)

9. Risch (Rüsch, Rischott)   21 (2%)

   Toni (Antoninus, Thonny)   21 (2%)

11. Jöri (Jörg)   20 (2%)

    Simon   20 (2%)

    Uolrich (Uolli, Uollrysch)   20 (2%)

14. Caspar   19 (2%)

15. Claus   18 (2%)

16. Dis(ch) (Matthis, Mattli)   15 (2%)

17. Bart(o)lome/Bärtsch (Bartli)   13 (1%)

    Lutzi   13 (1%)

19. Rüdi/Rüdolf (Riet)   12 (1%)

20. Flury   11 (1%)

    Lienhard   11 (1%)

22. Hainrich/Heintz   10 (1%)

    Steffan   10 (1%)

24. Fridryg/Frid(li) (Fritsch)   9 (1%)

    Vallentin   9 (1%)

26. Bernhard (Berni)   7

    Cunrad (Curedin, Cuntz, Kuni)   7

    Doman   7

    Ott   7

30. Lentz (Lorentz)   6
31. Nigg(o)   5
32. Ga(u)dient (Gudientg)   4
    Härtly (Hard)   4
    Os(ch)walt   4
    Silvester (Saluester)   4
36. Bastian   3
    Cristoffel   3
    Donawli   3
    Galli/-us   3
    Ludwig   3
    Margg(in)   3
42. (two each) Adam, Albrecht, Bendict, Bläsy/ Blasch, Duffli(n), Götz, Gorius, Jochum, Liechert, Michel, Mynsch, Wölffli/Wolf, Yegen/Jeger
55. (one each) Algoss, Bali, Brosy, Burkart, Cyper, Dietdiägen, Egli, Gabriel, Hiz, Johannes, Killian, Lerch, Niclas, Pauli, Pelay, Philipp, Rinard, Schnider, Sweikli. Tûtsch, Urbanus, Werly, Wilhälm, Xander.

WOMEN (250):

1. Anna   54 (22%)
2. Greta/Margareta   38 (15%)
3. Elsi/El(i)sa   32 (13%)
4. Cristina (Stina)   29 (12%)
    Urs(ch)(u)la   29 (12%)
6. Barbla (Barfla, Barbara)   10 (4%)
7. Nesa   9 (4%)
8. Menga   8 (4%)
9. Catherina (Trina, Drina)   7 (3%)
10. Cya (Lucya)   5 (2%)

Dorothe	5 (2%)
Eva/Effa	5 (2%)
13. Afra	2
Tûnia	2

15. (one each) Adelheide, Agatta, Aurea,
Burkanessa, Dinna, Efrosia, Frenna,
Fronegga, Künga, Madlena, Otylia,
Porga, Sabina, Vyda, Zillia.

f) Other Pre-Reformation Names

Miscellaneous name collections are available from
other parts of pre-Reformation Graubünden and will now
be briefly compared with the naming trends established
above. Early lists are found from Walser colonies in
the Safien Valley and Tavetsch in the Oberland.[60] In
addition, a collection of names from the Zehngerichtenbund reveals the progress of Germanization in the Herrschaft, Prättigau, and Schanfigg in the fifteenth century. The latter names will be examined first because
of their close relationship with those of Prättigau.

1) The Zehngerichtenbund

The Zehngerichtenbund was formed in 1436 by the
ten (later eleven) judicial districts formerly controlled
by Friedrich VII von Toggenburg. Its purpose was to
unite the districts against the division of the

Toggenburg property and to retain the rights and privileges granted them by the Toggenburg family. The
ten districts included Davos, Klosters, Castels (central Prättigau), Schiers/Seewis, Malans, Maienfeld,
Outer Schanfigg, Inner Schanfigg, Churwalden, and Belfort (including part of the Albula Valley). Later the
Chorherrengericht in Schiers became a member of the
alliance. The cultural composition of the Zehngerichtenbund was quite varied, including towns in the
Rhine Valley, Walser colonies, and Romansh-speaking
communities in the Albula Valley in addition to the
two main Walser-Romance contact zones in Prättigau and
Schanfigg.

The 204 names gathered from the Zehngerichtenbund
in 1447-1451 (Jecklin-Muoth AV) represent well this
cultural potpourri. Hans/Hensli (25%) appears here
nearly as often as in the Herrschaft (28%); yet a large
number of Romance speakers is evident from the popularity of Jan(ut) (15%). The frequency of Nigg(o) and
Claus together (9%) nearly equals that of (Ni)Clau(s)
in the Unterengadin (10%). These four names have suppressed the "Walser" Cristan, which appears in only
eighth place (3%) among the mixed population. German
names are borne by 17% of the men, somewhat higher
than the percentage established for the Walser-Romance
zone of contact in Prättigau (15%).[61] Especially

noteworthy is the meager representation of <u>Ulrich</u> and
<u>Conrad</u>, which are often used in Romance towns and in
the Rhine Valley, but which appear here a total of
only three times.

2) <u>Safien</u>

The upper Safien Valley was settled by Walser from
the Rheinwald, who migrated north over the Löchli Pass
and settled in the high tributary valleys of the Rabiusa River. From these higher regions at the southern
end of the valley Walser colonization proceeded gradually downstream, eventually including the area already
occupied by Romance speakers. Kreis (<u>DW</u> 78) believes
that the Romance speakers were quickly absorbed into
the Walser community, and that the Germanization of
the valley was complete by the mid-1300's.

A document from 1363 (GA Safien no. 51) mentions
a <u>Jenni</u> von Kamânen, and a <u>Jan</u> Gella appears in 1385
(GA Safien no. 98). These two men are the only bearers of Romance names recorded in pre-Reformation Safien.[62] A tax list from the Cazis monastery in Domleschg (Joos <u>SU</u>) shows that a century and a half after
the Walser settled in the lower valley all traces of
a Romance name-giving tradition in Safien had been
extinguished. The most popular of 150 names in Safien

in 1502 were:

<u>Hans</u> (Jung Hans, Hanschii, Hensli)	25%
<u>Peter</u> (Jung Peter, Peterman)	12%
<u>Cristen</u>	8%
<u>Hainrich</u> (Hayne, Heintz)	5%
<u>Jörg</u> (Jöry, Gory)	5%
<u>Michel</u> (Lang Michel)	5%
<u>Andres</u>	4%
<u>Caspar</u>	4%
<u>Jacob</u> (Jäcklin)	4%
<u>Thoma(n)</u>	4%

The isolated position of the Safien Valley within the Romance Oberland is evident from the Safien names. Favorite Romance forms such as <u>Jan/Jon</u>, <u>Giacon</u>, <u>Durisch</u>, <u>Padrut</u>, <u>Curau</u>, <u>Menisch</u>, and <u>Raget</u> are totally absent from the Cazis tax lists. <u>Cristan</u>, attested only three times in the Oberland, is borne by 8% of the Safien Walser. <u>Martin</u>, which is perhaps the most character-istic single element of the Oberland name vocabulary, appears only twice in Safien. In addition, the fre-quency of German names in the valley (11%) betrays a Walser onomasticon similar to that of Davos (8%) and quite unlike that of the Oberland (24%). The five favorite names in each area clearly show the "Walser" traits of the Safien group:

Davos	Safien	Oberland
Hans	Hans	Jan/Jon/Hans
Cristen	Peter	Martinus
Marti	Cristen	Jacobus
Peter	Michel	Uolricus
Jöry	Jöry	Petrus

These fundamental differences are explained by
the lack of contact between the two areas in the Oberland. Whereas Prättigau formed an important east-west
trade route between the Romance Unterengadin, Walser
Davos, and the Rhine Valley, the Safien residents were
completely isolated from the Romance Oberland by the
impassable Versamer Tobel at the north end of the valley and traded largely with the Walser Rheinwald to
the south. Not only did minimal contact exist with
Romance speakers to the north, but the continuous
communication with the Rheinwald reinforced the onomasticon which the Safien Walser had brought with them
in their initial migration north over the Löchli Pass.

3) Tavetsch

The most interesting evidence of onomastic contact
in pre-Reformation Graubünden comes from Tavetsch, one
of the earliest Walser colonies. Tavetsch is located
near the source of the Vorderrhein, just east of the
Oberalp Pass on the old via romana which led west from

the Rhine Valley through the Urserntal to the Rhone valley of Wallis. As a part of the Roman province of Raetia, Wallis was always closely connected with the Urserntal and the valley of the Vorderrhein to the east.[63] Walser chose this ancient pass connection as the first route of migration into Graubünden and seem to have settled in the high valleys of Medels and Tavetsch by the end of the twelfth century (Kreis DW 63).

Little is known about the subsequent history of Tavetsch. Like a few other isolated Walser settlements (Fidaz, Flix, Sblox), it failed to maintain the expansive energies characteristic of the settlers in the Davos and Rheinwald colonies and gradually became absorbed into the Romance environment. German has not been spoken in Tavetsch for several hundred years, and the only clear evidence that it is a former Walser colony has consisted of isolated Medieval documents mentioning residents of the Urserntal who settled there[64] and of place names of German origin.

The exact time of final Romanization is not known. Tavetsch was exclusively Walser in the fourteenth century (Joos WW 302) and probably for some time afterward; Zinsli (WV 91) believes that the Romanization was still taking place during the seventeenth and eighteenth centuries.

The <u>Jahrzeitbuch</u> of Tavetsch[65] from about 1450
shows that although Tavetsch was quickly becoming
Romanized in the fifteenth century, a naming tradition
was still in use which preserved with astounding clar-
ity those names brought by the first German speakers
from Wallis some three centuries earlier. Romansh
forms abound: <u>Gugli</u> (< <u>Wilhelm</u>), <u>Turrich</u> (< <u>Ulrich</u>),
and <u>Petrusch</u> in addition to the assuffixed <u>Jenat</u>/<u>Jannet</u>,
<u>Jakmet</u> (< <u>Jacob</u>), <u>Pedrut</u>, <u>Anthoinet</u>, <u>Ragett</u> (< <u>Hein-</u>
<u>rich</u>), <u>Barlott</u> (< <u>Bartholome</u>), <u>Mengot</u> (< <u>Dominicus</u>),
and <u>Tuffet</u> (< <u>Theophil</u>/<u>David</u>). But this Romance dis-
guise cannot hide the fact that in the Tavetsch names
the late Medieval onomasticon of Wallis is preserved
more faithfully than in all other Walser colonies in
Graubünden. The most popular names from Wallis (1200-
1280) and Tavetsch (ca. 1450) are remarkably similar:

Wallis		Tavetsch	
<u>Willel</u>/<u>ermus</u>	16%	<u>Johannes</u>	28%
<u>Petrus</u>	15%	<u>Jäcklin</u>/<u>Jacob</u>	13%
<u>Johannes</u>	11%	<u>Marti(n)</u>	12%
<u>Jacobus</u>	6%	<u>Petrus</u>	9%
<u>Anselmus</u>	5%	<u>Willi</u>/<u>Wilhelm</u>	9%
<u>Aymo</u>	5%	<u>Anshelm</u>	5%
<u>Rodulphus</u>	5%	(An)Tŏni(us)	3%
<u>Walterus</u>	5%	Rŭdi/<u>Rudolf</u>	3%
(H)Enricus	4%	<u>Uoli</u>/<u>Ulricus</u>	3%
Ul(d)ricus	3%	<u>Heini</u>/<u>Ragett</u>	2%

The standardization which affected names throughout Europe after the Middle Ages, and which was only
beginning in thirteenth century Wallis, is evident in
the Tavetsch list, where the <u>Johannes</u> complex makes
up 28% of the onomasticon.[66] As a result of this
standardization the ten most popular names in Tavetsch
account for 87% of the men, compared with 74% in Wallis. This is one of the chief differences between the
two lists presented here, but must be understood as a
temporal and not a cultural difference: Standardization is a function of time and, as seen in the other
name groups earlier, is not characteristic of specifically Walser or Romance traditions.

The increased popularity of Christian names in
Tavetsch, also a temporal matter, accounts for the
other main difference between the two groups. <u>Petrus</u>,
<u>Johannes</u>, and <u>Jacobus</u> have begun to be popular in thir-
teenth century Wallis, where they are the only Christian names among the top ten. Not surprisingly, these
names account for three of the first four positions in
fifteenth century Tavetsch. Taken as a whole, 58% of
the Wallis names are of German origin; this figure de-
creases to 27% in Tavetsch. Yet the latter figure is
comparatively high for the later pre-Reformation period
in Graubünden and especially high in view of the proportion of German names in other Walser settlements

at the time (Davos 8%, Safien 11%).

The appearance of the <u>Johannes</u> group in first
place in Tavetsch is no surprise, for this is also the
case in every other part of Graubünden. The special
popularity of <u>Jacob/Jäcklin</u> is undoubtedly to be explained by the existence in Tavetsch of the religious
society "Fratres Sancti Jacobi," whose members in 1609
and 1616 are listed in folios 5a and 28 of the <u>Jahr-
zeitbuch</u>. <u>Martin</u> is popular in Tavetsch as in the rest
of the Oberland; here its favored position is probably
due to the presence of the ancient St. Martin's church
in Disentis, which is already mentioned in Tello's will
in 765 (Farner <u>KG</u> 66). The presence of <u>(An)Tŏni(us)</u>
among the ten favorite names in Tavetsch shows the influence of the St. Antonius cult, which came to Graubünden relatively late and seems to have spread from
monasteries such as that in nearby Disentis (Farner
<u>KG</u> 156). The name is not attested in thirteenth cen-
tury Wallis.

Because the female onomasticon is generally more
subject to change than is that of men (cf. above, p.
204f.), the women's names from the Tavetsch <u>Jahrzeit-
buch</u> do not closely parallel those from Wallis. Although the entire inventory is too small to permit
thoroughly reliable conclusions (only 98 women are
listed in Wallis), some general observations can

safely be made:

Ten percent of the women in Tavetsch bear German
names, compared with twenty percent in Wallis. Although this proportion is small, it is far greater
than that registered in Romance areas (4%) or the
Rhine Valley (5%). It is especially significant that
not a single one of the 159 Davos-Langwies women has
a name of German origin, whereas a substantial number
of women in Tavetsch are named according to the old
Wallis pattern.

The virtual absence of Anna in Tavetsch (only
twice among 144 women) represents a surprising depar-
ture from naming tradition elsewhere in the canton.
This lack of popularity is probably to be accounted
for by the absence of Anna among Wallis women. Elsa,
which is very popular in Davos and Langwies, appears
only twice in Tavetsch and once in Wallis as Elisabeth.
Ursula, another Davos-Langwies favorite, is not found
in Tavetsch or Wallis. Solomea, in fifth place in
Tavetsch (5%), is the third most popular name in Wallis
(10%). It appears only once each in Davos and the Oberland.

The Romance Oberland seems to have influenced the
women's name inventory in Tavetsch in only one case:
Menga is the third most popular name in Tavetsch, borne
by 11% of the women, just under the proportion who are

named <u>Mingia</u> in the Oberland (13%). <u>Menga</u>/<u>Dominica</u>
is not attested in Wallis.

The appearance of <u>Martin</u> and <u>Menga</u> and the plethora
of Romansh name forms unmistakably place the Tavetsch
onomasticon in the Bündner Oberland. In all other respects, however, the <u>Jahrzeitbuch</u> of Tavetsch truly
reveals an updated version of the name inventory which
the first Walser brought east across the Furka and Oberalp passes in the late 1100's: the high concentration
of German names among both men and women, the close
correspondences between the ten favorite men's names
in Tavetsch and Wallis, and the absence of names characteristic of other Walser settlements in Graubünden
(<u>Christian</u>, <u>Anna</u>, <u>Elsa</u>, <u>Ursula</u>).

V. Conclusion

Much of the early history of the Walser migration
from Wallis to the east has been obscured by the lack
of sufficient documentation. Yet the evidence of personal names recorded as much as four centuries after
the initial migration suggests the following hypotheses
about the Walser colonization of Graubünden:

1.   The Tavetsch settlement represents the ini-
      tial stage of the migration to the east by the
      Furka--Ursern--Oberalp route and the first contact

which settlers from Wallis made with Romance
speakers in Graubünden. No intermediate contact
with a non-German culture is plausible because of
the direct route taken east from Wallis and the
speed with which the colony in Tavetsch seems to
have been established.

These factors contributed to the highly archaic onomasticon of Tavetsch and thus make obvious its direct derivation from that of the Rhone
valley. Both the arrangement of popular names and
the high percentage of names of German origin make
up a conservative name inventory virtually free of
non-Walser influence and characterize what may be
called the Walser onomasticon par excellence of
Graubünden. Because it is certain that Tavetsch
was colonized directly from Wallis by way of the
Urserntal, the composition of the name vocabulary
of Tavetsch can effectively be used to construct
theories about the settlement of other Walser
colonies in Graubünden.

2.   It was shown above that only 8% of the Davos
Walser and 11% of the Walser in Safien bore names
of German origin, whereas the archaic Tavetsch
onomasticon produced a far higher figure (27%).
It was also shown that the popular Tavetsch names
from 1450 were remarkably similar to those in use

in Wallis in 1200-1280 and that the Davos and
Safien name inventories bore no such resemblance
to that of the Rhone valley.[67] The fundamental
differences between these groups suggest that the
Walser in Davos and Safien did not come directly
from Wallis.

This is, of course, known to be true for
Safien, for the settlers there came from the Rheinwald. It is also known from the oldest Rheinwald
document from 1274 that the Rheinwald Walser came
to Graubünden not immediately from Wallis, but
from the Val Formazza and Bosco-Gurin. Here they
came into contact with Romance speakers, and it
was probably here that in the course of a few
generations they exchanged much of their Wallis
name vocabulary for the heavily Christian onomasticon of the Italian Piedmont. When they settled
in the Rheinwald they again encountered Romance
speakers in the outer valley (Medels, Splügen,
Sufers), and the Christianization of their names
was continued. The first Walser to leave the
Rheinwald for Safien to the north thus took with
them an onomasticon which had been considerably
weakened by Christian-Romance contact. Fifty-
eight percent of their ancestors in Wallis had
borne German names less than 150 years before;

by 1502 only eleven percent of the Safien men
had German names.

3.   Absolutely nothing is known about the route
taken east by the first Davos Walser; they are
simply "illi de Wallis . . . in Tafaus" (CD II,
165), and the first settlers, those gesellen of
Wilhelm de(r) ammen, were probably recruited directly from lower Wallis by Walter V von Vaz.   But
the Davos colony grew swiftly and expanded into
Schanfigg and Prättigau; it is widely--and doubtless correctly--supposed that later settlers came
to Graubünden to aid this expansion, and yet it
is generally assumed that all of these settlers
came directly from Wallis.   In view of the low
percentage of German names and the absence of
other characteristic elements of the Wallis onomasticon among the Davos Walser, it is probable
that many who later came to Davos came not from
Wallis itself, but from one of the secondary colonies in the Italian Piedmont, where for several
generations they had been exposed to the Christian
naming tradition of the Romance environment--a
tradition which was far stronger in Italy than in
Graubünden.[68]

4.   The low percentage of German names in Davos
is thus tentatively attributed to the same cause

for the appearance of few German names in Safien:
contact with Romance speakers in the Italian Piedmont.   But what of the onomasticon of Langwies,
a daughter colony of Davos, where 20% of the men
have German names?   The Langwies names compare
favorably with those of the Romance Oberland and
the Unterengadin (22%). It is possible that the
Langwies Walser from Davos encountered a different
naming tradition in Romance Schanfigg and adapted
themselves to it just as other Walser had done in
the Italian colonies. Yet it is also possible
that Langwies, originally settled from Davos, later
received most of its settlers from Wallis, and that
these latecomers brought with them an onomasticon
which contained a larger proportion of German names
than did that of Davos.

VI. Footnotes

[1] "Graubünden" (adjective: "Bündner") has existed
since 1471, when the Zehngerichtenbund, the Gotteshausbund, and the Oberer Bund (Grauer Bund) were
finally united to form a single political body. In
1803 this alliance joined the Swiss Confederation
as a single canton. The term "Graubünden" is used
here very freely to apply in general to the period
following the Walser colonization. Unless otherwise
indicated, "Curraetia" or "Raetia" then refers to
the pre-Walser period before the late 1200's. The
terms inevitably--and incorrectly--overlap in this
study, but this imprecision may be forgiven on the
one hand because the formation of the single political alliance plays no part in onomastic-develop-
ments, and on the other hand because the use of
"Graubünden" or "Curraetia (Raetia)" clearly ob-
viates the necessity of further specifying pre-Walser
and post-Walser eras. "Raetian name-giving" thus
antedates the Walser migration, and "Name-giving in
Graubünden" took place after the late 1200's.

[2] A typical document from Gremaud is reproduced in
the Introduction. Gremaud's formidable collection
is supplemented.by three documents in Wartmann RU
478-481. The terminal date of 1280 was chosen because by then a large number of Walser had migrated
out of Wallis to the south and then east to the Rheinwald and Davos.

[3] The hypocoristic forms Peronetus, Perrinus, and
Perretus are included under Petrus, just as Johan-
netus and Janinus are combined with Johannes, and
Jaquemetus and Jaquetus with Jacobus. The forms of
these and other names were highly unstable at this
time, producing scribal uncertainties such as "Jaquemetus vel Jacobus" (Richard UG 156f.). As late as
the nineteenth century birth and death registers in
Graubünden recorded Johannes, Johann, Hans, Hansi,
Hensly, and so on for the same person.
   The popularity of Petrus is strikingly illustrated in a Gremaud document from 1214 (no. 241), which
mentions among six witnesses Petrus de Turre, Petrus
de Cherpinnie, Petrus de Saxo milites, Petrus Bochi,
Petrus Pia de fer, and Petrus de Leuca.

[4] Richard's study of personal names in Geneva (UG)
shows that name-giving in this center of Romance

culture during the fifteenth century closely paral-
leled the tradition established for Sitten/Sion during
the 1300's. Twenty-two percent of the men in Geneva
bore German names. Most popular among 900 men in
Geneva between 1409 and 1461 were:

Petrus (Peronetus, Perretus, Perrinus)	24%	
Johannes (Janinus, Johannetus)	23%	
Franciscus	6%	
Guillermus	5%	
Jacobus (Jaquetus, Jaquemetus)	4%	
Nicodus	4%	
Antonius	3%	
Amedeus	3%	
Mermetus	3%	
Stephanus	3%	
Henricus	3%	

The worship of local saints may account for the
apparent discrepancy in name popularity between the
Geneva and Sion lists. Most important is the proportion of men bearing names of German origin in these
communities—22% and 17%—which suggests that a Romance onomastic tradition may be posited for this
corner of Switzerland. This tradition should have
been available to German speakers in Wallis through
the bishopric of Sitten at the Romance end of the
valley; yet the German population of Wallis, while
not altogether rejecting the Christian name vocabulary
more popular in Romance territory, seems to have
retained its inherited name inventory with remarkable
fidelity.

5   Meyer (AW 206 note 11) equates Valix with Wallis
and assumes that the name would have been given only
after the father left Wallis, making him 'Johannes,
the one from Wallis'; but why did only this man re-
ceive the name if all other settlers in the Val Formazza were from Wallis as well? Another uncertainty
is the reference—if the name really is "Wallis"—to
the entire valley of Wallis when all others from there
are more closely identified (de Sempiono, de Briga).
In any case, the name itself doubtless comes not from
Wallis, but from the Italian Piedmont somewhere,
either in or near the upper Val Formazza.

6   Only the sons mentioned are counted. It is not
known if any of the fathers listed for the purpose
of identification also came to the Rheinwald. The
first man mentioned, Jacobus de Cresta . . . f.q.
ser Petri de Rialle, is not included in this figure
because he is already cited in the document of 1274.

7   Meyer (AW 203 note 5) supposes that Rossinus is
the Italian equivalent of Röttiner, which is attested
in Davos in 1300; yet assuming that this transfor-
mation is linguistically valid, the name appears only
as a Zuname in "Walthero de Wallis dicto Röttiner"
(CD II, 165). At no time is Röttiner attested as a
first name in Wallis or any of the Walser settlements. It would seem more reasonable to associate
Rossinus with Italian rossino 'reddish,' perhaps
after the widespread custom of naming children according to unusual physical characteristics. Röttiner is probably best derived from Rüti/reuten,
from the land-clearing activity of the Walser: i.e.
'Walther (dictus) the land-clearer' (cf. Chapter I,
note 41; RNB II, 477).

8   Hereafter Gemeindearchiv will be abbreviated GA
according to the practice adopted by contemporary
Swiss publications (BM, JHGG, etc.).

9   A fixed yearly sum of 56 young sheep, 473 cheeses,
1000 fish from the Davosersee, and 168 ells of cloth.

10   This is the only reasonable assumption which
can be made at this point; but see pp. 218ff. below
for evidence to the contrary.

11   Maiensässe: The second stage of the typical three-
stage living and pasture arrangement used by Swiss
Alpine farmers. In the early summer hay is cut and
stored in the area around the main living quarters
(stage one) and is eaten during the following winter
by the cattle which have to stay at this low elevation. In the late spring the cattle are driven to
the high pastures (stage three), where they remain
until the first snowfall. In the late summer hay is
cut from the Maiensässe, or intermediate meadows
(stage two), and stored in small barns there for the
cattle which are forced to retreat downward from the
smow in the fall. Temporary living quarters are
arranged in these barns for the farmers and their
families. By mid-December the cattle are brought
down to the lowest elevations (stage one), which

still may be as high as 2000m. If a shortage of
hay develops in late winter the farmers must bring
more down from the Maiensässe on large sleds. In
the early spring the cattle are again taken to the
barns in the Maiensässe and fed until the last snow
has disappeared from the highest pastureland (cf.
Schw. Id. VII, 1381f.).

12

For this reason the names from the Davos archives and those of the Landammänner (above) were
also examined for the period ending about 1560.

13

The name Johannes is attested in Davos in nine
different forms, but never as Johannes. Often names
are transcribed in birth, marriage, and death records
in their "official" form, especially if the writer
has some formal schooling and is intent on producing
"correct" records. Thus a man may be registered in
church archives as Johannes at birth, Hänsly when he
marries, Henni in a land transaction, and so on, according to who the scribe may be. If father and son
are both named Hans, the father becomes Grosshans
and the son becomes Kleinhans or Knabenhans and remains so even after the father's death. (This method
of differentiating bearers of the same name is not
confined to German-speaking areas. Two men from
Lugnez (Oberland) are mentioned together in the Jahrzeitbuch from Pleif (p. 4) in 1499 as Gion Pitschen
and Gion grond'st, the Romansh equivalents of Kleinhans and Grosshans. Pitschen 'small' is a common
family name in the Davos Spendbuch, where the name
Gross Hanss Pitschen shows that the Romansh word
could no longer be understood literally, but must be
seen as a family name.)
The records can thus occasionally be quite confusing. In the Davos Spendbuch (24) Hansely Bül and
Hans Bül are both mentioned, but the context is such
that they are clearly not the same person. If they
were not named together, but on different pages, they
would seem to be identical and could be counted only
once. Another such case involves the name Bartholomeus (49): One Gallus Bassler owns land which "stost
abwert an Bertschy Plangis güt und usswert an Bertsch
Blangen güt." It is apparent that these last two are
not one and the same person, although this would have
to be assumed if they appeared in separate entries.
The utmost caution is required in these cases, especially when it is possible that brothers bear the
same name as in an earlier Davos listing of "Hänsli
Bråder und Hanns sin brüder" (Jecklin-Muoth AV 8).

Because of such uncertainties many names may have been treated here as belonging to one person, and the total number of men may be more than the 351 counted. Jecklin's generally unreliable register to the Spendbuch lists 410 men, including some 92 named Hans, but he has certainly counted several names twice when they actually belong to the same person. U. Senn (GH 290) estimates the number of landowners (men and women) to have been 450. A conservative total of about 400 seems, however, to be more accurate.

The use of nicknames in such records provides valuable evidence for possible cultural contact. Georg and Ulrich may appear as Gieri and Duri in Romansh communities and as Jörg and Uoli in German areas. Unfortunately, nicknames introduce some problems as well: Both Claus and Nigg appear in Davos, as in many other communities, and are both derived from Nicolaus. Similarly, Jan and Hensly both come from Johannes. When are such name pairs to be treated as two separate names, and when as variants of one name? The methodological assumption made in this study is that names of significantly different forms, such as the two pairs mentioned, are treated as independent units: Claus and Nigg are considered separately. But where can "significant" variation be found in the spectrum extending from Jon and Jan through Johann, Johannes, Hannes, Hans, Hansi, Hansli, and Hensli to Henni? This must be determined for each name and for each document. For Johannes, for example, no one named Jon or Jan is also called Hans in the records investigated, although both Jon and Hans may appear in hypercorrected form as Johannes. (The extremes of the Johannes spectrum are united in the name of the contemporary German author Hans Henny Jahnn.)

In the list of the most popular names from Davos in 1562 Jan (which appears once) has not been included under Hans; Risch (also mentioned once) does not count as Ulrich, which appears most commonly as Üli. Bertschy, Bartli, and Barttollome all count as one name.

14

The appearance of Ulrich and other German names presents a terminological problem. It was noted above (Chapter II, p. 84) that most German names have survived to the present day only because they were borne by people who were later canonized. The German names of saints were thus officially favored by the church and could maintain their popularity with the support of the new calendar and the growth of the holy orders. Thus Ulrich, Heinrich, Bernhart, Lienhart, and others

are as much saints' names as are <u>Georg</u>, <u>Antonius</u>, and
<u>Martin</u>. They will still be referred to as "German
names," however, since they are one criterion by
which differences and changes in the various onomastica of Graubünden can be measured.

15   A. Schorta concludes from the field names and
personal names of the Lüen <u>Stiftungsurkunde</u> that Lüen
supported twice as many farmers in 1084 as in 1900
(<u>NL</u> 110).

16   The area must have been as inhospitable to the
first Walser as the inner Rheinwald had been to the
settlers from the Val Formazza (cf. p. 122). In 1742
Sererhard described

> das andere zu Langwiesen gehörige
> Neben Thal . . . Sappün und Cupen, allda
> wohnen etliche Hausshaltungen über Jahr,
> ist aber so gäch und stozig, dz sie ob
> den Häussern und Ställen einen überhochen
> Vorschopf bauen müssen wegen der Leuwinen.
> (<u>ED</u> 232)

17   The case concerns

> Hans Niggen sun vnd sine sun an einem
> vnd Haintz Bregentzer vnd sine sun an dem
> andern tail all von der langen wisen vmb
> die stössz vnd misshellung, so sy gegen
> ainander gehept hond von ainer frowen wegen
> genampt Cristina Jenett Wincklers säligen
> eliche tochter gewesen vnd ires güts wegen.

18   Actual numbers, not percentages.

19   Ideally, tax lists and other material should be
investigated from villages in Prättigau and Schanfigg
which were known to be free of Walser influence in
the early centuries. The degree to which the Walser
later influenced Romance name-giving and the process
of Walser-Romance contact could then be measured most
accurately. As the brief survey of Walser colonization in Chapter I shows, however, such Romance villages cannot be found, for the extent of Walser colonization in Prättigau and Schanfigg even as early as
the 1300's was such that contact with Romance speakers
was always a distinct possibility. The degree of
contact at this early time cannot be measured, but
later documents from the two valleys exist from the

time when the contact is known to have been taking
place. These sources are treated below (p. 196ff.).

20   The Romanization of Fidaz was still not complete
in the eighteenth century. Sererhard, writing in
1742, reported that

>   Die Leuth reden dieser Orten beide
>   Sprachen, Teutsch und rumansh. Daher
>   die Pfarrer zu Flimsz ihnen monatlich
>   einmal teutsch predigen müssen. (ED 13)

21   Jahrzeitbuch von Pleif, GA Villa no. 4; Bertogg
LA; Jecklin TJ.

22   A Hensl Walser is listed in Ramusch as the son
of Jakob Mutt. The two may represent one of the
Walser families from Prättigau who later settled to
the north of the Unterengadin in the Paznauntal, now
a part of Vorarlberg in Austria.

23   The names given here are supplemented by those
from the Domleschg and the Albula Valley published
in: Jecklin PK 47-56, ZP 42ff., and Cloetta BH 275ff.
The Landammänner and Landschreiber of Bergün are
listed up to 1600 because the Reformation was fully
accepted there only very late in the sixteenth century (Camenisch BR 470ff.).

24   Farner (KG 63ff.) outlines the tight network of
churches in the Oberland consecrated to St. Martin.

25   Other names present similar difficulties. Gyll/
Gielly in the Oberland could be Aegidius (cf. Aegidius (Gilg) Tschudi) or Julius (cf. Gilli Maissen,
Landrichter of the Oberer Bund in 1558). Duff may be
derived from either Theophil or David and Thiefel
from Theophil or Diebold. Jos/Josch is cautiously
assigned to Jodocus because Joseph is not yet attested
in its full form. Hercli could be either Hercules or
Hartwig/Hartmann/Hart-li with the common Romansh
shift of -tl- to -cl- as in Lat tabulatum + -aceu >
Clavadetsch (family name in Prättigau) (RNB II, 336).
Hercules von Salis (1503-1578) is often recorded as
either Hercli or Hertli.

26   Unterengadin: Rigatz, Rigott (< Heinrich);
Stschkern (< Sigisher?); Wartram; Ritschen; Oberland:
de Lut; de Ca Rigenzaus.

27   Cf. the list of farmers in Lüen in 1084,
Chapter II, p. 96.

28   Very few of the first names found in the Oberland
and the Unterengadin are of non-Christian origin.
Most of the German names in use had been incorporated
into the Christian vocabulary: Ulrich, Konrad, Heinrich, Wilhelm, Bernhard. Egino, Albert, Albrecht,
Rudolf, Parcziual, Orttwein, Ezzelo, Marcolf, Giselo,
and a few others managed to survive as non-Christian
names, as did the native Theophil, Fortunatus, Vigilius, Clement, Fidell, and Metardus.

29   The final thrust of Germanization took place in
similar fashion in Bonaduz, west of Chur in the Rhine
Valley. In 1908 the town was destroyed by fire and
was rebuilt largely by German and Italian speakers.
The fire not only destroyed the town, but also virtually severed every connection with the Romansh past:
Papers, pictures, and other mementos had represented
a culture separate from that of the rest of the Chur
basin. German was the language of trade and communication during the rebuilding, which reversed the pre-
vious ratio of German to Romance speakers in the
village: In 1900 there were 286 German and 488 Romansh speakers in Bonaduz, but in 1910 522 German and
230 Romansh speakers (Cavigelli GB 216-255).

30   Pult suggests that Romansh survived into the
eighteenth century in Chur because family names appear
at that time in Romansh masculine and feminine forms.
The author of a song book from 1756 was one Mengia
Violanda, nata Bisazia, whose surname was feminized
from Bisaz (HU 193). This practice was not restricted
to the Romance population: cf. Chapter II, note 11.
    In the Jahrzeitbuch of the St. Amandus church in
Maienfeld in 1475 (Jecklin SA 63) a Hainrich Zimmer-
mann is mentioned with his mother "matris dicte
Zimmermänni" (p. 70); the name of a relative, Ursula
Zymermennyna, appears with both German (-yn) and
Romansh (-a) suffixes.

31   Jecklin ZP 27-34; PK 16-23, 27-37, 62-66; JS.

32   Jecklin SA; ZP 36-41, 52; PK 23f., 39; Castelmur LB.

33   Mann appears only as a suffix in other areas:
Heintzman in Langwies (1488-1500), Hansmann in Davos
(1545), and Uoliman and Pettermann in Chur in 1481.
If the suffix -mann in Davos and Langwies is con-
nected with Amandus, it may be because these Walser
colonies were associated with the Herrschaft in the
Zehngerichtenbund whereas the other towns in the
Rhine Valley belonged to the Gotteshausbund with

Chur. Less daring, however, is the supposition that
Hansmann, Heintzmann, etc., were formed by analogy
to other names in -mann such as Hermann, Hartmann,
and the family name Allemann. The appearance of
Peterman in Safien (1502) suggests that the latter
is more reasonable.

34   Hübscher BO, SZ; Jecklin ZP 34f., PK 37f., HH.

35   Unfortunately, the scope of this study and the
lack of sufficient source material prohibit such a
thorough treatment of the entire canton. This investigation is intended more as a preliminary survey--
a feasibility study--of such a project.

36   The appearance of the form Johannes must be dis-
counted in considering these two nomemes, but is of
course included in an accounting of the entire complex: The Romance sources name 25% Johannes, including Jan (11%), Hans (11%), and Johannes (3%).

37   Gugliam, like Guigs (< *wig- ?), shows the Romance treatment of German w- as in OHG werra: Rrom
guerra, Go wida: Rrom guida, etc. Wûdencz, in the
Unterengadin, is an attempt to restore Gaudentius to
a more "correct"--but nonexistent--German form by a
scribe aware of the Romance w-/g- correspondence.
Heinreich and Ulreich are other Unterengadin examples of overcorrection, in which both members of the
Middle High German doublet -rich/-rîch are treated
as accented forms and diphthongized to -reich according to the written (but not spoken!) language (cf.
the confusion in early New High German between the
forms of -lich and -lîch).

38   This brings up the question of the naming of
churches: Why is one consecrated to St. Johannes
and another to St. Ursula? Originally churches were
built over the grave of a saint, such as the St.
Elisabeth church in Marburg, and later some relic
brought from this central church was sufficient to
consecrate a new place of worship. Eventually churches were simply dedicated to the honor of a saint,
after which an attempt was made to legitimize the
claim to the saint's name by acquiring holy relics
for the church (Farner KG 3f.). But did it also
happen that a Romance name (for example Vitalis) already popular in a community could later be applied
to a newly-built church and thus be perpetuated as
part of the Christian onomasticon? Although this

question, like that of the chicken and the egg, has
no ultimate answer, the problem involved may be kept
in mind.

39
Richard (UG 157) reaches the same conclusion in
his study of name-giving in Geneva.

40
Maria, Johanes ewangelista, lucius rex, theodolus,
vrsula, emerita, Katherina, barbara, dorothea, agatha,
margareta, jeorius, maria magdalena, steffan, leon-
hardus, sebastian, nicolaus, and laurentiuss (GA
Langwies no. 23: 13 April 1477).

41
The existence of such a name group accounts for
the striking similarity between the Davos-Langwies
names and those of Geneva (cf. above, p. 141f. and
note 4). Berger's study of naming traditions in German-speaking Frutigen in central Switzerland reveals
an onomasticon for the period 1200-1400 very much like
that of Romance Graubünden (NF 56f.). The distribution of the most popular names in Frutigen was:
Johannes (120), Peter (60), Niklaus, Rudolf, Konrad
(30 each), Ulrich (24), and Heinrich (14), followed
by Thomas, Walter, Christian, Anton, Jakob, and Martin.

42
The name of his sister, Emerita, appears in pre-
Reformation Graubünden as Meretta (Davos) and later
as Möritha/Mierta during the 1600's, when it becomes
more popular along with Maria and Drina (< Catharina).

43
The theory that the Walser brought the cult to
Graubünden, and that it is purely a Walser affair,
has justifiably been largely discredited. Theodor
is worshipped in Geneva, Basel, St. Gallen, and especially in central Switzerland (Zinsli WV 128). Yet
a special attachment to St. Joder is clearly evident
in Walser areas, and Zinsli argues with good reason
that the term "der Walser-Heilige" is essentially a
correct evaluation of the Theodor cult in Graubünden
(WV 130). The HBLS (IV, 410), indulging atypically
in a bit of local chauvinism, attributes the family
name Joos (and thus the first name Jos as well) to
the Walser saint Theodor. In doing so it overlooks
the more obvious derivation from Jodocus or Joseph.
The former is found in both Walser and Romance areas:
Cf. "Jodochus gen. Jost Bertsch aus Avers" in 1580
(Salis-Soglio RP 97) and Judocus de Vettano in the
Unterengadin (1353 or 1390); the latter appears
commonly in the Rhine Valley.

44
     It is still difficult to imagine a community in Graubünden in which the most popular name is not some form of <u>Johannes</u>. For this reason Stoffel's comment, doubtless supported by his pride in the Walser tradition of Avers, seems somewhat suspicious.

45
     Among Germans mentioned in Maienfeld in 1092 by Meinherz (<u>MBH</u> 220f.).

46
     The Schanielatobel was practically impassable for centuries. Only in 1898/99 was a permanent road built from St. Antönien to Küblis (Escher <u>SA</u> 6).

47
     From Schanfigg? Cf. Clavadetscher <u>WD</u> 387.

48
     It must be remembered that the Walser did not settle in the uninhabited alpine regions because they cared so much for the hardships which they inevitably faced there. The heavily populated valleys forced them to the higher altitudes where they at first had room for their herds. Later a variety of natural catastrophes (avalanches, floods, droughts) combined with animal diseases and war to send them into the lower valleys as miners, blacksmiths, masons, soldiers, etc. (Cf. Kreis' excellent discussion of the depopulation of the Calfeisental in <u>DW</u> 287ff.) Yet their greatest problem was undoubtedly their own overpopulation, which had already forced them out of Wallis and the main colonies in Davos and the Rheinwald. Zimpel calculates that the population in the Walser colonies of Graubünden reached a high point between 1530 and 1565. By this time the settlements housed and nourished as many people as could sustain themselves with the Walser methods of alpine farming (<u>EW</u> 135).
     But where were they now to find room at lower elevations if the valleys were so densely settled? Room was made for them by the Black Death, which decimated the Romance population and vacated vast amounts of land on the valley floors (Schorta <u>PZH</u>). The plague which destroyed one-half of the population of Bern in 1349 also killed all but two of the monks in the Disentis monastery (<u>HBLS</u> V, 401; Iso Müller, <u>Disentiser Klostergeschichte</u>, Einsiedeln/Köln, 1942, 154). Ardüser reports 5000 dead from the Black Death in Graubünden from Easter to Christmas in 1585 (Theus <u>SU</u> 17). The plague killed over a thousand people in Chur within three months in 1629, striking hard in the remote valleys as well (Sprecher <u>PG</u> 25-32) The Black Death combined with the slaughter and hardship wrought by the Thirty Years War (for example,

the bloody Austrian invasion of Prättigau in 1621)
and with the infamous witch trials in Prättigau,
where at least fifty people were hanged or burned
in Klosters alone during the 1600's (Thöny PG 120),
to decimate the Romance population of the valley.
    The Walser were not unaffected by these events.
But those communities which did not succumb to the
plague seem to have recovered quickly from their initial setbacks, perhaps with the help of late settlers
from Wallis. Many Walser now left their high villages to take over land below which the remaining
Romance speakers were unable to cultivate. Some Walser settlements were spared great hardship: Avers
had its largest population (498) immediately after
the epidemics of the early 1600's (Zimpel EW 136).
By 1640 Danusa was largely depopulated. The land
was divided between Furna and Jenaz, which had already
absorbed a large proportion of Danusa's former population (GA Furna no. 19). Stürvis, which once boasted
some fifty buildings, died out in 1629 as the plague
eliminated the few Walser who remained there (Mooser
WM 54).

49
    There were other means of enjoying the agricul-
tural privileges of the valley population: Walser
were repeatedly fined because they violated the grazing rights of their Romance neighbors (cf. GA Jenaz
no. 1 and passim). (The entire problem of Walser-
Romance contact is reviewed in Chapter V.)

50
    Tschudi reported in 1560 that German and Romansh
were spoken in Davos (!), Klosters, Jenaz, and
Schiers (AR 41). Lehmann (1799) set the date of Germanization somewhat earlier: "Anno 1500 und selbst
noch zur Zeit der Reformation bediente sich das Volk
der romanischen Sprache." Bergmann (1853) agreed with
Tschudi: "Die Prätigauer, wie auch die stammver-
wandten Muntafuner (in present-day Vorarlberg), hat-
ten die dt. Sprache vor ungefähr 300 Jahren ange-
nommen" (Kuoni RL 306).

51
    Curiously, nearly all Medieval castles in Prät-
tigau bore Romance names: Solavers, Castels, Montas,
and so on. This contrasts with the castles in the
Romance Oberland and Domleschg, which had German
names (Schorta PZH; Poeschel BB map).

52
    It should be mentioned here that the Reformation
undoubtedly helped to suppress the use of Romansh in
Prättigau. Because most of the peasant population was
illiterate, the new religion was transmitted orally:

small pamphlets from Zwingli's forces in Zürich were
read aloud at public meetings, and Luther's teachings
were proclaimed by German-speaking ministers throughout the valley. Protestant citizens of Graubünden
established contact with sympathetic religious leaders
to the north and west. In Romansh communities the
communiqués with Zürich were translated into Romansh
and read aloud; in contact zones such as the Bündner
Herrschaft or Prättigau translation was no longer
deemed necessary for half-Germanized audiences, and
communication with the center of Protestantism was
maintained solely in German (Meinherz MBH 226). (The
Reformation in Graubünden is discussed more fully in
Chapter IV.)

53   "Fragment eines Prätigauer Zinsrodels aus dem XIV.
Jahrhundert" in Jecklin UP 39f.

54   GA Klosters no. 1-12 (1475-1533); Sprecher ZS;
Jecklin UP.

55   GA Conters no. 1-12 (1371-1545); GA Saas no. 1-2
(1482, 1491); GA Küblis no. 2-27 (1423-1545); GA
Fideris no. 3-69 (1443-1547); GA Jenaz no. 2-30 (1399-
1539); GA Schiers no. 1-42 (1411-1547); GA Fanas no.
1-3 (1481-1533); GA Seewis no. 11 (1539); Jecklin ZG
(1443-1504), SB; "Fragment eines Prätigauer Zinsrodels (der Kirche ·zu Luzein?) um 1500" in Jecklin
UP 41f.

56   The GA Grüsch contains no pre-Reformation documents.

57   This presupposes, of course, that the pre-Walser
name vocabulary of Klosters-Serneus was indeed similar to that established for other Romance areas in
Graubünden; there is no reason to believe that it
was not.

58   A meaningful comparison between Prättigau and
Davos women is made difficult by the small number of
women listed in Davos (68). It will therefore be
helpful to add Langwies names to those from Davos to
obtain a more dependable distribution.

59   It is unfortunate that more women's names from
Prättigau are not available for the pre-Reformation
period, for their appearance in great numbers during
the fourteenth century would certainly betray the
first signs of contact with the Walser. Yet just as
women's names can be useful in indicating the presence

of new naming customs, so can the conservative nature
of men's names yield information about other aspects
of name-giving. Among the ten favorite men's names
in Prättigau there appear three which are represented only occasionally elsewhere. Andreas is borne
by only 1% of the Davos Walser and by fewer than 1%
of the Romance men. Jos accounts for fewer than 1%
of the men in both areas. Risch appears a total of
twice among 1191 Walser and Romance speakers, yet 21
times among 871 Prättigau men.

The lack of St. Andreas, St. Joseph/Jodocus, and
St. Ulrich churches in Prättigau discounts the probability that local saints influenced the popularity of
these names. Could it be that an onomastic substratum
of some sort accounts for their appearance? Such a
proposal can be suggested seriously only on the basis
of more evidence than is available in the limited
material presented here. The idea parallels the suggestion by R. Hotzenköcherle that a linguistic substratum, "das wir vorläufig das Prätigauerisch-Schanfiggerische nennen wollen" (BV 511), may have existed
which produced certain linguistic phenomena found in
the German of Prättigau and Schanfigg but common to
neither the dialect of the Rhine Valley nor that of
Davos. Yet a linguistic substratum certainly does
not automatically presuppose an onomastic one, and
the proposal remains an unanswered question.

60
In addition, names of 42 men and four women from
the Walser settlement in Tschiertschen (Schanfigg)
are published by C. Camenisch in ST. These few names,
however, can hardly be compared with other onomastica:
The most popular name, Hans, appears only seven times,
and Claus and Cristan six times each.

61
Unfortunately, the relatively small number of
names can easily produce statistical variations when
none are really present. Thus it would be too risky
to propose that the slight increase in German names
in the entire Zehngerichtenbund is due to the presence of Rhine Valley (German) and Albula Valley (Romance) names among the collection, although this is
entirely possible. An inventory ten times as large
would help matters considerably.

62
In 1439 a Menisch Feraguden appears, but it is
unclear whether he is a resident of the valley because he is mentioned with "der from knecht Hänsly
Buchly von Safyon" (GA Safien no. 175).

63   Place names and other linguistic evidence indicate early contact between the Romance dialect of
the Oberland and Franco-Provençal to the west, perhaps during the Carolingian period (Planta OS 91f.).

64   Among German speakers serving in the Disentis
monastery in 1285, for example, were: Joannes de
Moesen (Moos in the Urserntal), Hans de Hospenthal,
Nicolaus de Glurinchen (Gluringen in Upper Wallis),
homines de Ursaria (Ursern), homines de Tivez (Tavetsch) et dominus Hugo, miles de Pultaningen (in
Tavetsch) et Wilhelmus frater suus (CD II, no. 28).

65   Jahrzeitbuch von Tavetsch: photocopy of unpublished manuscript in the Staatsarchiv Graubünden
AB IV 6/119.

66   The Jan and Hans nomemes are united with Johannes
for the purpose of this comparison with the Wallis
names, where no nickname for Johannes is given.
Jann/Jenni (Jenat, Jannet, Jenal) alone accounts
for 49 names (21%). Hans (Henni) appears eleven
times (5%) and the neutral Johannes six (3%).

67   Professor Zinsli's supposition that the Walser
brought a characteristic name vocabulary from Wallis
to Graubünden (cf. above, p. 109) has thus been confirmed for the Tavetsch Walser and proven incorrect
for the settlers in Davos and the Rheinwald (Safien).

68   R. Hotzenköcherle notes in a discussion of the
linguistic geography of Graubünden (SD 159) that if
an intermediate stage of colonization is to be assumed for the Davos group (and the present study
shows that it should be), not the eastern Italian
colonies (Pomat, Bosco-Gurin), but the western settlements around Monte Rosa (Gressoney, Alagna,
Macugnaga) should be considered.

CHAPTER FOUR

POST-REFORMATION NAME-GIVING IN GRAUBUENDEN

I. The Reformation in Graubünden

At the middle of the nineteenth century the Protestant population of Graubünden outnumbered the Catholic by some 14,000 out of about 90,000 (Theus SU 109).
According to the 1960 census the situation has been
reversed in the course of the past century to produce
a thin Catholic margin of about 5,000 out of a total
population of 147,458.[1] The confessional division of
the population is now nearly even, but a distinct distribution of Protestants and Catholics has been
achieved over the last four hundred years: The Engadin,
Prättigau, Davos, Schanfigg, Avers, the Bündner Herrschaft, the Heinzenberg, and the Safien Valley are pre-
dominantly Protestant, and the Oberland, Oberhalbstein,
and the Albula Valley are mainly Catholic. "Neutral"
zones are found in the Fünf Dörfer, the Oberengadin,
and in isolated areas throughout the canton.

This distribution according to confession is not
confined to Graubünden, but is characteristic of
Switzerland as a whole. In the very structure of public life are reflected the long-standing differences

which have separated families, towns, and entire districts from their neighbors for centuries. Catholics
and Protestants have different dress for festive occasions, and fields can be prepared for planting and
cultivated in a Catholic or a Protestant manner (Weiss
VS 310). Religious lines are drawn up even on the
linguistic level: In Remsen (canton Schaffhausen)
Catholics and Protestants differ in such fundamental
words as Motr/Mueter 'mother' and de Kcha'fee/s 'Kchafi
'coffee' (Weiss VS 254); in Protestant areas the most
common greeting is a form of Grüsse euch/Grüezi, whereas Catholics in central Switzerland use the older guten
Tag/guten Abend (Weiss VS 270; Geiger-Weiss ASVKo II,
5). Today Protestants in the Bündner Oberland say
glergia 'glory,' perder 'lose,' and Dieu 'God,' but
Catholics there use gloria, piarder, and Dieus (nom.)/
Dieu (oblique). In each case Protestant usage coincides with that of the Engadin dialects (glüergia,
perder, Dieu) because Protestant ministers in the Oberland had to be recruited from the Engadin, the only
Romance area in the canton which did not remain Catholic.

The confessional lines along which the population
of Graubünden is divided today were established during
the Reformation in the 1500's and shifted perceptibly
during the Counterreformation of the following century.
The term "Reformation" must be understood here in its

broadest sense, embracing not only religious, but also vast social, economic, and political reform as well. The foundations of this reform movement were firmly laid by the time the influence of Luther and Zwingli was felt in eastern Switzerland in the 1520's.

One of the most influential feudal landowners in Graubünden at that time was the Bishop of Chur, for his spiritual office was inseparably connected with secular responsibilities and powers. The Bishop owned land in all parts of the canton; hardly a community existed which did not feel the burden of taxation by the head of the church. Little sympathy was felt among the peasants for the Bishop, who was traditionally chosen from foreign aristocratic families and who felt responsibility only for the 'widening of his influence in secular affairs. The formation of the three Bünde in 1471 (cf. Chapter III, note 1) strengthened the resolve of the peasant population to change this situation and gave them the political influence which they needed to hasten the end of the feudal order in the canton (Vasella UR 402ff.).

The city of Chur, unlike other urban centers in Europe, held no political authority over the rural communities. On the contrary, Chur joined the strong alliance of peasants opposed to the continuation of corrupt church practices in religious as well as secular affairs (Vasella BR 4). With substantial political power and independence in the hands of the rural communities, the canton was ripe for the introduction of Zwingli's teachings from Zürich.

The corrupt practices attacked by the reformers had already been partially undermined by the large numbers of Bündner who studied theology in Zürich, Basel, and Germany. Martin Luther's lectures in Wittenberg, of course, were given special attention. Intimate friendships developed between the Bündner reformers and Zwingli and Bullinger in Zürich, and the first men who preached the new religion in Graubünden received substantial moral and material support from the cultural center of the Swiss Confederation.[2]

Extraordinary meetings of representatives of the three Bünde in Ilanz in 1524 and 1526 established a legal basis for the introduction of reforms in religious matters. The important Ilanzer Artikel of 1526 took virtually all secular rights from the Bishop (coinage, judicial authority, etc.) and granted the individual communities in the canton the right to hire their own ministers and priests. In addition, the Artikel proclaimed that only natives of Graubünden be elevated to the office of bishop (a blow to Austrian dominance in religious affairs) and that no more novitiates be accepted into the monasteries in the canton (Pieth BG

132ff.). The most important of these reforms was the
stipulation that the communities were free to choose
their own religion.

Protestantism was quickly accepted by the Zehngerichtenbund and the Grauer Bund. With the exception
of Chur the Gotteshausbund hesitated for a time because
of the influence of the Bishop and the resistance of
the noble family Planta in the Engadin (HBLS III, 650).[3]
The communities of the Zehngerichtenbund illustrate
well the eagerness with which the Reformation was adopted elsewhere. In the Herrschaft Fläsch was the first
town to become reformed (1524); Maienfeld followed in
1529 and Jenins and Malans in the late 1530's (Camenisch
BR 203-213). St. Antönien was the first town in Prättigau to accept the Reformation (1523) and did not enjoy a favorable relationship with the neighboring towns
until the new teaching took hold elsewhere in Prättigau
in the following years: The inner and middle valley
were reformed by 1530, but it took Schiers over thirty
years to gain a Protestant majority. Catholicism held
out in Seewis until about 1590 due to the influence of
the family von Salis-Seewis (Rupp GK 123ff.; Camenisch
BR 241ff., 248ff.). The monastery St. Jakob in Klosters
closed in 1525 when its abbot became reformed, married,
and moved to Chur (Thöny PG 67ff.).

243

The reform movement took hold in Schanfigg about 1527 (Langwies) and, with the exception of Maladers, was carried through by the middle of the century. Maladers, allied with the Catholic church in Chur, did not become Protestant until the 1630's (Camenisch BR 251ff.). The Davos valley was reformed in 1526 by the same minister who had introduced the new religion in St. Antönien three years earlier.

In the Oberer Bund Ilanz was first to reform (Camenisch BR 264) and was followed by the Safien Valley, the Heinzenberg, Thusis, Schams, and the Rheinwald. Reform came to the Unterengadin about 1540 and to the Oberengadin between 1554 (Zuoz) and 1577 (St. Moritz and Celerina) (Pieth BG 149).

Walser colonies nearly unanimously embraced the Reformation: Only Vals, St. Martin, and Obersaxen (all in the Oberer Bund) remained Catholic. The sudden rise of Protestantism among the Walser was in part due to the pre-Reformation union of Walser colonies with distant churches whose congregations consisted chiefly of Romance speakers. Walser in Mutten, for example, went to church in Romance Stierva in Oberhalbstein, where they were forced to hear sermons in Romansh (Zimpel EW 135 and note 9). The independence granted individual communities by the Ilanzer Artikel of 1526 and the prospect of hiring someone to deliver sermons in German undoubtedly caused the shift to Protestantism in many cases. In addition German-Romance enmity, such as that between the Walser in Vals and the Romance speakers in Lugnez (cf. Chapter V), was avoided by the establishment of separate church communities.

Strange as it may seem, the religious differences wrought by the Reformation did not sharply divide the population during the early 1500's. Catholics visited Protestant services and vice-versa. Even the Bishops Iter and Planta were on friendly terms with the Protestant population of Chur (Pieth BG 151; HBLS III, 652). This all changed dramatically, however, with the Counter-reformation of the late 1500's and early 1600's, which demanded that the Catholics regain what they had lost to the Zürich reformers.

Graubünden now became unwillingly involved in the struggle between the Austria-Spain axis and France-Venice, who wanted to prevent a political alliance between the Habsburgs and Milan. Catholic Bündner sided with the Habsburgs; Protestants sided with France. Even some residents of the Protestant Zehngerichtenbund sympathized with Austria: Dietegen von Salis-Seewis was an Austrian Landvogt in Prättigau from 1557 to 1573 and naturally opposed the Reformation (Rupp GK 127); in 1607 Landvogt Georg Beeli was executed in Prättigau as an Austrian sympathizer (Thöny PG 83).

The year 1621 was decisive for the restoration of Catholic supremacy in Graubünden. Capucinian monks from Italy began missionary activities which eventually brought the progress of the Reformation to a halt and regained many communities for the church of Rome (Camenisch BR 561f.). Spurred by the persecution of Catholics in the Zehngerichtenbund, 8000 Austrian troops pressed through the Unterengadin and Davos and invaded Prättigau in late October of 1621. The conquering army burned most of the villages in the valley[4] and left behind occupation troops who confiscated food and forced many to starve during the following winter (Thöny PG 85ff.). The Austrian occupation and the reinstatement of Catholicism in Prättigau were ended the following spring by a popular uprising.

Graubünden became a battlefield in the mid-1620's, with Austrian, Spanish, and French forces all dependent on the local population for food and shelter. The citizens of Graubünden were rewarded for their services by the introduction of the Black Death by the 20,000 Austrian soldiers who marched through the canton to the west to help Spain in its war against France (Thöny PG 103ff.). A pitiful account of the religious conflict is contained in Folio 12a of the Tavetsch Jahrzeitbuch:

Item in Jar 1620. sin vil ufrhur, rebelion
vnd zwittracht entstanden in vnseren landen vnd
gemeinen drien pünten zwischen den Catholischen
und luterischen Herren vil landgericht einer
wider den andren vfgebracht, vil verretery an-
gericht vm gwins vnd vmb den geltgiz willen,
dar durch den gemeinen man vnd armen puren mit
den fenlin vfgemannt vnd gezwungen vnder den
falschen schin, ess sige vmb den glauben zu
thun, aber niit vs gericht. Die armen puren
vnd das ganz land ist verfürd vnd betrogen worden, in vnmercklichen kosten, schaden und schul-
den gerothen. Fünff Fendlin von den catholischen fünf orten schwizers volk sind vnss zu
Hilf kommen in Herpst vnd haben ihr Winter-
leger in vnseren landen vfgeschlagen biss in
nachkomendē frieling. in nachfolgenden Jar
1621. sind vil scharmüzlen geschechen zwischen
den catholichen und lutirischen zu Zizers, zu
Chur, zu Thusis zu Waladas vmb daselbst vmen
vil blud vergossen, gar vil Volk vmkomen, vil
fürnemen Herren geistlich vnd weltlich gar
schandlich hin vnd wider ermörd worden von den
luterischen. in denselben früeling in merzen
sin wir Catholischen in oberen Landeren von
den Vndersten luterischen pundsleüten gechlich
Vberlaufen worden, vs vnseren landen und gren-
zen jung vnd alt, Wib vnd Kind verjagt vnd ver-
triben, sie haben aber alles vnser gut ver-
schleiz, verderbt vnd vfgefressen, wir sind
aber bald wider in vnseren land komen, gros-
mechtige schaden erliten.

Thus it was not so much the Reformation itself as
the restoration of Catholicism which brought about the

deep religious divisions still extant in most of
present-day Graubünden.[5]

Most important for this discussion is the effect
of the Reformation on Walser colonies. It has been mentioned that the Graubünden Walser maintained contact
with the residents of Wallis long after the migration
to the east was initiated in the thirteenth century. A
public proclamation in Obersaxen in 1730, for example,
declared the days of St. Anton of Padua and St. Joder
holidays in honor of the Wallis homeland (Joos **WW** 301;
cf. Chapter III, note 43). When nearly every Walser
settlement in Graubünden became Protestant, however,
the close relationship with Catholic Wallis was abruptly severed. Further immigration from the Rhone valley
was now prevented for religious reasons (Zinsli **WV** 53).

Within Graubünden only three Walser colonies--Vals,
St. Martin, and Obersaxen in the Oberer Bund--remained
Catholic. For Vals this meant that the close contact
which had always existed with the Safien Valley and the
Rheinwald virtually ceased to exist.[6] Some residents
of Obersaxen, surrounded by Catholic Romance speakers,
decided that religious confession was more important
than language differences and began intermarrying with
their Romance neighbors. This immediately brought Romance speakers into the community;[7] similar circumstances probably brought about the final Romanization of

the Walser in Tavetsch, outer Lugnez, and Tersnaus
as well (Zimpel EW 135).

II. The Reformation and Name-giving

The Reformation demanded an end to corruption in
the church and the expulsion of elements in the mass
which were not directly supported by the Bible. Thus
the Catholic saints of non-Biblical origin (Georg,
Theodor, Emerita, etc.) were allowed no place in the
new Protestant theology.

Many Protestants, such as the Bavarian historian
Johannes Turmair (1477-1534), sought to expel the
"Catholic" names:

> Diese Namen Peter, Georg, Hans, Paul, Anna,
> Katharina, Margaretha usw. seynd bey den Teu-
> tschen neuwe; es haben sie unsere Vorfahren
> nicht gebraucht, haben erst nach Keyser Frid-
> richs des Andern Tode eingedrungen, nachdem
> das H. Röm. Reich in Abfall ist bracht worden
> durch Anrichten der röm. Geistlichkeit, durch
> welcher List die Christen noch heutigen tags
> uneins sind. (Bach DN I, 2, 43)

The rejection of saints' names led in some quarters
to the glorification of German names (Turmair: ein
"kostbarer Schatz bedeutungsvoller alter Namen, die zu
Tugend und kühner Tat reizen und spornen") and to the
promotion of a new body of names taken only from the
Bible. A new Christian calendar appeared in Zürich in

1527 which contained only Biblical names. Calvin's
church in Geneva persuaded the city legislature to dis-
allow any non-Biblical names, and Protestant ministers
there refused to baptize with any of the names of Catholic saints. Among Presbyterians in Geneva there appeared the unlikely names Tötediesünde and Stehfestim-
glauben; even entire Bible verses were used as first
names (Vetter PN 31).

These, however, are exceptional cases and represent
attempts by a few enthusiastic reformers to change a
popular Christian naming tradition which by the 1520's
had not only achieved widespread use among the lower
classes, but had also become extremely durable and resi-
stant to change. Although promoted by the most dogmatic
Protestants, the increased use of German or Biblical
names was not generally accepted on the popular level.
Studies of name-giving in Leipzig (Kietz PN 245f.),
Tirol (Finsterwalder FT 11 note), Zürich (Richard UG
242ff.), and Frutigen (Berger NF 63) show that in urban
and rural areas alike onomastic traditions were on the
whole undisturbed by the commotion of Reformation and
Counterreformation. Berger (NF 130, 133) notes that a
few new names appeared in Frutigen after the Reformation: Abraham, David, Elias, Gabriel, Isaak, Jochen,
Joseph, Manuel, Salomon, Theophilus; yet he points out
that the total number of these names accounts for no

more than one percent of the entire onomasticon of
Frutigen.

*   *   *

It now remains to be determined whether name-giving
in Graubünden was also unaffected by the Reformation and
how Walser-Romance contact proceeded during the seventeenth century.

III.   Name-giving among Walser and Romance Speakers
       in the Seventeenth Century

In view of the separate name-giving traditions
established in Chapter III for Walser and Romance regions in Graubünden, at least five main cultural divisions should be made in the canton for the post-Reformation era. The Romance-speaking population now includes
both Protestant and Catholic communities, and Walser
colonies may be found in both confessional areas as
well. In addition, the important contact zones in Prättigau and the Rheinwald present culturally mixed regions
which became Protestant. (A Catholic Walser-Romance
contact area did exist in Vals-St. Martin, but the lack
of documentation unfortunately excludes it from the
present investigation.)

The information upon which this study of the post-
Reformation onomasticon of Graubünden is based is taken
from the birth, marriage, and death records kept in
church registers in the archives of the individual communities. These records, compared with the tax lists
and Jahrzeitbücher consulted in Chapters II and III, are
not what may be called "old." Never are we fortunate
enough to find baptism records dating back to the 1520's,
when the Reformation was introduced. The earliest registers list births, marriages, and deaths in Davos from
1559 and in Ilanz from 1595, and marriages in Bergün
from 1586. Other church records seem to have been destroyed during the Counterreformation of the 1620's,
and for this reason the word "old" acquires a relative
meaning: Registers beginning in the 1630's and 1640's
become significant discoveries which must alone shed
light on local onomastic practices during the post-
Reformation era.[8] Too often the first pages of an important church book have fallen prey to careless hand-
ling and primitive methods of preservation: The church
register from St. Antönien, for example, began relatively late in 1680, and its value has been further
diminished by the loss of the entries for the years
between 1680 and 1696. Because the terminal date for
the present study was arbitrarily set at 1700, the few
names collected during the last four years of the

seventeenth century reveal little about the post-Reformation onomasticon of this important Walser colony.

The large number of names available from these
church registers during the 1600's makes up for the unfortunate lack of material for the crucial period immediately following the Reformation. In Chapter III a
more careful selection of communities in Graubünden was
prevented by the availability of a very limited number
and variety of sources. Also, some of the pre-Reforma-
tion·material did not offer enough names to assure an
absolutely rigid statistical base. Now, however, the
post-Reformation sources from Walser areas make possible
a detailed survey that precludes significant numerical
variations. The selection of materials from the most
important areas is surprisingly good: Although the
post-Reformation church registers begin for the most
part in the mid-1600's, they still contain over 16,400
names from Walser and Walser-Romance areas alone.

The chief source of onomastic information from pre-
Reformation Davos was the Spendbuch of 1562 containing
about 400 names. By contrast, the baptism records of
Davos from 1559 to 1700 name 6795 people, an astounding
statistical balance of 3397 men and 3398 women. The
investigation of pre-Reformation Rheinwald names could
show that the traditional belief in the "purity" of that
Walser colony was unjustified (Chapter III, p. 120ff.),

253

but the lack of material from 1300-1500 precluded a
study of name-giving there. Now, however, church
records from 1628 to 1700 list 2196 Rheinwald residents
and permit important conclusions about Walser-Romance
contact at the headwaters of the Rhine. Other archives
virtually silent before the Reformation (Obersaxen, the
Oberengadin) yield important material from the 1600's.
In the most fortunate cases towns investigated in Chapter III (Davos, Langwies) can now be revisited, and the
onomastic repercussions of the Reformation can be measured by the use of earlier material. Most important,
the evolution of naming tradition in Prättigau can be
further observed throughout the seventeenth century.

In Chapter III it was deemed necessary to compare
Walser and Romance names with those of the Rhine Valley
in order to establish the relationship between name-
giving and cultural history. This comparison showed
that three different naming traditions did indeed exist
and that the names of the Rhine Valley, unlike its dialect, failed to penetrate to the east beyond the Chlus
dividing Prättigau from the towns in the Herrschaft and
from the Fünf Dörfer. For the question of Walser-
Romance contact in Prättigau this comparison need be
carried no further. For the post-Reformation period
examples of name-giving are taken from sources in only
Walser, Romance, and Walser-Romance (i.e., Prättigau,

Schanfigg, and the Rheinwald) communities.

a)   <u>Romance Protestant</u>

Some Romance communities which accepted the Reformation are found in the Oberengadin (<u>Samedan</u>, <u>Bevers</u>)
and the Albula Valley (<u>Bergün</u>) as well as in the pre-
dominantly Catholic Oberland (<u>Trins</u>, <u>Flims</u>, <u>Ilanz</u>).

Although Samedan and Bevers are situated together
in the Engadin, their onomastica show characteristic
differences:

<u>Samedan</u> (1639ff.)		<u>Bevers</u> (1656ff.)	
<u>Jan/Nuot</u>	18%	<u>Jan/Nuot</u>	27%
<u>Peider</u>	9%	<u>Jachiam</u>	17%
<u>Jachiam</u>	8%	<u>Peider</u>	7%
<u>Bathrumieu</u>	6%	<u>Töen(in)</u>	6%
<u>Andrea(s)</u>	6%	<u>Lüci</u>	4%
<u>Thoeni</u>	5%	<u>Emanuel</u>	3%
<u>Gudains</u>	5%	<u>Gudenz</u>	3%

Most apparent is the greater popularity of <u>Jan/Nuot</u>
and <u>Jachiam</u> in Bevers. <u>Lüci</u> (Bevers) does not appear in
Samedan, and <u>Emanuel</u> is attested only once among the 495
men there. <u>Bathrumieu</u>, in fourth place in Samedan, is
found twice among 161 men in Bevers, and <u>Andrea(s)</u> appears in Bevers only four times. What accounts for such
differences between towns only two miles apart? Bevers
is closer to the important St. Luzius church in Zuoz,

but can this explain the popularity of <u>Lüci</u> in Bevers
and its absence in Samedan? And if <u>Bathrumieu</u> in
Samedan could be attributed to the large number of St.
Bartholomeus churches in the nearby bishopric of Como
to the south (Farner <u>KG</u> 59), why is it not equally as
popular in Bevers?

The onomasticon of Bergün, to the north of the
Albula Pass, introduces other names (1586ff.):[9]

<u>Jan/Nutt</u>	28%
<u>Jacob</u>	11%
<u>Pedar</u>	10%
<u>Nicolaus</u>	7%
<u>Leonhart</u>	4%
<u>Cristoffel</u>	3%
<u>Paul</u>	3%
<u>Steivan</u>	3%
<u>Anthieni</u>	3%

The distribution of <u>Jan/Nutt</u>, <u>Jacob</u>, and <u>Pedar</u>
among the 678 men in Bergün represents a compromise of
the figures from Bevers and Samedan. These three names
seem to enjoy nearly unassailable popularity in this
part of Romance-speaking Graubünden. The next five
names in Bergün, however, clearly set this town in the
Albula Valley apart from those in the Engadin. Of these
five only <u>Nicolaus</u> (7%) is represented in reasonable
quantity in Samedan as <u>Clo</u> (2%) and does not even appear
in Bevers. (It will be remembered that <u>(Ni)Klaw(s)</u> was

second in popularity only to the Johannes group in the Albula Valley and the nearby Unterengadin before the Reformation.)

Other Romance communities only further confound any attempt to categorize the names together in one group. Ilanz, Flims, and Trins in the Oberland present onomastica which not only differ dramatically from those to the southeast, but also appear to be completely un-related:

Ilanz (1650ff.)		Flims (1672ff.)	
Jon	8%[10]	Jon	11%
Jacob/Jac(h)um	7%	Casper	8%
Christ	6%	Hans	5%
(Chri)Stoffel	6%	Marti	5%
Jeri/Jöri	4%	Andris	5%
Balzer	3%	Risch	5%
Hans	3%[10]	Christ(ian)	4%
Risch	3%	Gieri	4%
Luci(us)	3%	Michel	4%
Lienart	2%	Cuorat	4%
		Hercli	4%

Trins (1666-68, 1681ff.)	
Jon	15%
Jacob	9%
Barcāzi	8%
Hans	8%
(Chri)Stofel	7%
Flisch	6%
Balzar	5%

Peter	4%
(Du)Risch	3%
Jerimaun	3%
Raget	3%

Most striking in this comparison is the fact that only Jon, Hans, and (Du)Risch are common to both Flims and Trins in spite of the location of the towns on the same side of the Vorderrhein only four miles apart and their common judicial administration since the Middle Ages (HBLS III, 173).

Other indices of naming tradition which were established in Chapter III fail to show a convincing onomastic relationship between Ilanz, Flims, and Trins, or among the other three Romance Protestant towns under investigation. The proportion of names of German origin in Flims is 16%, but in Ilanz 12%, in Trins 8%, in Bergün 8%, in Samedan 8%, and in Bevers 4%. In Bergün only two compound names (Hans Jacum, etc.) are attested during 114 years. Samedan produced 39 and Bevers only two compound names during the 1600's. By far the highest percentage of compound names is recorded in Ilanz, where fully 15% of the men bear them between 1650 and 1700.

It is apparent that no reasonable basis exists for grouping together the names from Ilanz, Flims, and Trins in the Oberland; nor is there a compelling reason for

combining these names with those from Bergün and the
Oberengadin villages. Such a combination would of
course be possible, but it would be virtually meaning-
less in presenting a name vocabulary to a large degree
foreign to each of the six towns involved.

Do women's names differ as greatly from town to
town (Bevers-Samedan, Trins-Flims) and from area to
area (Oberengadin-Oberland)? The following lists show
that women's names in Romance Protestant communities
present a more unified picture than do their male counterparts:

Bevers		Samedan	
Ursina	18%	Anna	20%
Maria	16%	Ursina	17%
Anna	14%	Maria	13%
Chiatrina	13%	Cathrina	8%
Barbla	10%	Clergia	5%
Malgiaretta	5%	Barbla	5%
Clergia	4%	Laina	5%
Maritta	4%	Malgaretta	4%
Vintüra	4%	Mierta	4%
Cilgia	4%	Neisa	2%

Bergün		Ilanz	
Anna	25%	Anna	13%[11]
U(o)rschla	15%	Maria	10%
Barbla	11%	Barbla	9%
Catharina	9%	Urschla	7%
Mengia	5%	Thorothe	7%

Greata	5%	Nesa	6%
Maria	5%	Me(i)ng(i)a	5%
Anglina	4%	(Cār̄i)Stinna	4%
Mierta	3%	Ma(r)gretta/	4%
Nŭ̊tt(in)a	2%	Greicli	
		Cat(a)rina	4%

Flims		Trins	
Urschla	19%	Onna	19%
Onna	11%	Magreta	13%
Barbla	10%	Mengia	10%
Greitli	8%	Urschla	10%
Maria	8%	Barbla	8%
Mengia	7%	Nesa	7%
Turte	5%	Maria	6%
Trinna	4%	Torcle	5%
Gietta	4%	Fren(n)a	4%
Nesa	4%	Eulscha	3%
		Zilgia	3%

Although the proportion of female names varies from town to town, the same group of names is drawn from in each case. Some local variants exist, of course: Clergia appears only in the Oberengadin and the popular Catharina/Trina is not attested in Trins. Maria is less common in the Oberland and Bergün than in the Oberengadin. Maritta/Mierta (< Emerita) is lacking in both Oberland communities. Greitli/Greicli/Magreta/Gietta is much more popular in the Oberland (12-13%) than elsewhere (4-5%).

In spite of these differences the same names appear in each town, and a cautious grouping of the women's onomastica in Protestant Romance communities seems to be justified. Among 2304 women are:

Onna/Anna	20%
Urschla/Ursina	14%
Barbla/-ara	9%
Maria	9%
Trina/Č(hi)at(a)rina	7%
Ma(r)gretta/Greicli	5%
Mengia	5%
Elisabetha (Lisa, Elsi, Eulscha)	3%[12]
Nesa (Neisa)	3%
Dorothe(a)	3%
Madleina (Laina)	2%
Mierta (Maritta)	2%
Christina/Stina	2%

It now remains to be seen whether men's names are as varied and women's names as similar among the other cultural groups.

b)   Romance Catholic

The choice of only two Romance Catholic communities for these names was determined by the relatively small number of archives found to be productive or available for study. Of the towns in Catholic Oberhalbstein

(extending south from the Albula Valley to the Julier
Pass) only Salouf (1641ff.) could be investigated. In
the Oberland only one source was fruitful: the church
records from Siat above Ilanz from 1632ff.

Among 299 men from Salouf are:

Jo(h)annes	19%	Carolus	2%
Jacobus	11%	Waltherus	2%
Georgius	6%	Crist(i)anus	2%
Peter/Petrus/	6%	Matius/-as/-eus	2%
Pedrot		Melch(i)er/	2%
G(a)udentius	4%	-or/-ar	
Stefanus	4%	Christophorus	2%
(Steffphfanus)		Janet/Gian(n)et	2%
Antonius	4%	Mauritius	2%
Franciscus	3%		

As a rule, Catholic records were conscientiously
kept in Latin. Gieri was listed as Georgius, Jacum
as Jacobus, and so on. Occasionally popular forms are
registered (Janet, Melcher), and sometimes a deliberate
attempt has been made to construct Latin forms from popular nicknames: Duri(g) was reconstructed to a properly
classical Doricus, far from the correct Ulrich (< *Odal-
ric).[13] On many occasions the attempted reconstruction
is etymologically false, such as the Salouf entry in
1695 which names "Otto seu vulg Nutt."[14]

The most popular names among 209 men from Siat in
the Oberland differ considerably from those found in
Salouf:

Joanes (Gion, Jon, Gienones)	16%	Petrus (Piader)	3%
Jacobus (Jacum)	12%	Bartholomeu/-s (Barclamiu)	2%
Christianus	12%	Blasius/Plasch (Blesi)	2%
Julius (Jülɏ)	8%	Ambrosius	2%
Georgius/Gieri (Jerɏ)	6%	Casparus	2%
Mathias	4%	Giosch (Josch, Josephus)	2%
Melchior (Melschior, Melcher)	3%	Martinnus	2%
Florinus	3%		

The Salouf names from Gaudentius through Waltherus
are not attested once in Siat, nor are Christophorus
and Mauritius: Eight of the sixteen most popular names
in Salouf do not even occur in Siat. Similarly, Julius,
Bartholomeu(s)/Barclamiu, Blasius/Plasch, and Ambrosius
are not used once in Salouf. As in the Protestant Romance communities, no reasonable basis seems to exist
for grouping these Catholic men's names together. Do
women's names in Salouf and Siat justify such an association?

Salouf (301 women)		Siat (178 women)	
Maria	24%	Anna	20%
Anna	19%	Maria	19%
Catharina	9%[15]	Ursula	12%
Ursula (Ursina)	8%	Margaritta/ Magriatta	6%
Barbara	7%	Dominica/ Me(i)ngia	6%
Margaretha	6%	Brigida	5%
Magdalena	3%		
Agnes (Nesa)	3%		

Elisabeth(a)	3%	Barbara	5%
Dominica	2%	Catherina	5%
Angelica	2%	Elisabeth	5%
Perpetua	2%	Emerita	3%
		(Chri)Stina	3%
		Agnes	2%
		Dorothea	2%

Again a standard body of women's names seems to
exist for both communities. Of the first ten names in
Salouf only Magdalena does not occur in Siat. Angelica
and Perpetua, which together account for eleven women
in Salouf, are not attested in Siat.[16] Brigida, Emerita, and Dorothea, totalling 10 in Siat, do not occur in
Salouf. Apart from these minor differences the groups
are quite similar and appear together in this configuration:

Salouf-Siat (479 women)[17]

Maria	22%
Anna	19%
Ursula	10%
Cathᵉrᵉina	7%
Barbara	6%
Margareta/ Magriatta	6%
Dominica/ Me(i)ngia	4%
Elisabeth(a)	3%
Magdalena	2%
Agnes (Nesa)	2%

*   *   *

Six Protestant and two Catholic communities have
now been examined. Among men's names no especially
close correspondences were found in either Protestant
or Catholic areas. Jan/Nutt, Jachiam (Jacob), and
Peidar (Pedar) are clearly favored in the Protestant
regions to the southeast (Engadin-Bergün), but Jacob
and Peter do not appear among the eleven most popular
names in Flims, and seven names precede Peter in the
Trins list. The appearance of Hans in third and fourth
place in the Oberland towns compares unfavorably with
only twelve attestations among 678 men in Bergün and
two among 656 men in Samedan and Bevers.[18]

The Protestant towns do not appear to be as closely
related as the Catholic Siat and Salouf, where not only
Joanes and Jacobus, but also Georgius, Mathias, Melchior, Florinus, and Peter provide at least some ground
for common agreement. The differences between the Catholic towns are nevertheless substantial. If it were
not for the appearance of Georgius in Salouf and Siat,
these towns would resemble one another no more than they
individually resemble the Protestant communities. Other
indices used above (p. 257) are inconclusive: The Salouf onomasticon is 9% German, but in Siat only three
men out of 209 have German names. (Two of these,

<u>Uldalricus</u> and <u>Uldaricus</u>, are of the noble family Vin-
cenz; the other name, <u>Durisch</u>, was surely no longer
recognizable as German in 1691.) Double names are not
clearly favored by one religious group and seem to have
been used sporadically by the nobility during the first
half of the seventeenth century. Their increased popularity in the 1680's and 1690's does not appear to have
a religious basis.

A dramatic reason for differentiating Catholic and
Protestant men's names among Romance speakers is thus
not apparent. Local differences seem to overshadow any
confessional similarities which might exist.

Whereas men's names are similar in their great di-
versity from town to town, women's names in Protestant
and Catholic Romance communities provide an amazingly
unified picture:

<u>Protestant women</u> (2304)		<u>Catholic women</u> (479)	
Onna/<u>Anna</u>	20%	<u>Maria</u>	22%
<u>Urschla</u>/<u>Ursina</u>	14%	<u>Anna</u>	19%
<u>Barbla</u>/<u>-ara</u>	9%	<u>Ursula</u>	10%
<u>Maria</u>	9%	Cath$\overline{\text{a}}$rina	7%
<u>Trina</u>/ C(hi)at(a)rina	7%	<u>Barbara</u>	6%
Ma(r)gretta/ Greicli/<u>-tli</u>	5%	Margar$\overline{\text{e}}$ta/ Magriatta	6%
<u>Mengia</u> (Menga)	5%	Dominica/ Me(i)ngia	4%
<u>Elisabetha</u> (Lisa, Eulscha, Elsi)	3%	<u>Elisabeth(a)</u>	3%

Nesa (Neisa)	3%	Magdalena	2%
Dorothe(a)	3%	Agnes (Nesa)	2%
Madleina (Laina)	2%	Brigida (Breida)	2%

The prominent position of Maria among women in
Salouf and Siat constitutes the only noteworthy difference between the two groups of names. The lists are
virtually identical except for two cases: The "Protestant" Dorothe(a) is attested only three times in Siat
and is lacking in Salouf; the "Catholic" Brigida (Breida) appears only in Siat and is not used once in Salouf
or in the Protestant communities.

c) Walser Catholic

The only Catholic Walser community which has
church records from the 1600's is Obersaxen, a chain
of small settlements located on a fertile terrace high
above Ilanz and the Vorderrhein in the Oberland. Obersaxen forms an island of German speakers in an otherwise completely Romance environment. The nearest Walser settlement to the south or east is Vals, which also
remained Catholic, but the two areas are separated by
Romance Lugnez. The Walser in Tavetsch, west of Obersaxen near the Oberalp Pass, probably became completely
Romanized shortly after the Reformation (Zimpel EW 135).

The baptism register from Obersaxen lists 524 children from 1625 to 1649 and 769 children from 1665 to 1700. (No names are recorded from 1649 to 1665.[19]) The most popular men's names are:

Johannes/Hans	17%
Christianus / -en	14%
Martinus	9%
Georgius/Jöri	9%
Petrus	8%
Casparus	7%
Melher/-ior	4%
Jacob	3%
Baltasar/-tzr	3%
Thoma(s)	3%

A suggestion that Obersaxen has a Walser, and not a Romance, population is found in the popularity of Christian/-en. In the investigation of pre-Reformation names Christian seemed to be a certain onomastic characteristic of Walser areas, appearing in second place behind Hans in the Davos Spendbuch of 1562 (Chapter III, p. 132) and indicating the presence of Walser in Prättigau.[20] Christian ranked nineteenth among pre-Reformation Romance names and is attested among post-Reformation Romance speakers only in modest numbers in Ilanz (6%) and Flims (4%). Here in Obersaxen the name appears in first place in the first half of the seventeenth century but drops in popularity during the second half.

Does this indicate that <u>Johannes</u> never occupied first
place in Obersaxen until the mid-1600's? If so, the
popularity of <u>Christian</u> there is striking indeed.[21]

    Among other Obersaxen names the appearance of
<u>Martin</u> (9%) is noteworthy. <u>Martin</u> was found to be the
second most popular name in the Oberland before the
Reformation, yet the brief survey of Catholic and Protestant Romance communities in the Oberland above showed
that the name had fallen into disfavor in all but Flims
(5%). Is the popularity of <u>Martin</u> in Obersaxen to be
attributed to the old (since 765: Farner <u>KG</u> 66) St.
Martin church there? If so, why did the St. Martin
churches in Flims and Ilanz fail to direct more attention to <u>Martin</u> in .those communities? The popularity of
<u>Martin</u> in post-Reformation Obersaxen is the same as it
was in the pre-Reformation Oberland as a whole (9%) and
seems to point to a degree of onomastic conservatism
not apparent in the Romance communities below on the
important trade route of the Vorderrhein.

    Only four percent of Obersaxen men's names are of
German origin, and compound names appear only seven
times among 682 men.

    The inventory of 611 women's names in Obersaxen
is virtually identical to that established for the
Romance Catholic communities:

Maria	24%
Anna	18%
Catarina/Trina	8%
Barbara/Barbla	8%
Dorothea	7%
Margareta/Greta	7%
Ursula/Urschla	5%
Agnes(a) (Nesa)	5%
Christina/Stina	4%
Elisabeth(a)/Elsi	3%
Ma(g)dalena (-leina)	3%

Again, only the pronounced popularity of Maria distinguishes these names from those in Protestant Romance towns (cf. above, p. 265f.).

List One: Obersaxen Names

MEN (682):

1.	Joannes/Hans	118	(17%)
2.	Christian/-en	98	(14%)
3.	Marti(n)	63	(9%)
4.	Georgius/Jöri	58	(9%)
5.	Petrus	55	(8%)
6.	Caspar	46	(7%)
7.	Melcher/-ior	24	(4%)
8.	Jacob	21	(3%)
9.	Baltasar/Baltzer	17	(3%)
	Thoma(s)	17	(3%)
11.	Nicolaus/Claus	13	(2%)
12.	Mati(as)	12	(2%)
13.	Andrea(s)	10	(1%)

	Antonius (Thöni)	10	(1%)
15.	Gaudentius (-enz)	9	(1%)
	Michael (Michel)	9	(1%)
	Paulus	9	(1%)
18.	Wolffgang (Wolff)	8	(1%)
19.	Albreht	7	(1%)
	Josephus (Joes)	7	(1%)
21.	Lucius	6	
22.	Joder (Gioder)	5	
	Mauritius	5	
24.	Bartolomeus	4	
	Christophorus (Christophel)	4	
	Gregorius (Gorgas)	4	
	Sebastian (Baschli)	4	
28.	C(u)onradt	3	
	Fluri	3	
	Gallus	3	
	Placidus	3	
32.	Leonhardus	2	
	Philippus	2	
	Ru(o)dolph	2	

35. (one each) Albertus, Alexandrus, Davit, Fridolin, Hainricus, Hercules, Joanrich, Laurentius, Meltz, Otto, Sigisbertus, Simon, Urich, Valentinus.

Compound Names:

Joan(n)es	5
Lucius	1
Urich	1

WOMEN (611):

1. Maria	145	(24%)
2. Anna	110	(18%)
3. Catarina/Trina	50	(8%)
4. Barbara (Barbla)	48	(8%)
5. Dorothea	43	(7%)
6. Margareta/Greta	41	(7%)
7. Ursula/Urschla	31	(5%)
8. Agnes(a) (Nesa)	28	(5%)
9. Christina/Stina	22	(4%)
10. Elisabeth(a)/Elsi	20	(3%)
11. Ma(g)dalena (-leina)	19	(3%)
12. Menga (Dominica, Monica)	12	(2%)
13. Agat(h)a	5	(1%)
Fron(ic)a (Veronica)	5	(1%)
15. Brigida	3	
16. Cilia/Cilgia	2	
Emerita/Mierta	2	
Malia	2	

19. (one each) Bolonia, Eulscha, Finia, Frena, Gilgia, Helena, Julia, Martina, Maxina, Meyide, Mona, Thelgia.

Compound Names:

Maria	6
Anna	4
Agnes	1

d) Walser Protestant

The only Protestant Walser settlements in which little or no contact with Romance speakers took place through the 1600's, and whose archives contain available early church records, are Davos and Langwies. Mutten would be another prime subject for investigation, but the church registers there begin in 1772.[22]

The first three books of baptism records from Davos (nos. 73 and 73a) list a remarkable balance of 3897 men and 3898 women for the years from 1559 to 1647 and from 1649 to 1700.[23] The extraordinary number of names collected from the Davos registers makes possible more precise and reliable conclusions about Walser name-giving than would be possible if only a few hundred names were available. The twelve most popular men's names in Davos between 1559 and 1700 are:

Hans	921	(24%)
Christen/-ian	410	(11%)
Peter	244	(6%)
Andres/Enderli	224	(6%)
Jöri (Jörg, Georg)	177	(5%)
Caspar	149	(4%)
Jacob	135	(3%)
Conrad	132	(3%)
Claus/Nigg(o) (Nicolaus)	118	(3%)
Paul	118	(3%)
Uolrich/Ul(d)rich	115	(3%)
Marti(n)	108	(3%)

These twelve names were borne by nearly three-fourths of Davos men and form a distinct group. The

next name on the list, <u>Meinrad</u>, appears only 58 times
(1%), and the less popular names form a continuum
descending from fifty to one. Because of the large
body of material investigated, the relative position
of the first six names seems to be secure: If there
were twice as many men in Davos it is doubtful that
the order of these names would change. But <u>Jacob</u> appears only three more times than does <u>Conrad</u>, and their
relative positions are thus quite unstable. Similarly,
only ten attestations separate <u>Claus</u> and <u>Marti(n)</u>, and
this order might well have turned out differently if
name-giving practices had been different in only one or
two families. The relative order of the <u>Jacob</u>-<u>Conrad</u>
and <u>Claus</u>-<u>Marti(n)</u> groups, however, is more stable.

As usual, <u>Hans</u> is by far the most popular name.
It should be mentioned that <u>Johannes</u> appears 34 times
and <u>Jann</u> four times as well, but the addition of these
names to <u>Hans</u> raises the <u>Johannes</u> group only one point
to 25%.

Only fifty men out of 3897 have compound names,
and 42 of these are formed with <u>Hans</u>. The 450 names of
German origin account for 12% of the male onomasticon.

The Davos and Langwies material available for both
the pre- and post-Reformation eras offers a valuable
opportunity for evaluating the effect of the religious
upheaval on naming traditions in Graubünden. A

comparison of the two name groups shows that the name-
giving traditions in Davos and Langwies changed somewhat after the Reformation:

1289-1562 (715 men)

1. <u>Hans</u>, etc. (cf.   22%
   Chapter III, p. 144)
2. <u>Peter</u>   6%
3. <u>Cristen</u>/-<u>an</u>   6%
   <u>Marti</u>   6%
5. <u>Claus</u>/<u>Nigg</u>   4%
   (Niclaus)
6. <u>Jacob</u> (Jagg,   4%
   Jägli)
7. <u>Jöry</u>/-<u>ig</u> (Georg, 3%
   Georyus)
8. <u>Casper</u>   3%
   <u>Heini</u>/<u>Heintz</u>   3%
   (Heinrich,
   Heintzmann)
10. <u>Üli</u> (Ulrich, Ütz) 3%
11. <u>Jos</u> (Jost, Jösch, 3%
    Jössly)
12. <u>Symon</u>   3%
    <u>Thöny</u>/<u>Töntz</u>   3%

1559-1700 (4008 men)

1. <u>Hans</u>   23%
2. <u>Christian</u>/-<u>en</u> 15%
3. <u>Peter</u>   6%
4. <u>Andres</u>/   5%
   <u>Enderli</u>
5. <u>Jöri</u> (Jörg,   5%
   Georg)
6. <u>Caspar</u>   4%
7. <u>Jacob</u>   3%
8. <u>Conrad</u>   3%
9. <u>Ülrich</u>/   3%
   <u>Ul(d)rich</u>
10. <u>Claus</u>/<u>Nigg(o)</u> 3%
    (Nicolaus)
11. <u>Paul</u>   3%
12. <u>Martin</u>   3%

The fate of three names is especially noteworthy:
<u>Christian</u>/-<u>en</u> rose from 6% to 15% to take a firm hold
on second place, and <u>Marti</u> dropped from third place
(6%) to twelfth (3%) after the Reformation. In addition
<u>Andres</u>/<u>Enderli</u> appeared in twenty-second place before
the Reformation (1%) but later rose to fourth place
(5%). Two German names exchanged positions: <u>Heini</u>/

Heintz fell from eighth place (3%) to thirtieth, but
Conrad filled this gap by rising from seventeenth place
to eighth. Jos, Symon, and Thöny dropped from positions eleven and twelve to 21, 27, and 28. Paul rose
slightly from fifteenth place to eleventh.

The women's names may now be compared briefly to
establish a broader basis for evaluating the causes of
these onomastic changes:

1454-1562 (159 women)		1559-1700 (4005 women)	
1. Anna	20%	1. Anna	19%
2. Elsa/Elsi	18%	2. Maria	15%
3. Gretta/ Margaretta	14%	3. Drina (Catharina)	12%
4. Urs(ch)la/-y	10%	4. Ursula/ Urschla	11%
5. Cristina	5%	5. Barbla	7%
6. Barbla/ Barbara	4%	6. Elisabetha (Elsbe(th), Elsa/e)	7%
Cilia	4%	7. Dorothe(a)	6%
Doritte/ Dorothe/ Dorle	4%	8. Greta/ Marg(a)reta	5%
9. Ag(a)tha	3%	9. Christina/ Stina	4%
Meretta	3%	10. Verena	2%
		11. Lena/ Ma(g)d(a)lena	2%

The most apparent differences are the appearances
of Maria and Drina after the Reformation. Maria, re-
presenting 15% of the Davos-Langwies women after the
Reformation, is not attested once in the earlier list.

<u>Drina</u> (Catharina) appears only twice in Davos-Langwies before the Reformation, but later rises to third place with 12%. <u>Elsa</u>/<u>Elsi</u> and <u>Gretta</u>/<u>Margaretta</u> fall from second (18%) and third (14%) place to more modest positions (7% and 5%). <u>Cilia</u>, <u>Ag(a)tha</u>, and <u>Meretta</u> each account for less than one percent of the post-Reformation names. <u>Verena</u> and <u>Lena</u>/<u>Ma(g)d(a)lena</u> appear respectively three times and once in the pre-Reformation era.

A certain degree of onomastic re-formation is apparent from the above comparisons. Is it necessary, however, to assume that the Reformation was responsible for it? An examination of the kinds of names used before and after the Reformation should answer this question. Of special interest will be names of German origin and Biblical names, since these two groups offered onomastic alternatives to those reformers who wanted to avoid the use of the "Catholic" saints' names.

The pre-Reformation men's names from Davos and Langwies include 13% of German origin. Later this proportion drops to 11%, hardly a significant difference. It may, however, be worth noting that taken separately the groups show opposite treatment of German names. Pre-Reformation Langwies sources revealed an onomasticon which was 20% German; later this figure dropped to 9%. In pre-Reformation Davos only 9% of the men had

German names, but later the proportion rose to 12%.
It would be foolish to propose that one group of
people in Langwies suddenly did away with German names
while another group in Davos promoted their use for
religious reasons. Because both towns fully accepted
the Reformation at the same time, it is highly unlikely
that the introduction of Protestantism had anything to
do with the apparently random onomastic changes which
affected German names.

The promotion or rejection of the "Catholic" onomasticon from one religious era to the next poses questions about the fate of several individual names. The
sudden popularity of Christian/-en after the Reformation
(from 6% to 15%) can hardly be attributed to the demand
for more Biblical names, because Christian is of Medieval origin (cf. Chapter II, p. 61) and does not appear
in the Bible. Drosdowski reports that Christian gained
popularity in Germany after the Reformation and especially among Protestants (LV 53), but this does not mean
that the religious reformers directly sponsored its
use.[24]

If Martin enjoyed increased popularity in Germany
after the religious activities of Martin Luther (Drosdowski LV 150), the opposite seems to have happened in
Davos and Langwies. The reason for the decline of Martin's popularity from third place to twelfth is not

clear. Nor is it apparent why Andres/Enderli suddenly
ascended to fourth place from twenty-second. If it
might be supposed that Thöny dropped in Protestant
Davos-Langwies because it is the name of a saint, why
did the Biblical Jos (< Joseph) and Symon lose popularity as well? And if saints' names fell into disfavor
in Protestant areas, why did Conrad (St. Conrad, Bishop
of Constance) increase in popularity while Heini/Heintz,
not a saint's name, decreased?

Women's names present similar puzzles. The popularity of Maria is certainly the result of Biblical
association, and yet the name can by no means be termed
"Protestant" because of its leading position among Catholic women in Romance towns (22%) and Walser Obersaxen (24%). If religious considerations were truly
important, it would seem that Protestants would reject
those names which Catholics especially seemed to favor.
Maria, however, is borne by 9% of Romance Protestant
women and by 15% of Davos-Langwies Walser.[25] The other
women's names which do not appear in similar proportions
in both lists seem to owe their popularity, or lack of
it, to factors every bit as unexplainable.

Finally, it should be mentioned that the Biblical
names attested in Davos after, but not before, the Reformation (Salomon (33), Elias (9), Gabriel (2), Sara
(1), and Rachael (4)) comprise less than one percent of

the 7795 men and women baptized in Davos between 1559 and 1700.

Thus there seems to be little or no connection between the introduction of the Reformation in Davos and Langwies and the first names which were popular in those communities during the sixteenth and seventeenth centuries.

*   *   *

The comparisons presented here illustrate what appears to be a basic characteristic of name-giving. It is evident from the studies cited above (p. 249) and from this investigation that Protestant parents no longer associated the names of their children with the Catholic saints whose glorification had promoted the names in the late Middle Ages. If a Protestant child bore the name of a Catholic saint, it was certainly not because the parents thought of the saint at the time of the baptism, but simply because the name enjoyed popularity in the community or in the family.

The Swiss Folklore Atlas shows that name-giving even today is one of the countless elements of folk culture passed from one generation to the next, and that the onomastic traditions of a community or a family no longer take into account the conscious "nomen est omen" philosophy of the Classical world or of Medieval society. In questions of name-giving in Switzerland, grandparents are consulted most often in present-day Graubünden (Geiger-Weiss ASVKo 344f.; Escher SA 22), where in most families the first son is named after the father's father, the first daughter after the mother's mother, and so on. Name-giving has traditionally been --and doubtless was at the time of the Reformation--a conscious process of renewing personal associations with the past, and family tradition is clearly more important in the eyes of the name-givers than a religious associa- tion which was never clear even in the crucial years of the Reformation and Counterreformation.

List Two: Davos Names

MEN (3897):

1.	Hans	921	(24%)
2.	Christan/-ian	410	(15%)
3.	Peter	244	(6%)
4.	Andres/Enderli	224	(6%)
5.	Jöri (Jörg, Georg)	177	(5%)
6.	Caspar	149	(4%)
7.	Jacob	135	(3%)
8.	Conrad	132	(3%)
9.	Claus/Nigg(o) (Nicolaus)	118	(3%)
	Paul	118	(3%)
11.	Ûlrich/Ul(d)rich	115	(3%)
12.	Marti(n)	108	(3%)
13.	Meinrad	58	(1%)

14.	Michel	50	(1%)
15.	David	49	(1%)
16.	Flori (Fluri)	47	(1%)
17.	Abraham	46	(1%)
	Stephan	46	(1%)
19.	Dichtus (Benedic(h)t)	38	(1%)
	Thoma(n)(-s)	38	(1%)
21.	Johannes	34	
22.	Laurentz (Lorentz)	33	
	Salomon	33	
24.	Luci	32	
25.	Berent/Bernet/ Bern(h)ardt	30	
	Töni (Anthoni)	30	
27.	Joss (Joseph)	27	
28.	Simon	26	
29.	Lienhart	25	
30.	Heinrich	23	
	Jochum	23	
32.	Tiss (Matthis)	22	
33.	Felix	19	
	Gaudenz	19	
35.	Erhart	17	
36.	Balthasar	16	
	Bartli (Bertli, Bartolome)	16	
	Lucas	16	
39.	Thobias	15	
40.	Bläsli (Blasius)	13	
41.	Dieble	12	
42.	Oswalt	10	
43.	Elias	9	
44.	Vit	8	
45.	Wallentin	7	

46.	Beat(us)	6
	(Gre)Gorius (Gorias)	6
	Rudolph	6
	Stoffel	6
50.	Fortunat	5
	Jochum	5
52.	Gebhart	4
	Jann	4
	Mauritz	4
	Wilhelm	4
56.	(Se)Bastian/ Baschli	3
	Daniel	3
	Dionys	3
	Gallus	3
	Joder	3
	Melchior	3
	Otto	3
	Sixtus	3
	Valentius	3
	Victor	3
	Zacharias	3
67.	Adam	2
	Fridericus	2
	Gabriel	2
	Gotthart	2
	Jeremias	2
	Theobaldt	2

73. (one each) Ambrosi, Badt, Bathart, Erassmus, Ferdinand, Hanibal, Hartmann, Hertli, Isaac, Jeronymus, Nutin, Parcifal, Pedrudt, Silvester.

Compound Names:

Hans	42	(1%)

Johann	4
Christen	1
Georg	1
Jörg	1
Ulrich	1

WOMEN (3898):

1. Anna	751	(19%)
2. Maria	581	(15%)
3. Drina (Catharina)	485	(12%)
4. Ursula/Urschla (Ursina)	427	(11%)
5. Barbla	283	(7%)
6. Elisabetha (Elsa/e, Elsbe(th))	259	(7%)
7. Dorothe(a)	248	(6%)
8. Greta/Marg(a)reta	203	(5%)
9. Christina/Stina	155	(4%)
10. Verena	95	(2%)
11. Lena/Ma(g)d(a)lena	83	(2%)
12. Apolonia	44	(1%)
13. Burga	38	(1%)
14. Fida	35	
Lucia/Zya	35	
16. Meret(a) (Möretga, Mörtesa, Emerita)	30	
17. Sina (Syne)	24	
18. Ag(a)tha	15	
(Ce)Zilia	15	
20. Cleophe	14	
21. Clara	11	
22. Marta	7	
23. Agnes	5	
24. Berta	4	

Eva	4
Menga	4
Rachael	4
Salome	4
29. Regula	2

30. (one each) Annotha, Fila, Frosemunda, Isabella, Jacobea, Julia, Ottilia, Perpetua, Resa, Sara, Sedonia, Sibilla.

Compound Names:

Anna	11
Catharina	5
Dorothea	2
Barbara	1
Maria	1
Thrina	1

e) Walser-Romance Protestant

Two separate contact zones contain church records which shed light on post-Reformation name-giving. In Prättigau the mixture of Walser and Romance speakers was well under way by the Reformation, and the entire valley was German-speaking by the late 1500's (cf. Chapter III, p. 191ff.). Few early records are preserved from the Rheinwald, but it was shown in Chapter III (p. 120ff.) that a considerable degree of Walser-Romance contact there should be assumed for the pre-Reformation era. Both of these contact zones accepted Protestantism, Prättigau by about 1590 (Camenisch BR 250 and the Rheinwald by 1530 (Issler GR 20).

1) Prättigau

Post-Reformation sources from Prättigau[26] show the most popular names among 3398 men to have been:

Cristen/-ian	17%
Hans	15%
Peter	8%
Andris/-e(a)s// End(er)li (Endris, Andreyen)	6%[27]
Jacob	6%
Jöri (Georg, Giöry)	4%
Jan	4%
Cla(u)s (Niclas)	3%
Marti	2%
Caspar	2%
Flury/Flori	2%
Bartli (Bärtsch, Batt, Batrug)	2%

Hans appears here for the first time in second place behind Cristen/-ian, but the entire Johannes complex (Hans, Jan, Johann(es), Nuttli) accounts for 20% of the names.[28]

The most apparent change in the Prättigau onomasticon after the Reformation is the rise in popularity of Christen/-ian from 8% to 17%. As in Davos, no explanation for this increase seems plausible for religious reasons. Also striking is <u>Jan</u>'s decline in popularity from second place (12%) to seventh (4%). The fact that this decrease is not accompanied by a corresponding rise in the proportion of <u>Hans</u> attestations is further evidence that these two different forms of <u>Johannes</u> were not considered·to be one and the same name (cf. Chapter III, note 13). If a high incidence of <u>Jan</u> is truly a characteristic of the Romance onomasticon, then the decrease in its popularity in post-Reformation Prättigau is a sign that the Germanization of the valley affected not·only the language of the native inhabitants, but other aspects of their culture as well.

The decline of <u>Jan</u> was accompanied by the rise of <u>Peter</u>, <u>Andre(a)s</u>/<u>Enderli</u>, <u>Flury</u>, and <u>Bartli</u> and the decline of <u>Risch</u>. None of these changes can be explained satisfactorily on confessional grounds.

Women's names in Prättigau[29] include among 1762 women:

<u>Anna</u>	19%
<u>Elsa</u> (Elsbetha, Lisa, Lisebeth)	12%
(Mar)<u>Greta</u>	10%
<u>Maria</u>	8%
(Ca)<u>Thrina</u> (Drina)	7%
<u>Barbla</u> (Barbara, Barffla)	7%
<u>Ursula</u>/<u>Urschla</u> (Ursina)	6%
(Chri)<u>Stina</u>	5%

As in Davos, the main difference between these
names and those of the pre-Reformation period is the
appearance of Maria. In Prättigau, however, the new
name did not attain the high position which it gained
in Davos (15%, second place). Greta, Christina, and
Urschla all declined in popularity and Catherina/Thrina
rose after the Reformation. No confessional reasons
seem plausible for these changes; even if one were to
assume that the increased popularity of Christian had
a religious basis,[24] the decline of Christina from 12%
to 5% proves the assumption to be ill-founded.[30]

Other possible indications of a religious influence on name-giving in Prättigau are inconclusive.
German names among men do not increase in popularity,
but decline from 15% to 8%. Biblical names not attested before the Reformation (Isaac, Solomon, Zacharias,
Juditha, Sara, etc.) account for only 18 of 5160 Prättigau men and women.

List Three: Prättigau Names

MEN (3398):

1. Cristen/-ian	591	(17%)
2. Hans	512	(15%)
3. Peter	263	(8%)
4. Andris/e(a)(s)/ End(er)li (Endris, Andreyen)	207	(6%)

5.	Jacob	199	(6%)
6.	Jöri (Georg, Giöry)	137	(4%)
7.	Jan	126	(4%)
8.	Cla(u)s (Niclas)	89	(3%)
9.	Marti	82	(2%)
10.	Caspar	80	(2%)
	Flury/Flori	80	(2%)
12.	Bartli (Bärtsch, Batt, Batrug)	75	(2%)
13.	Thöni (Anthoni)	62	(2%)
	Urich (Ulli, Ul(d)rich)	62	(2%)
15.	Jos (Josep)	51	(2%)
16.	Lutzi	49	(1%)
17.	Thoma(n)	46	(1%)
18.	Lienhart	45	
19.	Val(en)tin (Feldein)	44	
20.	Johann(es)	40	
21.	Rudolf (Rutsch)	33	
22.	Simon/Schamaun (Simen, Schamon)	31	
23.	Stäffen	29	
24.	Heinrich (Heintz)	28	
25.	Dis/Mattis (Dysch, Dusch, Mattli)	27	
26.	Fest(er)	22	
	Michel	22	
28.	Brose (Ambrosy)	21	
29.	Fidt	18	
	Kunradt (Curat, Kerandin, Guredyn)	18	
31.	Basch (Bastele, Beschian)	15	
	Lentz (Lorentz)	15	
33.	Felig	13	
	Ottli (Odman)	13	

35.	Fried(li)	11
	Luck(as)	11
37.	Adam	10
38.	Cyprian	9
	Risch	9
40.	Hartmann	8
	Palli	8
42.	Marckh (Märckh)	7
43.	Baltz (Beltz, Balthasar)	6
	Daniel	6
	Dietegen (Dietägi)	6
	Gadient (Gadäntz)	6
	Joder	6
48.	Bernet (Bernardt)	5
49.	Chiliass	4
	Dicht	4
	Gabbergel (Gabriel)	4
	Gall(us)	4
	Lem	4
	Oswald	4
	Wilhelm	4
	Xander (Alexander)	4
57.	Fort	3
	Gories	3
	Jochem	3
	Nauly	3
	Sixt	3

62. (two each) Abundi, Albert/Tutsch, Augustin/
Agenstin, Beat(us), Cilies, Franz, Gebhart,
Hercoles, Isaac, Jegen, Jeremias, Jeronimus,
Ludwig, Melch(er), Salomon, Theodorig, Wal-
ther/Wälthy

79. (one each) Abraham, Alle, Bleisch, Carly,
Claud., Crispinus, Dade, Dietrich, Diew,

Hand, Jelli, Jenart, Julius, Moritz, Nön,
Nuttli, Odmar, Perdold, Perttes, Stoffel,
Tobias, Urban, Wehrli, Wolf, Zacharias.

Compound Names:

Hans	28
Ulrich	3
Claus	2
Peter	2
Alberty	1
Jan	1
Johanness	1

WOMEN (1762):

1. Anna — 334 (19%)
2. Elsa (Elsbetha, Lisa, Lisbeth) — 209 (12%)
3. (Mar)Greta — 181 (10%)
4. Maria — 145 (8%)
5. (Ca)Thrina (Drina) — 123 (7%)
6. Barbla (Barffla, Barbara) — 121 (7%)
7. Ursula/Urschla (Ursina) — 113 (6%)
8. (Chri)Stina — 84 (5%)
9. Dorothea — 41 (2%)
10. Menga — 40 (2%)
11. Burga — 38 (2%)
12. Eva — 37 (2%)
13. Zia (Lucya) — 32 (2%)
14. Madlena (Lena) — 30 (2%)
15. Ag(a)tha — 28 (2%)
16. Tschina (Schina) — 27 (2%)
17. (Ap)Polonia — 17 (1%)

18.	Frena	15
19.	Merta (Meritta, Mortha)	13
20.	Clara	11
	Ros(in)a	11
22.	Cordula	10
23.	Nesa (Agnes(a))	9
24.	Künga (Cunigunde)	8
25.	Sina	7
26.	Petronella/Nella	5
27.	Fronegica/Negga	4
	Truta	4
	Zilia	4
30.	Cleophe (Clefa)	3
	Fida	3
	Johanina	3
	Lucretia	3
	Regina	3
	Sybilla	3
36.	Juditha	2
	Martha	2
	Salome	2
	Sara	2
	Susanna	2
	Zeda	2

42. (one each) Adelheit, Anastasia, Anthonia,
Ensa, Leda, Nutina, Ottilia, Petra, Regula,
Xillyana.

Compound Names:

Anna	10
Margareta	3
Maria	3
Ursula	2

Cordula	1
Regina	1
Rosina	1

2)   The Rheinwald

It was shown in Chapter III (p. 120ff.) that the
Walser who came to the Rheinwald in the thirteenth century encountered a sizeable number of Romance speakers
in the outer valley. Two possible directions were suggested for the onomastic development of the entire valley: The Romance names were supported and constantly
refreshed by contact with the Romance population south
of the Splügen Pass and to the east in Schams; or the
Walser expansion from the inner valley was so rapid that
no distinct Romance naming tradition survived.

The names from various post-Reformation sources in
the Rheinwald are compared with these alternatives in
mind. The onomasticon of the inner valley and that of
the outer valley[31] show that local differences are visible: Joder and Gorius are popular (4% and 3%) in the
inner valley during the first half of the seventeenth
century, but not during the second half. Lienhart appears during the late 1600's. Marti is more common in
the inner valley (12%) than in the outer valley (5%),
and Andre(a)s appears more often in Splügen, Medels,
and Sufers (7%) than in Nufenen and Hinterrhein (2%).

Antoni(us) and Alexander are attested more frequently
in the outer valley than in the inner valley. The inner valley differs from 1628-1666 to 1666-1700 as much
as it differs from the outer valley in both periods
combined. On the whole, it is impossible to establish
naming trends which separate the two halves of the
Rheinwald into two distinct onomastic units.

If Romance speakers continued to constitute a
culturally distinct minority in the Rheinwald after the
arrival of the Walser, this is not visible in the Rheinwald names (see below). Prättigau is known to have
contained Romance speakers until late in the sixteenth
century, and this Romance minority is reflected in the
names which appear there but not in Walser Davos:
Andreya, Batt, Batrug, Schamäun, Guredyn (< Conrad),
Beschian, and so on. The total absence of Romance name
forms in Rheinwald church records from the same period
suggests that the contact with Romance speakers in
Schams and to the south of the Splügen and San Bernardino passes did in fact not reinforce any Romance onomasticon which survived the immigration of the Walser.

List Four: Rheinwald Names

MEN (1120):

1. Christian/-en   161 (14%)
2. Hans/Johannes   158 (14%)

3.	Jöry/Georgius (Jeri)	98	(9%)
4.	Marti(n)	94	(8%)
5.	Jacob	87	(8%)
6.	Peter	85	(8%)
7.	Andre(a)s	56	(5%)
8.	Casper/-ar	50	(4%)
9.	Antoni(us) (Thönny)	28	(3%)
10.	Lienhart (Leonhart)	27	(2%)
	Michel	27	(2%)
12.	Alexander	22	(2%)
13.	Claus (Nicolaus)	14	(1%)
	Luci(us)	14	(1%)
15.	Ba/ertli (Bartlimo, Bartholomeus)	12	(1%)
	Lore(n)tz/Loritius (Räntz)	12	(1%)
	Mattli	12	(1%)
18.	Flori	9	
	Joder	9	
	Philipp	9	
21.	Thomas/-an	8	
22.	Jeremias	7	
23.	Bernhart	6	
	Gillius (Jilli)	6	
	Gorius	6	
26.	Bastian (Bastle)	5	
27.	(Chri)Stoffel	4	
	Cuonradt	4	
	Daniel	4	
	Paul	4	
	Sim(e)on	4	
	Stephan	4	
33.	Davidt	3	
	Eberhart (Eby)	3	
	Frid(e)rich(us)	3	

	Josephus	3	
	U(o)rich	3	
	Vincenz	3	
39.	Hartmann/Härtli	2	
	Hercules	2	
	Herman	2	
	Maax/Maximilianus	2	

43. (one each) Abraham, Albert, Bachli, Balthasar,
Banlius, Cornelius, Gallus, Gartman, Godtlieb,
Gentz, Horatz, Huldenricus, Josua, Rudolff,
Samson, Theophilus, Vallatin, Vitus, Wieland,
Zacharias.

Compound Names:

Hans	19	(2%)
Johann	7	
Christian	1	

WOMEN (1076):

1.	Anna (-li)	155	(14%)
2.	Maria	143	(14%)
3.	(Chri)Stina	100	(9%)
4.	Elsbeth/Elsa (Elsi, Elisabetha)	91	(8%)
5.	(Mar)Greta	89	(8%)
6.	Ursula/Urschla	80	(7%)
7.	Agatha (Acta)	70	(7%)
8.	Barbla/-ara	66	(7%)
9.	Fida	58	(5%)
10.	(Ca)Thrina (Chaiarina)	28	(3%)
11.	Cordula	24	(2%)
12.	Dorathe(a)	22	(2%)
13.	Ma(g)d(a)lena	19	(2%)

14.	Cilia (Cecilia)	11	(1%)
	Verena/Frena	11	(1%)
16.	Regula	10	(1%)
	Rosa	10	(1%)
	Susanna	10	(1%)
19.	Acola	4	
	Felicita	4	
	Martha	4	
22.	Agnes (Nesa)	3	
	Sara	3	
24.	Eva	2	
	Frona	2	
	Violanda	2	

27. (one each) Ammalia, Burga, Eleonora, Elsta, Englina, Jacobea, Johanna, Lucia, Menga, Sabina, Salome, Thomoshea, Uohta, Virgo.

Compound Names:

Anna	28	(3%)
Maria	6	
Catharina	2	
Cordula	2	
Madalena	2	
Margreth	1	

f) Conclusion

In Chapter III the percentage of German names used in the various regions of Graubünden was an important index of the concentration of Walser and Romance speakers in any given area. Compound names such as Johann Ulrich normally indicated the presence of noble families in a community.

The investigation of post-Reformation Romance
sources shows that German names no longer occur in
characteristic proportions in either Catholic or Protestant communities; nor is this true for Walser or
Walser-Romance areas. Catholic and Protestant, Walser
and Romance cannot be distinguished in any way by the
German names present in their onomastica.

Compound names are also ineffective in characterizing either Walser or Romance areas or confessional
groups; they also are not always used by the nobility.
Compound names early in the 1600's are normally those
of noble families: Cordula Magdalena is the daughter
of D(ominus) Signifer Christianus Georgius (of the noble
Schorsch) and Dna (Domina) Anna Maria Elmeriana in the
Rheinwald in 1631. Later, however, they become fashionable among all segments of the population. In Salouf,
where only two compound names are recorded among men
from 1641 to 1691, eleven appear among undistinguished
families between 1692 and 1700.

Although German names and compound names provide
no clues to the identification of Romance or Walser
populations, other elements in the onomastic vocabulary
of Graubünden show that two kinds of name-giving remain
clearly visible throughout the seventeenth century.

1)   Romance Names

The study of pre-Reformation Graubünden showed
that a uniform onomasticon existed from which, with
some local variations, Romance speakers chose their
names. Both the names used in Romance areas and the
proportion of German names remained relatively constant.

Later developments, however, produced an entirely
different picture. Not only the proportions of German
names, but also the "standard" onomasticon was found
to vary from community to community regardless of confession in Romance areas. No single criterion could
be found by which Romance men's names could be defined
as a group. (Romance women's names were found to be
remarkably similar, but cannot be called exclusively
"Romance" because they are shared by Walser women as
well.[32])

Soon after Christian names were introduced into
Raetia a number of them were standardized and used by
the Romance population as a whole. Up to the end of
the 1400's little local variation had taken place, but
this soon changed. By the seventeenth century random
choices seem to have been made in each Romance community
which produced a variegated onomastic picture of Romance
Graubünden characterized as a whole only by its remarkable disunity. It is doubtful that the Reformation had

anything to do with the dissolution of the Romance
onomasticon, for no confessional lines are clearly
visible. More probable is simply the universal factor
of local preference, or Namenmode: If a man was highly
regarded, his name became popular (cf. Julius (Gilli)
Maissen in the Oberland); if someone was looked down
upon, his name was condemned as well (cf. Catharina
in Salouf). Combined with the time difference between
the 1400's and the 1600's, this factor of local popularity gains considerable importance and seems to be
the sole explanation for the breakdown of the Romance
name vocabulary even between pairs of towns as close
together as Bergün-Samedan and Trins-Flims.

2)   Walser Names

The opposite seems to have taken place among the
Walser. A comparison of the Rheinwald names with those
of Davos and Prättigau shows a remarkable uniformity
among these three areas. The Rheinwald names differ
just as much from the Davos names as do those in Prättigau: The three groups are similar, yet vary in characteristic respects. A schematic representation shows
the similarities and differences:

Davos		Prättigau		Rheinwald	
Hans	24%	Christian	17%	Christian	14%
Christian	11%	Hans	15%	Hans	14%
Peter	6%	Peter	8%	Jöri	9%
Andres	6%	Andres	8%	Marti	8%
Jöri	5%	Jacob	6%	Jacob	8%
Caspar	4%	Jöri	4%	Peter	8%
Jacob	3%	JAN	4%	Andre(a)s	5%
CONRAD	3%	Claus	3%	Caspar	4%
Claus	3%	Marti	2%	ANTONI	3%
PAUL	3%	Caspar	2%	MICHEL	2%
ULRICH	3%	FLURY	2%	LIENHART	2%
Marti	3%	BARTLI	2%	ALEXANDER	2%
				Claus	1%

(The underlined names in each list are those which occupy a special position in relation to the other lists: Hans is relatively popular and Jacob relatively unpopular in Davos, Jöri and Marti enjoy special favor in the Rheinwald, and Caspar is somewhat less common in Prättigau than elsewhere. The names in capitals in each list are those which do not occur among the favorites in both of the other areas. The appearance of JAN, FLURY, and BARTLY among the top twelve names is characteristic of Prättigau, and so on.)

These three lists treat the three most important concentrations of Walser culture in post-Reformation Graubünden. Especially in view of the similarities

identified in these areas, the onomasticon of Catholic
Obersaxen (above, p. 269ff.) acquires considerable importance as well.

The most common names in Obersaxen show essential
agreement with the Davos, Prättigau, and Rheinwald lists.
Three names appear in Obersaxen which are not among the
favorites elsewhere: Melher/-ior, Baltasar/-tzr, and
Thoma/-s. These names, however, are attested in moderate frequency in the other areas. Most important,
seven of the first eight names in Obersaxen appear among
the first eight elsewhere as-well (with the exception of
Caspar, which is tenth in Prättigau). All of these
areas--Walser Protestant, Walser Catholic, and Walser-
Romance Protestant--have unmistakably similar onomastica.

In the discussion of Obersaxen names above, special
attention was called to the prominent position of
Christian there. Its popularity in Obersaxen contrasted
strongly with its relative absence in Romance communities in the Oberland and suggested that a connection
existed between Obersaxen and other Walser areas, where
Christian was common.

Marti, although prominent before the Reformation,
later fell into disuse in the Romance communities in
the Oberland. In the Davos group of Walser colonies to
the east Marti was only moderately popular both before
and after the Reformation. Although early Rheinwald

names are lacking, the absence of a St. Martin's church
in the valley would seem to indicate that <u>Marti</u>, if at
all popular there, was not as common as it was in the
Oberland, where Farner (<u>KG</u> 53ff.) established the presence of a well-developed St. Martin cult. But the
post-Reformation Rheinwald names include <u>Marti</u> in fourth
place with a respectable 8%. What source for this popularity is apparent but conservative Obersaxen, where
even during the 1600's <u>Marti</u> still appears in third
place with 9%? The borrowing from Obersaxen to the
Rheinwald, of course, would have to have taken place
before the Counterreformation because of the later lack
of contact between Catholics and Protestants. Assuming
that <u>Christian</u> is found in Obersaxen as the result of
contact with Vals (< Rheinwald), Obersaxen seems to have
reciprocated by "supplying" <u>Marti</u> to the Rheinwald. And
not only <u>Marti</u> was available for borrowing: <u>Jöri</u>, appearing in fourth place in Obersaxen (9%), is found in
third place in the Rheinwald with the same percentage
and exists in Davos and Prättigau in lesser proportions.

*   *   *

It is appropriate here to return to the often-posed
question, "Is there such a thing as a Walser name?" The
survey of Walser, Romance, and Rhine Valley name-giving
undertaken in Chapter III showed that "Walser names" did

indeed continue to be used in Tavetsch, one of the
oldest Walser colonies in Graubünden. The sources just
investigated suggest that one might justifiably speak
of a Walser onomasticon for the post-Reformation period
as well. However, it must be remembered that these
constitute two different name groups.

The names brought by the Walser to Tavetsch were
not found in any of the material available from other
Walser areas during the pre-Reformation era. (Whether
these Tavetsch names survived to 1700 is unfortunately
not known because no church records exist there for the
first two hundred years after the Reformation.)

The second group of Walser names represents a
development from the Christian onomasticon widely used
throughout Graubünden before the Reformation. (These
names are found at that time in Davos and Prättigau,
but their existence in a largely unified configuration
in the Rheinwald and Obersaxen as well after the Reformation by no means indicates that the impulse of their
popularity emanated from Davos or Prättigau. Pre-
Reformation material from the Rheinwald and Obersaxen
is simply not available.[33])

Especially in view of the diverse collections of
men's names in Catholic and Protestant Romance communities, the first names in each of the Walser areas seem
to have been chosen from a central onomasticon. It is

highly unlikely that such a selection was made consciously; the image of community elders or other leading
citizens determining the names to be used at any given
time is utter fantasy. Yet such choices may quite plau-
sibly have been made unconsciously by the individual
name-givers in Walser colonies where inter-settlement
communication was a common--and often necessary--fact
of life. The existence of a more or less standard
Walser onomasticon which remained unchanged even by
religious upheaval (cf. Obersaxen) suggests that a considerable degree of intercommunication was maintained
by the Walser long after they came to Graubünden. Not
only was the contact close among Walser neighbors such
as those in Safien and the Rheinwald, but it seems to
have reached far beyond immediate geographical limits
to bring together the members of the Davos and Rheinwald
groups as well.[34]

The general agreement of Obersaxen names with those
in the Rheinwald (and, by association, with those in
Vals as well) inevitably leads to speculation about the
general onomastic history of Obersaxen, which might have
been something like the following:

> The Walser who came to Obersaxen represented
> a further stage of the Furka-Oberalp-Tavetsch mi-
> gration. As long as Tavetsch (and possibly Versam
> and Valendas to the east) was the only Walser

neighbor in the Romance environment, the Obersaxen Walser retained the archaic Walser name vocabulary brought from Wallis and well preserved in the Tavetsch _Jahrzeitbuch_ of 1450. When other Walser later appeared in the Oberland (Vals, Safien), however, contact with the new colonies slowly began to change the onomastic structures in Obersaxen just as the names used in Prättigau changed with the arrival of the Walser from Davos.

The Reformation led to the Romanization of Tavetsch and forced the Obersaxen Walser into a closer cultural association with the Walser in Vals. The friendship between the two settlements is reflected in the significant fact that Obersaxen, Vals, and the small intermediate colony in St. Martin are the only Walser communities which did not become Protestant. The Reformation, which was rejected in these three colonies, did not change the naming traditions of the Walser settlements where it was accepted. For these reasons the names found in Davos, Prättigau, and the Rheinwald do not differ significantly from those in Obersaxen.

What accounts for the apparent tendency of the Walser to maintain close communication between small colonies often separated by considerable distances? The methods by which the first Walser were settled in their

new surroundings (appropriation of land from native
Romance speakers) and the legal favoritism granted them
("herkommen Lütt, die da fry oder Walser sind..."[35])
in the feudal age make it not only likely, but probable,
that a considerable degree of animosity existed between
them and the Romance speakers who formed the native population. If problems arose between the Romance natives
and the newcomers, and there is every reason to suppose
they did, the Walser were forced together as a measure
of self-preservation in an alien and occasionally hostile environment.

This supposition explains the uniformity of Walser
names and the dissimilarity of Romance names (cf. Flims
and Trins) in the post-Reformation period. Romance
speakers, being the cultural majority, felt no need for
the close intercommunal relationships which the Walser
were forced to maintain. It should be emphasized here
that the close contact between Walser colonies is not
satisfactorily explained by a mystical feeling of cama-
raderie which is often proposed by enthusiasts who wish
to honor the accomplishments of this extraordinary
people. The basic need to survive as a cultural and
economic entity assured the maintenance of strong ties
which transcended the physical boundaries demarcated by
the native population of Romance Graubünden.

IV. Footnotes

1

Eidgenössische Volkszählung 1. Dezember 1960,
Bern, 1964, XI, 50.

2

The influence of German-speaking Zürich on bilingual areas in Graubünden has been mentioned above
(Chapter III, note 52).

3

In 1616 Haldenstein in the Fünf Dörfer became
the last town in Graubünden to accept the Reformation
(Poeschel KG VII, 363).

4

Of the towns on the river only Fideris and Jenaz
were not destroyed. Jenaz and its archives burned
some years later.

5

The Fünf Dörfer, which remained Catholic until
the early 1600's, still present a confused picture of
religious parity. Until recently schoolchildren in
Mastrils attended either the Catholic or the Protestant school in spite of the fact that the community
is hardly large enough (1960 population = 387) to support one schoolteacher. Mixed marriages have traditionally resulted in the estrangement of the marriage
partners from their families, yet were already so
common in the seventeenth century that the nearby
canton of Schwyz passed the following law in 1691
regarding the religious training of the children of
a Catholic-Protestant union:

> Erstlich wann zwey Ehemänschen zuosamen
> khämend, undt dass ein Catholisch undt das
> andere Evangelisch were undt Kinderen bey
> einanderen erzeugeten, ohne andere Heyraths
> Pacten, so sollen dann die Söhn in der Re-
> ligion dem Vater nachvolgen, undt die Döch-
> teren der Mutter nach, bis dann die Kinder
> in das Alter khommen auf 16 Jahr, undt dann
> füro hin soll es den Kinderen in der Reli-
> gion frey stehen. (Maissen EK 319)

The Fünf Dörfer subscribed to this law, often with
tragic consequences. If a Catholic father died, his
Protestant wife could prevent the sons from being
raised by the father's Catholic relatives by arranging
for the sons to be kidnapped and taken to a "safe"
Protestant refuge such as Zürich. The converse, of
course, was also true (cf. Maissen EK).

6   According to oral tradition in Vals the acceptance
of the Reformation was put to a vote which resulted in
a tie. At this moment of indecision an old Valser
goatherd came down from his alp and broke the tie with
a vote for the rejection of the new religion (Jörger
WV 21).

7   A girl born in Obersaxen in 1628, for example, is
the daughter of "brabara (sic) von grüneck aus lug-
netz"--from Romance Lugnez just over the mountain to
the south.
     Iso Müller offers conclusive evidence that Ober-
saxen contained a significant number of Romance speakers in the seventeenth century (VV 295): In 1635 the
church community in Obersaxen petitioned the Bishop of
Chur to send a Romansh-speaking priest to the Walser
town. In 1670 a Lugnezer, Gieli Demont, published a
missal containing German as well as Romansh texts.

8   Because some of these registers date from the late
1500's and others from a century later, their comparison might at first seem to be of questionable value
on temporal grounds. Can Davos names from the 1560's
be accurately compared with St. Antönien names from
1696? In order to answer this basic question sample
communities are analyzed from each of the cultural
areas: Salouf (Romance Catholic), Bergün (Romance
Protestant), Obersaxen (Walser Catholic), Davos
(Walser Protestant), and Prättigau and the Rheinwald
(mixed Protestant). The degree of change--the role
played by Namenmode--is analyzed in each area; the
details of each random investigation are presented in
the sections below.

9   In order to estimate the role played by Namenmode
in Bergün the marriage registers are investigated for
the periods 1586-1625 and 1626-1700. Because the Reformation was fully accepted in Bergün by about 1590,
the first group reflects names of Catholics as well
as Protestants; the second group begins in 1626, giving all those children who were born after the Reformation came to Bergün a chance to reach marriageable
age. The second group should therefore include only
Protestants.
     Neither the temporal difference between the two
groups nor the coming of the Reformation seems to
have changed the onomasticon of Bergün appreciably.
Jacum drops from second place (14%) to fourth (8%)
and Leonhard rises from twelfth (2%) to sixth (6%);
the relative frequency of other names remains virtually

the same. These slight changes do not seem to have taken place for religious reasons: Neither was <u>Jacob</u> scorned by the reformers nor was <u>Leonhard</u> consciously promoted by them.

10

    The addition of 39 <u>Jon</u> and 31 <u>Hans</u> combinations (<u>Jon Gori</u>, <u>Hans Luci</u>, etc.) raises these low figures from 8% (3%) to 14% (11%).

11

    The addition of the 39 <u>Anna</u> compounds (<u>Anna Maria</u>, etc.) raises this figure to 19%.

12

    Apparent variations of <u>Elisabeth(a)</u> in the eight Protestant and Catholic Romance towns cause some confusion. <u>Elsa/-i</u>, popular in Davos and Prättigau, appears in Bergün, Flims, Ilanz, and Trins; <u>(E)lis(a)-beth(a)</u> is common to all communities, Romance and Walser. One name characteristic of Romance regions is <u>Jeulscha</u> (Flims and Trins)/<u>Jelscha</u> (Bergün)/<u>Jelza</u> (Bevers); <u>Eulscha/Euscha</u> appears in Salouf and seems to have been assuffixed to <u>Schetta</u> in Bergün. <u>Jeltscha</u> is attested in Thusis in 1651 (Haffter <u>ST</u> 225). The <u>Rätisches Namenbuch</u> (II, 552) assigns <u>Eulscha</u> (and, therefore, these other forms as well) to <u>Elisabeth</u>, but other women's names obscure this association to such a degree that other sources for the shortened form might profitably be considered.

    The following men's names appear in Romance areas with their abbreviated forms: <u>Julius</u> (Jüli, Jilli), <u>Aegidius</u> (Gilg, Gellÿ), <u>Georgius</u> (Gieri, Jiere, Jeri, Jöri), <u>Jeremias</u> (Jeri, Jöri), and <u>Gregorius</u> (Göri, Gory). Female forms of two of these names (<u>Julia/Jülia</u> and <u>Gilgia</u>) are attested in Flims, Ilanz, and Siat; or do these forms represent more than two names? Examples of -<u>r</u>-/-<u>l</u>- exchange in Romansh areas are commonplace: <u>Margreta</u> > <u>Malgiaretta</u>, <u>Wilhelm</u> > <u>Guglerm/Goulerm</u>, and so on. Thus an entire name complex of <u>GVl-/GVr-</u>//<u>JVl-/JVr-</u> (V = vowel) is open to consideration and could even include <u>Urschla/Oschla</u> (cf. <u>RNB</u> II, 603). It would be surprising if <u>Eulscha</u> and its other forms were not in part inspired by this wide-ranging onomastic association.

13

    The variations of <u>Ulrich</u> among both German and Romance speakers in Graubünden illustrate well the contortions to which many no longer intelligible German names were subjected. The most common derivative of *<u>Odal-ric</u> in late Medieval texts is <u>Ulrich</u> (von Montfort, etc.). From this form are derived U(o)rich (cf. Obersaxen 1637) and the ever-popular U(o)li.

In Romansh-speaking areas *Odal-ric can become Uldal-
ric and then Uldaric (Siat 1671 and 1683), which is
syncopated in both Romansh and German areas to Uldrich
(Davos 1679). (The -d- in Uldrich may also simply be
a glide consonant easily inserted between -l- and
-r-.) A somewhat pietistic touch is added to the name
when Gmc *ōþal- 'riches, treasure' becomes Huld 'grace'
in the imaginative forms Huldenricus (Splügen-Medels-
Sufers 1642 and passim) and Huldrich (Langwies 1696
and 1698).

The loss of the first syllable (under Romance
stress of the second) produces Durig as well as the
Latinized Doricus in Salouf (1653). -rig is then
treated in two ways as the -g is palatalized and lost
in Duri (cf. the historian Duri Campell) and spiranti-
cized in Durich (Bergün 1695) and Durisch (Siat 1691).
By the time Risch develops (cf. Prättigau in pre- and
post-Reformation sources) any popular association of
the nickname with its ancestor *Odal-ric is purely co-
incidental. It will be recalled that a similar puzzle
involved the various forms of Johannes from Jan to
Nutt in the Davos Spendbuch as well as elsewhere in
Graubünden.

The treatment of German names by Romance speakers
was noticed in 1560 by Aegidius Tschudi:

> Item der tütsch nam Rŭdprecht / so von
> tütschen abkompt / ob ein Italianer den zŭ-
> namsen gefragt / wurd er vō anerborner art
> Robert namsen / dannenhar habend sy Robertus
> daruss gemacht / dañ sy kŏnnend nit Rŭdprecht
> nemen mit anderer stim. Dessglych vss Adel-
> brecht Albertus / Sigbrecht Simpertus / Wild-
> brecht Philibertus vñ dero noch vil / die wir
> wissend vss tütschen namen entsprungē. (AR 116)

14

The "corrected" form of Nutt, of course, is Johannes. The priest who recorded the names of children
baptized in Salouf hesitated to enter the nicknames
chosen by the parents. Compromises were made in some
instances, however: "Antonius seu vulgo Thieni" (1694),
"Christianus seu vulgo Christli" (1695), "Petrus vulgé
Pedrot" (1697), and "Petrus seu Patrut vulgo dictus"
(1697). The priest in Siat in 1665-66 reversed this
procedure by writing first the nickname, then the full
form: "Plasch (Plasius)," "Jüli (Julius)," etc. Obersaxen records include "Elsi vel Elisabetha" in 1691
and the Davos books record "Gorias (scripsit pro Gre-
gorius)" in 1688; in Seewis (1697) Thö- is stricken
and changed to Anthoni. An apparent popular etymology

is by chance correct in the Greek name <u>Dorothea</u> in
Splügen-Medels-Sufers (1661): "Dorothea i.e. Donu
Dei vel Donata à Deo." "Latiné Elisabeta" is written in Roman letters under "Elssbedt," which appears
in German script in the Rheinwald in 1658.

These entries are valuable, for they shed light
on aspects of name-giving which would otherwise have
to go unnoticed. From the Oberland baptism note in
1634 "nomine Theophilum aut Duff nostro idomate"
(Müller <u>VV</u> 302) the etymology of <u>Duff</u>< <u>Theophil</u> (not
<u>David</u>) seems to be clear (cf. also Muoth <u>BG</u> 40 note 3).

The 1695 entry from Salouf ("Otto seu vulg Nutt"),
however, shows that etymological mistakes can be made.
But is the <u>Otto</u>/<u>Nutt</u> confusion to be regarded as a
mistake on the part of the Salouf priest? It is clear
from his entry that the correct etymological relationship of <u>Nutt</u> and <u>Johannes</u> was not understood. Yet a
cardinal rule of informant work is that a word means
what its speakers think it means; this may justifiably
be extended to include names, which "mean" what the
name-givers intend. On the basis of this assumption
the priest made no mistake, but only if the parents
of Nutt agreed with the priest that the nickname came
from <u>Otto</u> and not from <u>Johannes</u>. This is now impossible to determine, but positive evidence is contained
in the excellent Oberländer Romansh-German dictionary
published by the Ligia Romontscha (R. Vieli and A.
Decurtins, <u>Vocabulari romontsch sursilvan-tudestg</u>,
Chur, 1962), which reports that <u>Nut</u> is the Oberländer
Romansh equivalent of German <u>Otto</u>. Thus an etymological myth seems to have been perpetuated as a popular
fact; but people, and not etymological dictionaries,
are the immediate sources of name-giving, and this
fact may well have been valid already in 1695.

The priest's helpful note introduces a further
question. <u>Gian(n)et</u>, <u>Janet</u>, and <u>Not</u> all appear in
Salouf, as do <u>Otto</u> (twice) and <u>Othones</u> (once). Because of the equation of <u>Nutt</u> with <u>Otto</u> most of these
names belong together etymologically; but should the
other occurrences of <u>Otto</u>/<u>Othones</u> be assumed to be
<u>Nutt</u> even if no connection is made in the church regi-
ster? Does the one connection justify grouping all
<u>Ottos</u> (here, luckily, there are only three) with
<u>Johannes</u>?

A similar case is found in the Davos baptism register (no. 73a), where a 1608 list of baptisms from
1559 to 1596 mentions the name "Nicodemus oder Nicco"
four times and "Nicolaus oder Claus" 23 times. <u>Nicco</u>
(which also appears as <u>Nigg</u>) can be derived from <u>Nico-</u>
<u>laus</u> as well as from <u>Nicodemus</u>, and the case is strong

for the former: <u>Nicodemus</u> is not attested in this form among any of the 20,000-odd names in pre- or post-Reformation sources examined in this study. <u>Nicolaus</u>, on the other hand, is quite common. This is one case in which the minister's correction must be viewed with a measure of suspicion, since it is highly doubtful that anyone but the minister associated <u>Nicco</u> with <u>Nicodemus</u>, a form probably unknown to the layman.

15   A rare example of <u>Namenmode</u> is found in Salouf. <u>Catharina</u>, <u>Maria</u>, and <u>Anna</u> all compete for first position until 1653. After this time the latter two names continue their popularity; but <u>Catharina</u>, having appeared fully twenty times among 96 women until 1653, accounts for only five out of 205 women for the rest of the century. The virtual banishment of <u>Catharina</u> from the onomasticon has no recognizable religious basis. It is probable that someone with this name committed adultery, murder, or some other crime serious enough to alienate not only herself, but her name as well, from the rest of the community. A frequently cited parallel is found in the sudden drop in <u>Adolf</u> attestations in post-war Germany.

16   In 1679 "Otthonia vulg Notegna" appears in Salouf, presenting the same difficulty as did "Otto seu vulg Nutt" in 1695. <u>Notegna</u> is a palatalized version of <u>Nutina</u>, which is simply the feminine of <u>Nutt</u>< <u>Johann-utt</u>. This note introduces the possibility that other occurrences of <u>Ott(h)onia</u> are "corrected" forms of <u>Nut(t)ina</u>.

17   An inventory of people killed by the Black Death in Catholic Schlans.(near Disentis) in 1631 (Muoth <u>RP</u>) shows close agreement with this composite of Salouf and Siat. Among 44 women are:

<u>Onna</u>	9	(actual number, not
<u>Maria</u>	6	percentage)
<u>Trina</u>	5	
<u>Ursula</u>	5	
<u>Griata</u>	4	
<u>Mengia</u>	4	
<u>Barbla</u>	3	

18
    The virtual absence of Hans in Samedan and Bevers
contrasts sharply with the position of Hans/Hensl in
the pre-Reformation Unterengadin, where it occupied
second place (ahead of Jan) with 13% among 512 men.
(Hans appeared among 5% of the men in the pre-Reformation Oberland, approximately the same proportion it
held during the 1600's.) Do the Bergün Hans attestations represent the remains of this pre-Reformation
popularity in the southeast? Probably not: Notes in
the Bergün baptism records from the 1600's show that
a number of families there came from nearby Davos, and
Hans may owe its modest popularity (3% from 1626 to
1700) to this Walser influence. The family names of
Hansett Riedi (1648) and Hans Müller (1696) point to
Davos, as does that of Hans Wÿldner (1654), which is
one of the few family names in this section of the
church book written in German script. The most convincing evidence of Davos influence, however, is "Hans
filg da Bernart Müsteinar da Tawo" in 1635.

19
    The lack of records for these fourteen years pre-
sents an opportunity to search again for Namenmode in
a Graubünden community. The same names appear in the
first and second halves of the seventeenth century in
Obersaxen, but their proportion varies. Christian
drops from 17% to 12%, Caspar drops from 10% to 5%,
and Georgius rises from 6% to 10%. Other names maintain their relative positions.

20
    Cf. Chapter III, pp. 202 and 206. Christian,
rare in other parts of Switzerland, was still the
most popular name in Graubünden in 1962; Peter and
Jacob were in second and third position (Geiger-Weiss
ASV 210).

21
    In spite of this tentative identification of
Christian as a "Walser" name it must be remembered
that the archaic onomasticon of the important Tavetsch
Jahrzeitbuch, which was closely identified with that
of Wallis, did not reveal Christian as a favored name
among the Tavetsch Walser. The prominence of Christian among the Davos and Safien Walser, and its virtual absence in Tavetsch, strengthened the conclusion
(Chapter III, p. 218ff.) that the Davos and Rheinwald
(> Safien) Walser shared a common intermediate home
in Italy during the migration east to Graubünden.
The popularity of Christian in Davos and Safien may
thus have its foundation in the Italian Piedmont.
    But what of Obersaxen, which was colonized from
the Furka-Oberalp route and still includes Christian

in a prominent position in its name vocabulary? It
is likely that close contact was maintained among the
Walser colonies for centuries after the initial migration was concluded in the late 1200's (Clavadetscher
WD 390; Zinsli WV 205). It is also probable that the
Obersaxen Walser, surrounded by Romance speakers and
sharing no common borders with other German speakers
(as did the Walser in Davos, Langwies, Vals, Safien,
and the Rheinwald), were especially anxious to cultivate a close relationship with the nearest Walser
colony. This colony was Vals/St. Martin, and it is
indicative of the intimacy which must have been established between Obersaxen and Vals that these colo-
nies--and these alone--followed a common path long
after the first migrations into Graubünden in resist-
ing the otherwise universal Walser conversion to Protestantism.

The popularity of Christian in post-Reformation
Obersaxen and the Rheinwald is, of course, no proof
that such a relationship did exist between Obersaxen
and the Rheinwald colony of Vals/St. Martin. To be
sure, no documentary evidence of a special Vals-Ober-
saxen friendship is known to exist. But few documents
reveal anything about the relationship among any of
the Walser areas, and for this reason mere shreds of
evidence, such as the appearance of Christian in Obersaxen, take on an importance which they could otherwise not possibly assume. The frequent attestations
of Christian in Obersaxen would indeed be insignificant if it were not for the lack of popularity of the
name in the Catholic Romance Oberland and for the
reasonable positing of a special Obersaxen-Vals relationship out of sheer cultural necessity. Onomastic
developments in Obersaxen and the proposal of contact
among the Walser colonies are investigated more fully
below, p. 304 f., and in Chapter V.

22   Because of heavy snows and avalanche danger Avers
could not be reached during the period of name collection, and the church register there (1645ff.) still
remains to be examined.

23   The number and variety of Davos names permit the
most extensive investigation of Namenmode among the
communities studied.
No significant differences in name-giving tradition are visible between 1559-1599 and 1600-1700. A
chart listing the frequency of each of 142 names in
each year between 1600 and 1700, however, reveals
subtle changes and trends. Christina appears 56 times
in the first 56 years of the century and only seven

times thereafter. <u>Elias</u> and <u>Marta</u> are <u>Modenamen</u>, attested only 1610-1619 and 1600-1607 respectively.
<u>Elsbeth</u> does not appear until 1639, but 32 times
thereafter. <u>Jöry</u> picks up gradually from the beginning of the century and becomes one of the favorites
after 1665. In three cases the passing of names from
generation to generation is quite clear: <u>Jochum</u> is
popular from 1632 to 1641 and from 1658 to 1669;
<u>Stina</u> is attested from 1629 to 1641, then reappears
in 1660 and is moderately popular until 1700;
<u>Ul(d)rich</u> is concentrated between 1600 and 1621,
1640 and 1645, and 1656 and 1673.

24   One might cautiously suspect that the name was
sometimes given by disgusted Protestants in the hope
that their children would lead Christian (i.e., non-
Catholic) lives, but this, of course, is speculation.
It will be recalled that <u>Christian</u> was one of the
many names given in the Middle Ages to remind their
bearers to live according to the example of Christ
(cf. <u>Benedictus</u>, <u>Clemens</u>, <u>Pius</u>, <u>Vitalis</u>).

25   Drosdowski (<u>LV</u> 148) attributes the unpopularity
of <u>Maria</u> in the pre-Reformation period to the extreme
respect for the mother of Christ and the unwilling-
ness to offend the holy figure by naming her directly.
This is similar to the well-known practice of naming
feared animals (bears, wolves) or natural objects
(sun, moon) by euphemisms ("honey eater," "grey one,"
etc.) in many societies.

26   GA Furna no. 15 (1601); church books from Seewis
(1644ff.), Fideris (1645ff.), Conters (1647ff.), Küblis (1648ff.), Schiers (1650ff.), Furna (1668ff.),
Grüsch (1685ff.), and St. Antönien (1696ff.). This
material is supplemented by a collection of the names
of all men liable for military duty (age 16 and over)
in Prättigau in 1623 (Gillardon <u>BG</u>).
    A comparison of names from the three judicial
districts in Prättigau (Klosters, Castels, Schiers/
Seewis) in 1623 with those found in church books from
1644 to 1700 reveals no substantial differences between
the two groups. <u>Cristen</u> accounts for 26% of the men
in the Klosters district, and <u>Hans</u> for 19%: high figures compared with those in Castels (16% and 13%) and
Schiers/Seewis (13% and 15%). The high percentages
in the innermost valley were continued in Conters
(20% and 18%) and Küblis (23% and 16%) in the second
half of the century.
    Although no <u>Modenamen</u> seem to develop in Prättigau
as a whole between 1623 and 1644-1700, local

preferences are visible from the church records of
the latter part of the century. <u>Lukas</u> is an unusual
favorite (6%) in Conters and <u>Rudolf</u> in Küblis (5%);
<u>Jann</u> is well represented in the outer valley (which
was the last area to be Germanized) but uncommon in
the inner valley.

27   <u>Andris</u>/<u>Enderli</u> appears in fourth place (6%) in
Prättigau, exactly the position and proportion it
held in Davos. Gillardon's collection of names from
neighboring Schanfigg in 1623 (<u>BG</u>) lists <u>Andres</u>/
<u>Enderli</u> only four times among 381 men. The name is
not attested among the 112 Catholic (1640ff.) or 145
Protestant (1669ff.) men listed in the church registers of nearby Churwalden, also a Walser settlement.

28   Information from Schanfigg (1637-1703) shows that
<u>Christen</u> (12), <u>Hans</u> (11), and <u>Peter</u> (10) were favored
among 83 men there as well (Caflisch <u>PS</u>).

29   Cf. the list of church records consulted above
(note 26). The 1623 collection by Gillardon, of
course, contains no women.

30   Possible short forms of <u>Christina</u>/<u>Stina</u> cause some
uncertainty about the popularity of the name. <u>Tschina</u>
is common in Prättigau during the 1600's, attested
most frequently in Furna (fourth place) and Conters
(seventh place). A possible connection with <u>Christina</u>
is understandable by analogy to a nickname of <u>Chris-</u>
<u>tian</u> which is still popular today: <u>Hitsch</u>. The com-
bination <u>Christian</u>/<u>Hitsch</u> could conceivably have produced <u>Christina</u>/<u>(Hi)Tschina</u>. Other names both confuse
and clarify the problem. <u>Otschina</u> in Langwies (1684)
and <u>Eutscha</u> in Bergün (eleventh place 1586-1625) suggest that some origin other than <u>Christina</u> might be
considered; but what?
        <u>Tschina</u> occurs commonly with <u>Schina</u>, and the two
names are counted together in List Three. Yet <u>Schina</u>
seems to be inseparably connected with <u>Sina</u>, which is
found in Prättigau and elsewhere as well. <u>Sina</u> is in
turn a nickname for <u>Ursina</u>, which is extremely common
(second place) in Samedan from 1639 to 1700; or is
<u>Sina</u> short for <u>Rosina</u>/<u>Rosa</u>, attested in Nufenen
(tenth place), Ilanz, and Prättigau? Both are pos-
sible, but the latter may be more plausible in view
of the 1608 entry in the Davos baptism register which
records "Eüphrosina oder Sina" twelve times between
1559 and 1596.

If the <u>Sina</u>/<u>Schina</u> relationship seems to be clear,
<u>Tschina</u>/<u>Otschina</u>/<u>Eutscha</u>, and the possible derivation
from <u>Christina</u>/<u>Stina</u>, are still very much a mystery.

31
    Inner valley: <u>Erblehen- und Spendzinsrodel der
Nachbarschaft Nufenen</u> (1602); church records from
Hinterrhein and Nufenen (1628-1666) and from Nufenen
alone (1666-1700); outer valley: church registers
from Splügen-Medels-Sufers, volumes one (1630-1662)
and two (1664-1700).

32
    The great similarity in women's names among Ro-
mance communities is puzzling in view of the general
disunity of the men's names. Perplexing, too, are
the close correspondences between Romance and Walser
women's names. A comparison of all name groups shows
only that <u>(Chri)Stina</u> is a common name in Walser
areas, corresponding to the popularity of <u>Christian</u>.
<u>Me(i)ng(i)a</u> is more common among Romance women than
Walser. <u>Maria</u> is the only visible mark of the Catholic onomasticon, accounting for 22% of Romance and
24% of Obersaxen Catholics and appearing less frequently elsewhere (Davos 15%; Rheinwald 14%; Protestant
Romance 9%; Prättigau 8%).
    A look at name variety reveals a surprising turn-
about in the proportion of men's and women's names in
general use. Before the Reformation it was found that
naming tradition among men was quite conservative, perhaps for reasons of dynastic identification. Women's
names appeared more subject to popular fashion (<u>Mode-
wellen</u>) and proved to be good indices of the emergence
of new naming trends. Consequently, the number of
men's names was small and the variety of women's names
seemed to be virtually unlimited.
    After the Reformation the reverse is true. This
is already apparent in the close correspondences between Romance and Walser women's names and the general
uniformity of the women's onomasticon in all communities. Men's names, on the other hand, are quite
varied. In Flims 31 names account for 272 women, but
a slightly higher number of men (311) requires twice
as many names. Six hundred forty women in Ilanz bear
47 names, but the 714 men there have over twice as
many (99). The same is true of Walser areas: The
statistical parity of men and women in Davos is belied
by the appearance of 94 men's names and 48 women's
names there.

33
    It is clear that the appearance of similar names
in pre- and post-Reformation Davos and the post-Reformation Rheinwald does not in itself point to a strong

influence of the former on the latter. Yet this
should be stated in view of an assertion made by
P. Issler in his study of the Rheinwald (GR).

Issler contends that many of the Davos Walser
came not from Wallis, but from the Rheinwald; this
may or may not be true, but his argument is at best
ill-reasoned. His proof is the existence of similar
family names in both areas:

> Heute noch in Davos lebende Walser-
> geschlechter sind: Wolf, Schuler, Hermann,
> Prader, Ruedi, Bandli etc. Obige Geschlech-
> ter lassen sich im 16. und 17. Jh. noch alle
> auch im Rheinwald nachweisen, müssen dann
> aber nach Davos ausgewandert sein. Aller-
> dings begegnen die gleichen Namen in Davos
> z.T. schon vorher; es sind das wohl Ver-
> treter von den ersten Nachschüben aus dem
> Rheinwald. (GR 30 note)

On the one hand it is well documented by the
materials investigated in the present study that
family names did not come into general use for centuries after both Davos and the Rheinwald were settled: Both before and after the Reformation people
were commonly known as "Schwartz Hanns," "Töni im
Wald," "Jon (the son of) Gieri (the son of) Jacum,"
and so on. On the other hand the family names cited
by Issler, as most family names in Graubünden, do not
point to a specific place of origin. The descendants
of a blacksmith became known as Schmid, those of an
especially small man were Klein (later entered in a
Prättigau church register as Parvus and transformed
to the present Barfuss), and those of men named Jacob
and Conrad acquired the family names Jecklin and
Kuoni. These names, of course, could arise anywhere
in the canton by spontaneous generation, or "poly-
genesis." Issler's family name Prader, for example,
could have its origin in any of the over 2000 field
names Praden/Prau (Romance 'meadow') in Graubünden.

It should be mentioned that Issler conceived his
theory before R. Hotzenköcherle established conclu-
sively the basic linguistic differences between the
Rheinwald and Davos, and that one should be merciful
in evaluating Issler's conclusions; yet the logic of
his argument demands refutation.

34   It was stated above (p. 253) that Rhine Valley
names need not be investigated for the post-Reformation period because their development had little to
do with that of names in Walser-Romance contact zones

Yet at first glance it seems irresponsible to declare
that the Walser had a name vocabulary of their own
without knowing what names were used in the Rhine
Valley. What guarantee exists that Rhine Valley names
and Walser names were not identical for the post-Reformation era? Unfortunately, time limitations precluded
an examination of the later names in the Fünf Dörfer
and the Herrschaft; the early names from these areas,
however, and the knowledge of the negligible onomastic
effects of the Reformation, indicate that the Rhine
Valley names remained unique.

Two possibilities exist for the further development of the Rhine Valley onomasticon. According to
the pattern, or lack of a pattern, seen in Romance
communities, the differences established between the
individual towns in the Rhine Valley could continue
to grow as each community unconsciously chose and promoted its own favored names. This development would
exaggerate the fundamental differences between Rhine
Valley and Walser names already apparent before the
Reformation.

Another possibility would have the Rhine Valley
names consolidating in much the same manner as did
the Walser names; individual developments in each town
would be stifled, perhaps as the result of increased
intercommunal contact. The Walser-Rhine Valley differences would, however, remain irreconcilable.

It is absolutely implausible that the Rhine Valley
communities would suddenly abandon their favored names
(something which even the Reformation failed to inspire elsewhere), and by coincidence abandon them in
favor of the very names used by the Walser. Such an
evolution would strain the limits of one's credulity.

35   Karl Wegelin, Regesten der Abtei Pfäfers, no.
650 (1467), in Theodor v. Mohr, Die Regesten der
Archive in der schweizerischen Eidgenossenschaft,
Chur, 1851, 79.

CHAPTER FIVE

GERMAN-ROMANCE CONTACT IN GRAUBUENDEN

As Weinreich points out in his dissertation, the
major portion of the German-Romansh language border in
present-day Graubünden is impassable (RP 102); areas of
contact between the two language groups are found largely
in the Oberland and the Heinzenberg-Schams region of the
Hinterrhein. In most other places where topographic
boundaries did not separate the two groups, the Romance
population has been Germanized by the Walser.

Some former Walser colonies became Romanized (Fidaz,
Scheia, Jux, Flix, Sblox, Tavetsch), but the inventory
of their field names clearly reveals that they once
supported a Walser population (cf. Szadrowsky AA, RN;
Zinsli MaWW, ZF). Similarly, in areas which are German-
speaking today (Davos, St. Antönien) Romance field names
attest the former presence of a Romance population. If
only a few Romance field names are available, the Romance
population may be presumed to have been sparse (Upper
Wallis, Davos); if there is a high percentage of Romance
names, then pre-Walser inhabitants must have existed in
significant numbers (Prättigau, Rheinwald). The more
common are Romance field names, the greater are the

chances that a given area was used intensively before
the Walser came, and the more probable is a relatively
long period of Walser-Romance contact (cf. Zinsli WV
325).

The facts of the Romance presence in Curraetia are
clear: Most areas were densely colonized, if not overpopulated. To be sure, the fertile Rhine Valley was
heavily settled; but even outer Schanfigg supported as
many farmers in 1084 as it does today (Schorta NL 110),
and Schams was so densely populated that some Romance
speakers were forced as high as 1582 meters to establish the colony of Lohn (Kreis DW 132). Land was
clearly scarce throughout the canton, and the Walser
were rarely able to gain a foothold below 1400 meters.[1]
Wherever conditions seem to have been favorable for
Walser colonization, and where the Walser did not
settle (Schams, Lugnez), one may reasonably assume a
concerted effort on the part of local farmers to keep
them out.

Research concerning the Walser has presented a confused picture of the Walser-Romance relationship. The
uncertainty about the nature of contact between the two
populations is largely the result of poor documentation
in the early centuries. On the one hand Gillardon supposes that jealous Romance speakers sought to marry
Walser in order to share their superior legal position

in feudal society (GZ 13); on the other hand Thöny

writes (PG 35f.):

>   Es wird auch nicht selten zu einer
>   Mischung von Romanen und Walser gekommen
>   sein, obwohl sich erstere oft, mitunter
>   sogar mit obrigkeitlichen Verboten, da-
>   gegen zu wehren suchten.

The study of names in Graubünden shows that Walser

and Romance speakers formed separate groups in at least

one important respect long after the initial coloniza-

tion; other cultural differences (architecture, folk-

lore, etc.) might be posited as well. The following

survey indicates to what extent mutual admiration, dis-

trust, or hostility existed between the two populations;

it also attempts to summarize the development of these

attitudes from the late Middle Ages to the present.

I. Mutual Observations

The relationship between Romance natives and the

first German speakers in Curraetia was probably one of

mutual tolerance. As has been mentioned, the pre-Walser

Germanization of the Rhine Valley, the Vorderrhein, and

Domleschg took place peacefully over a period of several

centuries (ca. 800-1200). Yet although the slow intru-

sion of nobles from Germany is not known to have caused

any violent reaction among Romance speakers, a Romance

saying, probably dating from the late Middle Ages,

indicates that the Germans of all social classes were
not welcomed wholeheartedly:

Tudeschg reschdan ils signurs e parlers

'Deutsch sprechen die Herren und die Landstreicher'
(Cavigelli GB 180f.). Language differences provided
the most apparent cultural division between the two
populations.

Within this bicultural framework there now appeared
the colonists from Wallis, settled in the highest valleys of Graubünden by the German nobles:

> Aes sind alls gross, schtarch Ma gsi
> mit rotä und blondä Haari und Bärt. Zu
> innä Poschtur hat au diä ruch, hert Schprach
> passt, wasch gredt hent. Das sind d'Walsär
> gsi, wa ubär Bärg und Tall gwandärät sind,
> ga schi äs Land syochä, wa nä Brot, Arbät
> und Friheit gäbi.

Romance speakers evidently felt culturally superior
to these German-speaking newcomers. In the first Engadin Romansh Bible translation, the Nuof Sainc Testamaint
from 1560, Jakob Bifrun explained the word Barbari
(Apostles 28:2) as "Barbari, lieud grussera, sco nus
dschain gualzers": 'grobe, rohe Leute, Walser, wie wir
sagen' (Liver WG 274). Gilg Tschudi suggested an etymology of the word Prättigau which was all but flatter-
ing to the German speakers in the valley:

Darzů sind ouch alda hohe oberste
pirg / ist villicht vss grobheit des
volcks / p der bůchstab zůgethon /
vnd vss Rhetico Pretticow gemacht. (AR 60)

Some two hundred years later the Romansh historian

Nicolin Sererhard remarked of the Walser in Avers:

Die Sitten der Einwohner sollen
ziemlich rauch seyn, die Frömdlinge
ärgeren sich ab ihren ungesalzenen
und manchmal unflätigen Reden. (ED 87)

The circumstances of initial Walser settlement in

Graubünden are now well known: The Rheinwald and Davos

were founded by members of the feudal nobility who wanted

the Walser to protect the periphery of their lands and,

if necessary, to subdue their Romance subjects as well

(Kreis DW 252). Yet oral tradition in Grüsch (Prättigau)

recalls another origin of the Walser:

Emal hed eina im Montafů ä Bock gstohla
und hed flüühe müässe. Dua ischt er überhäre
cho gä Grüsch und hed nümma hei törfa. No
lang-g sî z'Prdisla in ds Helde Hus ds Fähl
vom Bock ghanget. Där Montafuner isch dua
z'Grüsch bbliba, und vo dem stammend ali
Walser ab. Siter seid mä dä Walser "Bocker".[3]

It is significant that this tale of the origin of

the Walser is attested in Prättigau, where the Germani-

zation of the Romance population is known to have lasted

some three hundred years. This long period of intense

contact gave Romance speakers in the valley ample

opportunity to develop what may have been an entire mythology about the foreign newcomers.

Two other early accounts of the Walser as robbers reinforce the story from Prättigau. Gilg Tschudi reported in 1538 that the settlers in the Italian Walser colony of Ornavasso were also thieves:

> Es ist ouch in Lamparten nach by dem see
> Verbanus / yetz der lang see genant / noch ein
> dorff Vrnafasch genant / tütscher spraach / aber
> nit des alten harkomens / sonders inert ettlichen
> hundertjaren in eins tütschen Keysers Romfart /
> als Banditen sich dahin gesetzt / vnd darnach
> versünt worden / vnd jnen der flecken jngeben /
> mit gedingen vnnd satzungen / als sy darumb vom
> fryheyt habend jrs ursprungs. (AR 128)

The eighteenth century Engadin historian Gubert von Wiezel also indicated that the Walser were somewhat less than acceptable citizens and hinted that they became civilized only after establishing roots in Romance Graubünden:

> [The powerful family von Vaz attracted men
> of strong character:] unter diesen waren beson-
> ders die Walliser, deren Eifer und Treue denen
> Grafen so verdienstwürdig vorkamen, dass diese
> allen andern vorgezogen, ihnen viele Freiheit
> gestatteten, die sie zu Räubereyen verleiteten,
> bis die Anpflanzung der Wildnussen auf Davos,
> Langwies, Churwalden und anderen Orten sie zu
> arbeitsamen Einwohner machten. (HK 27)

Most interesting, however, is a lengthy account of the "wilde Leuth" in the "Vall Dafos" by Sererhard (ED 182-186):

> Diese wilde Leuth werden von den Alten
> beschrieben, dz sie den andern Menschen an
> Gestalt gleich gewesen, doch etwas kürzer
> und diker, am ganzen Leib mit Haaren über-
> wachsen, ausgenommen um die Augen oder im
> Angesicht nicht. Sie seyen von ungemeiner
> Stärke gewesen und schnell zum Laufen. Die
> Weiber nenten sie die Waldfänken oder auch
> Holzmütern etc. Die sollen so lange Brüst
> gehabt haben, dz sie solche über die Achslen
> hinwerfen können.

These strange creatures were believed by the valley residents to live in the "Felsen-Klüfte und Erdhölenen" of the highest mountains:

> Sie waren auch nicht durchgängig im Land
> anzutreffen, sondern nur auf etwelchen Parti-
> cular-Bergen.

The Reformation seems to have put an end to the race: "Vor der Reformation waren sie nichts Rahres, nach derselben ist ihr Geschlecht ausgestorben." The Protestant Sererhard supposes that they might have been phantasmata diabolica who died out after the Reformation because they were somehow used by the Catholic church to strengthen men's belief in supernatural beings; or, too, perhaps they were magic-mythical beings such as satyrs and nymphs.

Reports of these creatures were widespread in Prät-tigau and Schanfigg, and even the coat of arms of the Zehngerichtenbund showed a wildes Männli (Poeschel KG I, 262). Elsewhere in the canton the Waldfänken were

known to live in Davos, Safien, and the Rheinwald.[4] Not
by coincidence these five areas--Davos, Safien, the
Rheinwald, Prättigau, Schanfigg--were the very centers
of Walser culture or Walser-Romance contact in Graubünden.

The Waldfänk is attested not only in Graubünden,
but in Bavaria, Tirol, Liechtenstein, and Sargans as
well; in this Alpine environment, which until the eighteenth century inspired fear and wonder in its settlers,
the Waldfänk could appear as a dwarf or a giant (HdA II,
1184f.). Sererhard, for example, tells of giants who
lived in the Calfeisental in the canton of St. Gallen
(ED 204); they were no myth, he asserts, for local people
found uncommonly large human bones in the high valley
long after the giants had vanished. The Calfeisental
harbored one of the earliest Walser settlements in the
canton of St. Gallen, yet provided even the Walser with
such formidable natural obstacles that they were soon
forced to abandon the valley (Kreis DW 287ff.). Perret
briefly characterizes the relationship between the Walser
and the native population in the Sargans area:

> Die Walser bezeichnete das angestammte
> Volk als "alienigenae", d.h. Fremdlinge, "ad-
> venae", d.h. Neulinge, "peregrini", d.h.
> Fahrende, und als "Wilde" und "Barbaren".
> Die freiheitliche Vorzugsbehandlung dieser
> "fremden" brachte das dienende rätische
> Volk so auf, dass sich ein "Riese" zeitweise
> kaum allein in einer geschlossenen Ortschaft
> zeigen durfte . . . (RV 121)

Of considerable significance in Perret's statement is
the equation of Walser with "Riesen," which seems to
have been a common euphemism for "Walser" around Sargans
Are the giants' bones in the Calfeisental then really
those of the Walser who settled there?

Curious parallels are easily found between these
reports of giants and wilde Leuth and those of the Walse:
in eastern Switzerland. Both lived in the roughest, mos
inaccessible Alpine areas: the wilde Leuth in "Felsen-
Klüfte und Erdhölenen" and the Walser in "obersten wild-
enen höhinen" (Rheinwald) which were "gäch und stozig"
(Sapün). The wilde Leuth were known to the valley population chiefly as cowherds[5]; the Walser had to rely on
cattle as their sole source of income, whereas the Romance farmers grew grain, vegetables, and fruit on the
fertile land below. The wilde Leuth were not to be
found everywhere, but only "auf etwelchen Particular-
Bergen," and their stories are attested only in the
Walser strongholds of Prättigau, Davos, Schanfigg,
Safien, and the Rheinwald.[6] Huge bones found in the
Walser Calfeisental were believed to have been those of
a mysterious race of giants.

Finally, the wilde Leuth were common before the Re-
formation· but died out shortly thereafter. The Reformation represented a crucial stage in the Walser·expansion;
at this time Prättigau and Schanfigg finally became

Germanized, and Walser from the overpopulated high colonies in Prättigau (St. Antönien, Danusa, Valzeina)
began and completed their emigration to tertiary colonies in the Rhine Valley (Mastrils, Says). After this
final expansion the Walser no longer represented a totally foreign race of newcomers within the Romance environment, for they now lived among and intermarried
with the native population. The mystery of the <u>phantas-
mata diabolica</u> did not have a religous solution as
Sererhard suggested, but rather a sociological one.

It would be too daring to assert that the <u>wilde
Leuth</u> and the Walser were one and the same race of mountain dwellers, especially in view of the appearance of
<u>Waldfänken</u> in parts of the Alps which were not settled
by Walser. Yet the obvious contempt which the Romance
population felt for the Walser newcomers ("Barbari") has
a curious parallel in the proliferation of stories of
<u>Waldfänken</u> in areas inhabited by the German speakers.
It can safely be presumed that even if the Walser themselves were not the original subjects of these stories,
their presence helped considerably to reinforce' and
perpetuate the mythology in Graubünden.

*   *   *

There is very little evidence that the Walser were
so suspicious of their Romance neighbors. The few

existing indications of intolerance on the part of the
Walser involve the common phenomenon of language rivalry
The Walser chronicler Guler von Wyneck reported in his
Raetia in 1616:

> Ich habe noch alte leuthe im Walgöuw
> gekannt, die grob rätisch reden konnten.
> Sonsten ist an jetzo allein die Deutsche
> sprach bei ihnen breuchlich. (Zinsli **WV** 372)

The conception of Romansh as a "grob" language was apparently common among German speakers. Gilg Tschudi
remarked on the roughness of the Romance dialect and
explained that its harsh sounds were the result of the
primitive lives which its speakers led:

> Vrsach / warumb man Churwelsch nit
> schryben kan. Die Rhetijsch spraach ist
> nit gericht / das man die schryben könne
> / dan all brieff vnd geschrifften in jrm
> lande / sind von alter har in Latin / vnd
> yetz mehrteils zů tütsch gestelt. Es ist
> ouch nit wunder das die sitten vnd spraach
> by jnen ergrobet / dan als sie anfangs lange
> zyt allein die rühestē vnd obersten wildinen
> besessen / hat mengklich ruhe handarbeit
> thůn müssen / dann sy sunst nit jro narung
> gehaben / acht ouch / schůlen vnd leer
> meister schrybens vn̄ lesens / vnder den
> nachkommen nit gewesen / noch dero gepflegen
> / sonders allein rüthowen / mistgablen /
> vnd segentzen gebrucht / dardurch sie in
> künfftigem aller Grammatic / schrybens vnnd
> redens art entwonet / ye lenger ye vester
> zů grobem bruch / vnnd verbőserung der
> spraach komen / als noch vndern Tütschen
> vnd allen lannden gesehen wirt / das die
> in wildenen / von wegē das sy on alle leer
> schrybens vnd lesens wonend / vnd vffer-
> zogen werdend / mit grobheit vnnd verbőse-
> rung der spraachen / gantz vnglych andern
> dero nation geartet sind. (_AR_ 6f.)

Elsewhere Tschudi relates a remarkable custom
observed by Romance speakers in the Oberland:

> In obgedachter Riuier der Etuatiern
> [Tavetscher] / zů ylantz / Lugnitz / vnd
> in der Grůb / ist der sitt von heydnischen
> zyten harkoṁen / das sy zů ettlichen jaren
> gemein versamlungen hond / verbutzend sich
> / legend harnaṡch vnd gwör an / vnnd nimpt
> yeder ein starcken grossen stecken / oder
> knüttel / ziehend also in einer harscht mit
> einanndren von eim dorff zum andern / thůnd
> hoch sprüng vnd seltzam abenthür . . . .
> Sy louffend starcks anlouffs ineinandren /
> stossend vnd putschend mit krefften / ye
> einer an den anndern / das es erhilt / sy
> stopffend lut mit jren grossen stecken /
> daṅenthar werdend sy daselbsszůland die
> stopffer genempt / sy thůnds das jnē jr
> korn desterbass geraten sol / haltend also
> disen aberglouben. (AR 53f.)

Yet these observations by the sixteenth century
historian have little to do with Walser-Romance conflict. They are indeed made by a German speaker, but
not by a Walser: Tschudi was from Glarus. In neither
instance is the writer contemptuous. He is, rather,
slightly alarmed by the hardships endured by mountain
dwellers and at the same time is openly amused by the
antics of the superstitious Oberländer. Enmity toward
Romance speakers is not evident, for Tschudi remarks
that the "verböserung der spraach" took place in German
areas as well.

If the Walser were openly hostile toward Romance
speakers in Graubünden their feelings do not seem to

have been recorded. On the other hand, it is certain
that the Walser often met with suspicion and defiance
in the native population. This is wholly understandable, for the legal and social favoritism which were
granted to the newcomers by the feudal landowners ren-
dered even more hopeless the position of the Romance
natives. No means of legal redress was available to
those whose land was confiscated and given to the barbarians from the west; yet with the breakdown of the
feudal order in Graubünden the Romance population quickly found ways to bar the Walser from further expansion.

II. Legal Differences

Walser settlement in Graubünden was based on a
written contract between colonists and landowner
(Erblehenbrief). Because the German speakers were in
such demand, they could drive a hard bargain, and in
spite of their background as serfs in Wallis they ex-
tracted from the Raetian nobles three important concessions: The property on which they paid taxes, or
Erblehen, could be passed from one generation to the
next freely without a new contract and could be rented
or sold to others; the Walser were self-governing in
virtually all matters; but most important, they were
freemen (Branger RW 63ff.). The Erblehenvertrag

negotiated by "Wilhelm dem ammen" in Davos in 1289
says of the Walser: "und wenne si iren zins verrichtent
so sint si fry und habent mit nieman nût zu schaffen"
(Branger RW 162). The only difference between the legal
position of the Walser and that of the few Romance freemen in Graubünden was that the former did not own their
own land; yet the low taxes on any given colony were un-
changing no matter how many Walser lived there, and the
position of the Walser therefore constituted practical
ownership of the lands which they occupied.

It was clearly the intention of the feudal nobility
that the Walser should be granted these privileges, for
the services which the new colonists agreed to perform
demanded substantial rewards. It was also intended that
the land given in fief to the Walser remain only in
their hands. When the head of the Cazis cloister on
the Heinzenberg granted an Erblehen to the Walser Peter-
mann Buchlin in Safien in 1479, she stipulated that the
fief could be sold or rented to others as long as they
were neither nobles nor serfs (Joos SU 282). For all
practical purposes this meant that the land was to remain in the possession of Walser.

The freedom of the Walser as a recognized privilege
should not be underestimated. In a society where nearly
everyone was a bondsman, the nobility was determined
that the rare privilege of personal freedom should not

become widespread. Walser were thus encouraged by the
nobles to stay together. For example, when the Walser
from the Gonzenberg near Sargans moved into the valley
below, they lost their freedom; yet they could regain
it by moving back up the mountain (Zinsli WV 209; cf.
also Branger RW 69). If a Walser (with the exception
of those in Davos and the Rheinwald) married a non-free
native, the children had to follow "der ärgern Hand" by
assuming the less favorable legal position of the native (Branger RW 66ff.). Walser in closed colonies
governed themselves; those in mixed groups, however,
lost the right of self-government (Kreis DW 146). The
dissolution of the feudal structure after the Reformation brought an end to these stipulations and thus
furthered Walser-Romance contact.

In many cases the high valleys where the Walser
had first settled simply became uninhabitable as the
population increased. As the high forests were cleared
for pasture and the wood was used for building and fuel,
the heavy snows were no longer held back throughout the
seven-month winters and destroyed whole villages where
avalanches had never occurred before. Some Walser accepted the loss of their personal freedom as a welcome
alternative to the hardships in the mountains; the slow
migration to lower elevations began.[7]

At first there was no room for Walser on the more productive valley floors, and the resistance which they met there was strong. Maienfeld kept enforcing new restrictions to the pasture granted to the Walser from Stürvis who settled on the north slope of the Falknis (Zinsli WV 209). An often-cited case of conflict between the two groups is the contested election of an Ammann in Klosters in 1489, in which the Walser there wanted to choose the official from their own number. Naturally, Romance speakers protested. The argument was finally decided by the Austrian archduke, who reserved for himself the right to appoint the Ammann but declared that Walser and Romance speakers should hold alternate terms in office (Rupp GK 106).

Legal restrictions did not always favor the Walser In another attempt by the nobility to discourage intercultural contact Graf Hans von Sax-Misox, the entire population of Lugnez, and the local Vogt prohibited "die von vater stam Romonsh sind" from selling or renting land or buildings "an frömde die nit sind von vater stam Churwalhen dysenthalb den bergen oder gotzhuslüt."[8] Anyone who married an outsider lost his right to inheritance in the valley. These restrictions, initiated in 1457, were obviously directed against the Walser in Vals. Some two hundred years later Romance speakers in Lugnez were still hostile

toward their German neighbors. The few Walser who had
been settled in St. Martin (between Vals and Lugnez)
belonged to the church of Lugnez, but the Romance
speakers of Lugnez refused to grant them the right to
vote in community affairs unless they voted with the
majority (Muoth SPS 220).

The use of community pastureland on the Heinzenberg was disputed between Walser in Tschappina and
Romance speakers in Flerden and Urmein until the end of
the sixteenth century. Later individual landowners were
required to obtain the permission of the entire Romance
community before they could sell pastureland to the
Tschappina Walser (Liver WG 273f., WW 213; Kreis DW
283). In 1677 Walser who wanted to live in the Romance
town of Masein on the Heinzenberg were told that they
must not establish a "typical" Walser Einzelhof, but
must live within the closed community (Simonett BG
II, 224).

It can hardly be expected that the Walser always
obeyed these laws. Perhaps the first legal dispute between German and Romance speakers in Prättigau is documented in 1394, when Walser from Danusa violated the
borders of the Jenaz community pasture and were made to
return to their higher grazing lands (GA Jenaz no. 1).

In general, the Walser appear to have been understandably eager to gain a foothold at the more clement

and desirable lower elevations. One exception, however, was the community of Says above Trimmis in the Rhine Valley. In 1512 the Walser in Says separated the high and low pastures of Hintervalzeina (between Says and Danusa) and gave the lower to Trimmis while keeping the higher ones for themselves (GA Trimmis no. 13). In other documented arguments the Walser in Says disputed grazing rights (no. 11) and other local ordinances (no. 55) and refused to contribute more than a token amount of labor to the damming of the Rhine (no. 26). As the Trimmis historian J.U. Meng summarizes in a statement generally not applicable to the expansive energies of the Walser,

> Es erweckt den Eindruck, dass mit der Vermehrung des walserischen Einflusses in der Bergfraktion die Isolierungsbegehren besonderen Auftrieb erfuhren. (TH 60)

The legal defenses which the Walser often encountered in Graubünden were not unique within the Alpine environment. Because of the extraordinary population density of the Italian Piedmont, laws there forbade the sale or transfer of grazing land to strangers and effectively frustrated local Walser expansion from the intermediate colonies (Kreis DW 133).[9]

It has been seen that the Romance population of the Alpine area was generally opposed to settlement by the

Walser; yet if this defensive attitude was in part due
to the inevitable cultural differences which initially
separated the two groups, it was probably more immediately founded in the local knowledge that higher and
lower valleys alike were simply too overpopulated to
absorb an additional group of settlers.

III. A Common Culture

Much has been made of the existence of a Walser
house, a Walser room, a Walser oven, and domestic tools
which are "typically Walser." In the search for the
unique cultural trappings of Walserdom, parallels with
other Alpine populations have too often been overlooked
or dismissed as insignificant. No degree of nostalgia,
however sincere it may be, can conceal the fact that
although the Walser probably brought to Graubünden many
cultural elements unique to their Wallis homeland, all
traces of these elements have long since disappeared.
In the words of the eminent folklorist Richard Weiss:

> Wir finden bisher keine Sachkarte im
> ASV [Atlas der schweizerischen Volkskunde],
> auf welcher der sprachlich so deutliche
> Unterschied zwischen Deutschbündnern und
> Romanischbündnern oder insbesondere zwischen
> Walsern und Rätoromanen fassbar würde.
> Kein Brauch, kein Sachgut, innerhalb wie
> ausserhalb des ASV, das wir allein den
> Walsern oder allein den Rätoromanen zu-
> schreiben könnten. (DvS 12f.)

It was shown in Chapter III that the Walser brought
a standard inventory of first names to Graubünden
(Tavetsch), and it has been amply demonstrated by
linguists such as Jud, Szadrowsky, Zinsli, and Rübel
that countless linguistic phenomena characteristic of
the Bernese Oberland and Wallis found their way to
Graubünden with the Walser as well. These were undoubtedly not the only cultural features which the settlers
brought with them, yet today the Walser dialects of
Graubünden represent the only unique cultural remnant
of the original colonists.

In virtually all other respects the contact between
Walser and Romance speakers has produced a partial or
complete cultural symbiosis. Motifs from Oberwallis are
found among Romansh folk tales,[10] and methods of culti-
vating and harvesting crops vary not between language
groups, but between entire geographical regions and even
among their component villages. C. Simonett's comprehensive study of farmhouses in Graubünden indicates that
some criteria differentiate Walser and non-Walser houses
(BG II 80, 246); yet his ambition leads him astray when
he recognizes two groups of Walser houses (Prättigau-
Vorderrheintal-Tschappina-Rheinwald and Davos-inner
Schanfigg-Mutten-Avers) and declares that this arrangement corresponds to the linguistic geography of the
Walser colonies (BG II 242 and map I). Linguistically,

of course, Prättigau belongs with Davos and inner Schanfigg, and Mutten and Avers belong with the Vorderrheintal,
Tschappina, and the Rheinwald (cf. Chapter I, p. 25f.).

The cultural uniformity found in Graubünden today
has been in the making ever since the Walser first made
contact with the Romance population. The evidence presented by legal documents and other sources shows that
this contact did not always proceed without difficulty
in the initial centuries. As contact increased, the
final spectrum of Walser, Walser-Romance, and Romance
communities was established which has survived to the
present. With this contact came mutual tolerance:
Just as Walser were gradually accepted in Prättigau,
Schanfigg, the Rheinwald, and elsewhere, Romance speakers
began intermarrying with Walser and moving to Walser
settlements. Although the most inhospitable Walser
colonies died out (Stürvis, Danusa), most managed to
hold their own and occasionally even to increase in
population as the immigration of Romance speakers more
than balanced the Walser emigration.[11]

IV. Footnotes

1   Tavetsch: 1650-1850m; Rheinwald: 1530-1620m;
Davos: 1450-1860m; Obersaxen: 1200-1400m; Langwies: 1350m.

2   Hössli WR 15f.: 'They were all big, strong men
with red and blond hair and beards. The rough, rugged language which they spoke matched well their
physical appearance. These were the Walser, who
wandered far and wide to find a place where there
was sustenance, work, and freedom.' The legal historian P. Liver tells of the Safien Walser descending
from the Bischola Pass down the Heinzenberg to the
market in Thusis in the autumn:

        an diesen hochgewachsenen, weitaus-
        schreitenden Gestalten fielen mir am
        meisten die roten Vollbärte bei dunklem
        Haupthaar auf. (WG 260)

This is the standard picture of the Walser which
is fondly remembered in present-day Graubünden; similar observations are frequently made in the short
encomia which appear in the periodicals Wir Walser
and Terra Grischuna. The mystique of a strong, fair-
haired race of German speakers in an otherwise Romance
environment has inevitably inspired blood-group in-
vestigations and anthropological treatises on racial
purity; a high percentage of O negative blood in a
community allegedly indicates a strong Walser an-
cestry (cf. J.K. Moor-Jankowski, "La prépondérance
du groupe sanguin O et du facteur rhésus négatif chez
les Walser de Suisse" Journal de génétique humaine
III (March 1954), 25-70). Kreis, who enthusiastically
embraces the results of such investigation, notes on
the basis of blood-group studies made within the last
forty years that early Walser-Romance contact must
have been more common in Safien-Platz than in the more
remote regions of the Safien Valley, although Safien-
Platz is located only five miles north of the most
distant part of the valley (DW 78 note 44); he also
cites serological parallels (after Moor-Jankowski)
between Walser and Icelanders (278).

3   Büchli ML 166; 'Once a fellow from Montafon (just
over the mountain to the north in Austrian territory)
stole a billy goat and had to escape, so he came over
here to Grüsch and didn't dare go back home. For a

long time after that the goatskin hung in the Helde-
house in Pardisla (a community near Grüsch). The
fellow settled in Grüsch, and all Walser are descended from him. Since that time the Walser have been
called "Bocker."¹ This anecdote was related by the
82-year-old Magdalena Walser-Roffler in Grüsch in
1938; A. Büchli reports that the legend was still
known in Seewis twenty years later (ML 166).

4   E. Hoffmann-Krayer, Handwörterbuch des deutschen
Aberglaubens (HdA), II, Berlin/Leipzig, 1929/1930,
1184.

5   Cf. the collection of tales in Bündnerisches
Volksblatt, II (1830), 373-396.

6   It may be argued that stories of the wilde Leuth
or Waldfänken are common to high mountainous areas in
general, and that the appearance of Walser in these
inhospitable regions merely coincides with the place
of origin of the widespread myth. Yet tales of the
fantastic creatures do not appear in non-Walser areas
of Graubünden, even where some Romance towns are as
high as or higher than Walser colonies (Schams, Lugnez, Bergün, Oberhalbstein, the Oberengadin) and
where the Romance population had ample reason to suspect that their mountains were inhabited by wild men.

7   For an account of the gradual Germanization of
Prättigau see Chapter III, p. 191ff. and note 48;
cf. also Zinsli WV 84.

8   Wagner-Salis, Die Rechtsquellen des Kantons Graubünden, Zeitschrift für Schweizerisches Recht, neue
Folge, III, 245 and 326.

9   Writing in 1886, Julius Studer remarked that

    Für die (deutschen) Alagnesen zum Bei-
    spiel ist der Italiener der Welsche oder
    Wailschu, auch Wahle oder Wohu, d.h. der
    Fremde, der nicht Deutsche, ungefähr im
    Sinne der Barbaren für die alten Griechen
    und Römer. (cited by Zinsli WV 371)

Zinsli notes that at the turn of the present century the Walser in Salecchio still preferred to climb
over the Albrun Pass into Oberwallis to visit a phy-
sician rather than follow the easier path to a doctor
in Italian territory ("Wälschland") below. Whether
the decision of the Walser is to be attributed to

their allegiance to their ancient homeland or simply
to better or less expensive medical treatment cannot
readily be determined.

10   Leza Uffer, <u>Rätoromanische Märchen und ihre Er-
zähler</u>, Basel, 1945, 28. Cited by Zinsli <u>WV</u> 444
note 244.

11   Zinsli <u>WV</u> 206; note the surprising composition
of the population of isolated Mutten in Hotzenköcherle
<u>MM</u> 16ff.

CHAPTER SIX

CONCLUSIONS

I. A Brief Survey of Name-giving

    in Raetia/Graubünden

A regrettable lack of source material precludes
any extensive study of the naming customs in pre-Roman
or Roman Raetia. The cultural layering of this early
period is visible only in the thousands of Celtic,
Etruscan, Ligurian, Illyrian, and Roman place and field
names which have managed to survive to the present.
Only with the early Middle Ages do sources begin to
reveal the pre-Christian and Christian Romance onomasticon which was used among all segments of the Raetian population.

After political developments initiated the Germanization of Raetia, German names began to appear among
nobles in the late eighth century. By the tenth and
eleventh centuries German names were used almost exclusively by members of the secular and religious aristocracy; at this time it becomes impossible to differentiate German and Romance speakers by name alone,
because German names came into use even among the
Romance natives of Raetia. Romance names remained
popular with the lower classes.

The high Middle Ages ushered into use a new name
vocabulary as saint worship spread throughout Europe;
German names slowly began to lose popularity. The
German- and Romance-speaking members of the Raetian
nobility maintained their allegiance to German names
until the late 1300's, when Christian saints' names took
over and held the favored position which they still enjoy. German names were less popular among freemen and
serfs, whose onomastica were still partly Romance; the
wave of saint worship abruptly changed name-giving
practices among the lower classes before German names
could come into exclusive use. Up to this time the
post-Roman onomastic layering thus involved among the
aristocracy: Romance -- German -- Christian; among many
segments of the population, however, the change from
Romance to Christian names took place without the intermediate German stage.

In general, only those German names survived the
Middle Ages which were borne by saints (<u>Ulrich</u>, <u>Konrad</u>)
or powerful political dynasties (<u>Heinrich</u>, <u>Otto</u>). The
various segments of the Graubünden population all subscribed to the use of a single body of Christian names
which varied among the three distinct linguistic groups
in the canton: Walser, Romance, and Rhine Valley German.
These were largely the same names popular throughout
Europe at the time; local saints had little to do with

name-giving tradition in Graubünden.

The new Christian names had been in use for two to three centuries in Graubünden before the Reformation. By the time of the religious upheaval of the 1500's and 1600's the names were no longer associated with the saints whose worship had earlier introduced and promoted their use. The use and perpetuation of a fixed body of personal names had become such an integral part of the local culture that such an important event as the Reformation failed to have significant onomastic repercussions among Catholic or Protestant Bündner. At the same time family names finally began to assume standard forms and to come into general use among all parts of the population. With the final regulation of first names and family names throughout the canton the present system of name-giving was established.

II. The Value of Name Study in Graubünden

The study of personal names would seem to add little to what is already known about the early history of Raetia. After all, the political integration of the former Roman province into the Frankish kingdom is well documented. It is no surprise that German names came into general use among the Raetian aristocracy, and the very fact that they did become popular among these select

347

few is not relevant to the central question of contact
in this study. It is much more important to know just
how the German names were used: how quickly their use
spread and what people accepted them. These questions,
answered in Chapter II, involve another consideration:
How are cultural groups to be differentiated and the
influence of the one on the other to be determined on
an onomastic basis if both use the same name vocabulary?
In answering this question, it must be understood that
the estimation of intercultural contact requires only
the knowledge that one or more elements of one culture
were borrowed by the other. On the one hand, it is unfortunate that aristocratic Germans and Romance speakers
in Raetia cannot be differentiated solely by their names;
on the other hand, it is not important for the purposes
of this study that specific German- and Romance-speaking
individuals be identified for the pre-Walser period. It
suffices to know only that German names were consciously
and regularly used by Romance speakers of all classes.
Indeed, this is the only truly relevant consideration.

The phrase "the Germanization of Raetia" is not to
be understood to mean the increase in concentration of
Germans in Raetia, but rather to indicate the degree to
which elements of German culture, including language
and name-giving practices, were absorbed by the native
Romance population. The city of Chur did not become

Germanized by the high concentration of Swabians and
Franks there in the Middle Ages, but by the final acceptance of German as the majority language in the sixteenth century.

In the case of Curraetia as a whole, German influence during the Middle Ages can be very effectively
estimated by the rate of conversion of the native population from Romance to German names. The use of German
names, of course, did not involve Germanization in every
respect, but it does indicate that the gradual acculturization took place without a violent confrontation which
would undoubtedly have reduced the appeal of the new
onomasticon.

This is an instance in which an entire body of new
names contrasts strongly with a well-established name
vocabulary; the later meeting of saints' names and German names is similar. In both cases the historical and
cultural backgrounds are clear and the evidence of personal names merely confirms well-known facts.

The study of Walser names, on the other hand, offers new evidence and suggests new conclusions about
important historical and cultural phenomena which have
hitherto not been fully understood:

1. The examination and comparison of Tavetsch
and Wallis names showed that a Wallis onomasticon
was successfully transplanted to the Walser colony

at the head of the Bündner Oberland. The names
used in Safien showed that the Rheinwald (> Safien)
settlers used an entirely different set of names
although their ultimate origin was in Wallis;
because it is well documented that the Rheinwald
Walser had their immediate origin in the Italian
Piedmont, it could be assumed that the new names
used in Safien had been brought from Italy, where
the Christian onomasticon had achieved widespread
popularity before the Walser began emigrating from
Wallis.

    2. The close examination of the earliest names
from the Rheinwald suggests that there was a substantial number of Romance speakers or men of Romance origin among the first Walser who settled in
the inner Rheinwald. This fact, combined with the
likely presence of Romance speakers in the inner
valley and with the probability of close Walser-
Romance contact within the valley as a whole, casts
serious doubts on the contention that the Rheinwald
was a "pure" Walser area.

    3. The names used in pre-Reformation Davos do
not resemble those in Tavetsch or Wallis; therefore,
it is unlikely that the Davos Walser came directly
to Graubünden from Wallis. The Davos names do,
however, strongly resemble those of Safien. This

fact suggests that a) the immediate origin of the
Davos Walser was in the western Italian Piedmont,
where they paused long enough in their migration
to take on a body of Christian names not yet popular in Wallis; and/or b) the Davos Walser maintained close relations with the residents of the
Rheinwald for the first several generations of
their settlement in Graubünden. In any case, a
substantial degree of Romance cultural influence
should be assumed for both the Rheinwald and Davos;
both colonies are "primary" in the role of Walser
settlement in Graubünden, yet are really secondary
because they were established largely by German
speakers from the Italian Piedmont.

4. The names used in Langwies before the Reformation differ from those popular in Davos although
the first Langwies Walser came from Davos. Because
it is highly unlikely that name-giving traditions
could change so rapidly for no apparent reason,
perhaps the different Langwies names are the result
of a) a later immigration of colonists directly
from Wallis or b) contact with the Romance population in middle and outer Schanfigg.

5. Chapter V showed that the nobility of Graubünden had a vital interest in the absence of contact between Walser and Romance speakers. It was

also apparent that Romance speakers were contemptuous of and often hostile toward the German-speaking
intruders. Finally, it must be assumed that the
colonists from Wallis, virtually forced together
in their new environment, were interested in maintaining contact among their isolated settlements.
Aside from the apparent exchange of some family
names between Walser colonies (Zinsli **WV** 204f.), no
evidence has yet been presented that a special relationship did indeed exist among the Walser in
Graubünden. Personal names provide this evidence.
The hypothesis of a pre-Reformation Davos-Rheinwald
relationship suggested above is strengthened by the
appearance of similar first names in Obersaxen as
well. Moreover, a redirection of cultural allegiance from Tavetsch to Vals can be posited for
Obersaxen.

Unfortunately, these hypotheses are difficult to
test further. They are presented as an attempt to clarify historical events and cultural relationships which
are either poorly documented or not recorded at all. In
the case of the Germanization of Prättigau, the evidence
of personal names can only reinforce the well-known historical facts of German-Romance contact. In the absence
of any satisfactory documentation, however, name study

provides viable solutions to the problem of the general Walser-Romance relationship in Graubünden.

III.   "What's in a Name?"

Juliet's question requires different answers at different times; at all times, however, the significance of a name seems to be determined by its "meaning," its relationship to its bearer, and the function which it maintains in society.

Many names used in the early Middle Ages in Raetia probably did hold a specific meaning. This is true of German names (Frid-rich, Cuon-rat) as well as of some Christian formations (Clemens, Pius). It becomes impossible to assume a literal meaning of German names for a later time because name-building elements changed in form (partly under Romance influence: cf. Ulrich/Duri) and were forgotten. The "meaning" of saints' names also became obscure: After the Reformation Protestants continued to use the names of saints glorified by the Catholic church.

Among the earliest German speakers in Raetia names could be formed with or without regard to fixed patterns; variety was practically unlimited and repetition nearly nonexistent. The high Middle Ages witnessed a gradual narrowing of the onomastic perspective, first in the appearance of favored German names (Heinrich, Konrad,

Ulrich) and second in the widespread promotion of a
restricted body of saints' names. By the Reformation
the choice of men's names had narrowed considerably,
and fixed patterns, much like those established among
the Medieval nobility, became the rule among families,
towns, and cultural groups (Walser -- Romance -- Rhine
Valley). Early attempts to counter the conformity of
Christian names resulted in hybrids such as Leonhard
and Christhild; later members of the nobility of Graubünden named their sons Dionys, Thobias, etc., in order
to set them apart from the sea of Hans, Peter, and Jöry.

If in the Middle Ages names were felt to represent
an important part of an individual's being (cf. the
taboo of disclosing one's name to an enemy), they later
became a firm part of an entire cultural heritage and
were passed on unchanged from one generation to the next
just as other folk traditions. A cultural element formerly "owned" by the individual, or at most by his family, became community property.

Because the function of a name is to identify,
social groups soon seized upon a means of differentiating individuals identified by this "community property." At a time when everyone had a different name this
was not necessary; yet the presence of one Johannes for
every four or five males necessitated further identification. This resulted in the development of Zunamen

in formations such as <u>Schwartz Hanns</u> or <u>Gross Christen</u>
and eventually brought about the development of family
names.

Individual identification encompasses identification
both within a small community and within an entire cultural group. It was seen that post-Reformation Romance
names varied considerably from town to town. This reflects
well the observation of Paul Zinsli that

> Jede einzelne Siedlergruppe ist ... zu
> einer eigenwilligen Sondergemeinschaft mit
> zahlreichen ... Eigenarten im Bauen und
> Wohnen, Brauch und Arbeiten, im Wollen und
> Glauben mit einem eigenen "kulturellen Ge-
> sicht" geworden. (<u>WV</u> 135)

In other words, small community and cultural group were
identical. Walser names also reflect this "eigenwillige
Sondergemeinschaft," but on a broader scale: Not individual communities, but an entire cultural unit is visible
from the personal names used in Walser settlements.

Only massive social change seems to have been able
to produce corresponding onomastic changes. In early
Raetia the influx of German culture caused the gradual
acceptance of German names. At a later time the onomasticon of Prättigau changed not when Walser first appeared
in the highest regions, but when they moved into the valley, intermarried with Romance speakers, and eventually
brought about the final Germanization in the sixteenth
century.

This investigation has thus borne out the hypothesis proposed in the introduction: that because individuals are the ultimate locus of language contact--and because individuals are also the immediate sources of name-giving-the extent to which two cultures have interpenetrated can sucessfully be estimated by the willingness of individual members of each cultural group to use freely the onomasticon of the other.

BIBLIOGRAPHY

Bach, Adolf. Deutsche Namenkunde. I, part 1. Heidelberg, 1952; I, part 2. Heidelberg, 1953.
(DN)

Baesecke, Georg. "Das Althochdeutsche von Reichenau
nach den Namen seiner Mönchslisten," PBB,
LII (1928), 92-148. (AR)

Beck, Marcel. "Bemerkungen zur Geschichte des ersten
Burgunderreiches," SZG, XIII (1963), 433-
457. (GB)

Berger, Hans. Volkskundlich-soziologische Aspekte der
Namengebung in Frutigen. Bern, 1967.
Sprache und Dichtung, Neue Folge. XIV.
(NF)

Bertogg, H. "Das Luviser Anniversar," JHGG, LXXII (1942),
73-94. (LA)

Betz, Werner. "Namenphysiognomik," Namenforschung
(Festschrift für Adolf Bach). Heidelberg,
1965. 184-189. (NP)

Birlinger, Anton. "Liber Viventium et Defunctorum von
Pfäffers," Alemannia, IX (1881), 57-71.
(LV)

Boesch, Bruno. "Namenforschung und Landesforschung,"
Rheinische Vierteljahrsblätter, XXI (1956),
70-76. (NL)

Bohnenberger, Karl. Die Mundart der deutschen Walliser,
BSG, VI. Frauenfeld, 1913. (MW)

Branger, Erhard. Rechtsgeschichte der freien Walser in
der Ostschweiz. Bern, 1905. (RW)

Bruckner, Wilhelm. Schweizerische Ortsnamenkunde. Basel,
1945. (SO)

Brun, Leo. Die Mundart von Obersaxen, BSG, XI. Frauenfeld, 1918. (MO)

Büchli, Arnold. Mythologische Landeskunde von Graubünden. I. Aarau, 1958. (ML)

357

Buck, M. R. "Zu den welschen Namen des Liber Viventium et Defunctorum von Pfäffers," Alemannia, IX (1881), 175-186. (LV)

Büttner, Heinrich. "Geschichtliche Grundlagen zur Ausbildung der alemannisch-romanischen Sprachgrenze im Gebiet der heutigen Westschweiz," ZMF, XXVIII (1961), 193-206. (GG)

Caflisch, Christian. "Ein Pfandt- und Spendtbüchlein der Kirche zu St. Peter Schanfigg vom Jahre 1637," BM (1956), 221-247. (PS)

Camenisch, Christian. "Stiftungsurkunde der 'ewigen Mess' zu Tschiertschen vom Jahre 1488," BM (1899), 241-247; 265-272. (ST)

Camenisch, Emil. Bündnerische Reformationsgeschichte. Chur, 1920. (BR)

Campell, Ulrich. Raetiae Alpestris Topographica Descriptio. ed. C. J. Kind. QSG, VII. Basel, 1884.

Castelmur, Anton von. "Die Leibeigenen der III Bünde in der Herrschaft Maienfeld," BM (1929), 377-380. (LB)

_____. "Eine rätische Kirchenstiftung vom Jahre 1084," ZSK, XXIII (1929), 297-308. (RK)

_____. "Jahrzeitbuch und Urbare von Ruschein," JHGG, LVII (1927), 43-83. (JR)

Cavigelli, Pieder. Die Germanisierung von Bonaduz in geschichtlicher und sprachlicher Schau, BSM, XVI. Frauenfeld, 1969. (GB)

Clavadetscher, Erhard. "Die Walsersiedlungen Danusa, Furna und Valzeina im Prätigau," BM (1944), 375-395. (WD)

_____. "Zur Geschichte der Walsergemeinde Avers," BM (1942), 193-211. (GA)

Cloetta, Gian Gianett. Bergün-Bravuogn Heimatkunde. Thusis, 1954. (BH)

Dalbert, P. "Die ehemalige Walsersiedlung Batänien,"
BM (1950), 225-230. (WB)

Dauzat, Albert. "Les études d'anthroponymie en France,"
ZNF, XIV (1938), 113-128. (EA)

Decurtins, Casper. Rätoromanische Chrestomathie. II.
Erlangen, 1895. (RC)

Derichsweiler, W. "Aus dem Valsertal im Bündner Oberland," Jahrbuch des Schweizer Alpenclubs,
L (1914/15), 53-105. (VO)

Drosdowski, Günther. Duden Lexikon der Vornamen. Mann-
heim/Zürich, 1968. (LV)

Elsasser, Beatrix. "Neuere Ergebnisse zur Siedlungs-
und Wirtschaftsgeographie der bündner-
ischen Walserkolonien," Terra Grischuna,
XXVIII (1969), 287-290. (SW)

Escher, Walter. Dorfgemeinschaft und Silvestereinsingen
in St. Antönien. Basel, 1947. (SA)

Evans, D. Ellis. Gaulish Personal Names. Oxford, 1967.
(GPN)

Farner, Oskar. "Die Kirchenpatrozinien des Kantons Graubünden," JHGG, LIV (1924), 1-192. (KG)

Finsterwalder, Karl. Die Familiennamen in Tirol.
(Schlern-Schriften, LXXXI). Innsbruck,
1951. (FT)

Fleischer, Wolfgang. Die deutschen Personennamen.
Berlin, 1964. (DP)

Flom, George T. "Alliteration and Variation in Old Germanic Name-giving," Modern Language Notes,
XXXII (1917), 7-17. (AV)

Förstemann, Ernst. Altdeutsches Namenbuch. I: Personennamen. Bonn, 1901². (AN)

Gadmer, Nikolaus. "Davos und die Walser," Terra
Grischuna, XXII (1963), 8-14. (DW)

Gaudenz, G. "Herkunft und Verwandtschaft der Räto-
romanen," Terra Grischuna, XXVII (1968),
280-283. (HR)

Geiger, Paul and Weiss, Richard. Atlas der schweizer-
    ischen Volkskunde. II, part 1. Basel,
    1962. (ASV)

_____. Atlas der schweizer-
    ischen Volkskunde. Kommentar. II, part
    1. Basel, 1962. (ASVKo)

Geographisches Lexikon der Schweiz. I-VI. Neuenburg,
    1902-1910. (GLS)

Gillardon, Paul. "Die Bevölkerung der VIII Gerichte im
    Frühling 1623," BM (1930), 161-174; 193-
    218. (BG)

_____. Geschichte des Zehngerichtenbundes.
    Davos, 1936. (GZ)

Gremaud, J. Documents relatifs à l'histoire du Vallais.
    I (300-1255) Lausanne, 1875; II (1255-1300)
    Lausanne, 1876. (DV)

Grisch, Giatgen. "Zur Walserfrage im Oberhalbstein,"
    BM (1942), 118-124. (WO)

Grotefend, H. Taschenbuch der Zeitrechnung des deutschen
    Mittelalters und der Neuzeit. Hannover,
    1960. ·(TZ)

Haffter, Ernst. "Zwei Schnitzlisten der Nachbarschaft
    Tartar aus den Jahren 1651 und 1671," BM
    (1899), 224-226. (ST)

Herrling, Walter G. L. The Romanization of Raetia.
    Chicago, 1943. (RR)

Hesterkamp, Wilhelm. "Einflüsse sozialer Verhältnisse
    auf die Namenwahl," Muttersprache, LXXV
    (1965), 33-40. (EN)

Historisch-Biographisches Lexikon der Schweiz. I-VII
    and Supplement. Neuenburg, 1921-1934.
    (HBLS)

Hoppeler, Robert. "Untersuchungen zur Walserfrage,"
    JSG, XXXIII (1908), 1-54. (UW)

Hössli, Christian. "Die Walserkolonie Rheinwald," Wir
    Walser, V (1967), no. 1, 11-18. (WR)

Hotzenköcherle, Rudolf. "Bündnerische Verbalformengeo-
graphie," Sache, Ort und Wort (Festschrift
für Jakob Jud), Romanica Helvetica, XX
(1943), 486-543. (BV)

_____. Die Mundart von Mutten, BSG,
XIX. Frauenfeld, 1934. (MM)

_____. Review of Iso Müller, "Die
Wanderung der Walser . . . ," VR, III
(1938), 161ff.

_____. "Zur Raumstruktur des Schweizer-
deutschen," ZMF, XXVIII (1961), 207-227.
(RS)

_____. "Zur Sprachgeographie Deutsch-
bündens mit besonderer Berücksichtigung
des Verhältnisses zum Wallis," JHGG, LXXIV
(1944), 135-159. (SD)

Hübscher, Bruno. "Bündner Orte in den Pfäferser Abtei-
urbaren von 1447 und 1495," JHGG, XC
(1960), 1-82. (BO)

_____. "Die Steuergüter im Gericht Zizers um
1448," JHGG, LXXXIX (1959), 1-44. (SZ)

Hubschmied, J. U. "Alte Ortsnamen Graubündens," BM
(1948), 33-50. (AO)

_____. "Sprachliche Zeugen für das späte
Aussterben des Gallischen," VR, III (1938),
48-155. (SZ)

Ilg, Karl. Die Walser in Vorarlberg. Dornbirn, 1949.
(WV)

Issler, Peter. "Beziehungen zwischen den Walserkolonien
Rheinwald und Davos," Davoser Revue, XI
(1935/36), 261-267. (BW)

_____. Geschichte der Walserkolonie Rheinwald.
diss. Zürich, 1935. (GR)

Jahrzeitbuch von Pleif. GA Villa, Document no. 4 from
1443 with later additions.

Jahrzeitbuch von Tavetsch. Staatsarchiv Graubünden AB
IV 6/119.

Jecklin, Fritz. "Aus der ältern Geschichte der Herrschaft Haldenstein und ihrer Inhaber bis
auf die Zeit Heinrich Ammanns von Grün-
ingen," JHGG, XLVII (1917), 1-84. (HH)

_____. "Das älteste Churer Steuerbuch vom
Jahre 1481," JHGG, XXXVII (1907), 31-73.
(CS)

_____. Das Davoser Spendbuch vom Jahre 1562.
Chur, 1925. (DS)

_____. Das Jahrzeitbuch der Kirche Langwies.
Chur, 1919. (JK)

_____. Das Taminser Jahrzeitbuch. Chur, 1921.
(TJ)

_____. Jahrzeitbuch der St. Amandus-Kirche zu
Maienfeld. Chur, 1913. (SA)

_____. "Jahrzeitstiftungen der Schuhmacher,
Gerber und Metzger zu St. Martin in Chur."
Special supplement from Anzeiger für
Schweizerische Geschichte 1916. No. 2. (JS)

_____. Land und Leute des Unterengadins und
Vintschgaus im 14. Jahrhundert. Chur, 1922.
(LL)

_____. "Stiftung und Begabung der Kirche St.
Nikolaus in Küblis, 11. August 1464," BM
(1903), 221-224. (SB)

_____. Urbar der Propstei St. Jacob im Prätigau
(Klosters) vom Jahre 1514. Chur, 1910.
(UP)

_____. Urbar des Hospizes St. Peter auf dem
Septimer. Chur, 1915. (UH)

_____. Zinsbuch der Galluskirche in Fideris.
Chur, 1927. (ZG)

_____. "Zinsbuch des Praemonstratenserklosters
Churwalden," JHGG, XXXVIII (1908), 1-93.
(ZP)

_____. Zinsbuch des Prediger-Klosters St. Ni-
colai in Chur vom Jahre 1515. Chur, 1911.
(PK)

Jecklin, Fritz and Muoth, Giachen Caspar. "Aufzeich-
        nungen über Verwaltung der VIII Gerichte
        aus der Zeit der Grafen v. Monfort," JHGG,
        XXXV (1905), 1-94. (AV)

Jörger, Johann Josef. Bei den Walsern des Valsertales.
        Basel, 1947². (WV)

Jörger, Paula. "Zu einem Kaufbriefe der Alp Walletsch
        im Peiltal, Gemeinde Vals, aus dem Jahre
        1591," BM (1956), 205-210. (ZK)

Joos, Lorenz. "Die beiden Safien-Urbare des Klosters
        Cazis von 1495 und 1502 im Gemeindearchiv
        von Safien-Platz," BM (1959), 277-318.
        (SU)

_____. "Die Walserwanderungen vom 13. bis 16.
        Jahrhundert und ihre Siedlungsgebiete,
        Einzelhöfe und Niederlassung in schon be-
        stehenden romanischen Siedlungen gegen
        Ende des 15. Jahrhunderts auf dem Gebiet
        von Graubünden, St. Gallen und Liechten-
        stein," ZSG, XXVI (1946), 289-344. (WW)

Jud, Jakob. "Zur Geschichte der bündner-romanischen
        Kirchensprache." Special supplement, JHGG,
        1919. (GK)

_____. "Zur Geschichte der romanischen Relikt-
        wörter in den Alpenmundarten der deutschen
        Schweiz," VR, VIII (1945/46), 34-109. (GR)

Juvalt, Wolfgang von. Necrologium Curiense, das ist:
        Die Jahrzeitbücher der Kirche zu Cur.
        Chur, 1867. (NC)

Kessler, Heinrich. "Zur Mundart des Schanfigg," PBB,
        LV (1931), 81-206. (MS)

Kietz, Georg. "Die Personennamen und Familiennamen im
        Leipziger Lande zur Zeit Luthers," ZNF,
        XV (1939), 244-261. (PN)

Kreis, Hans. Die Walser. Bern/Munich, 1966². (DW)

Kuoni, Michael. "Restanzas dil lungatg romonsch, en las
        valladas della Landquard e della Plessur,"
        Annalas della Societad Rhaeto-Romanscha, I
        (1886), 305-337. (RL)

Liver, Peter. "Die Walser in Graubünden," BM (1953),
257-276. (WG)

_____. "Zur Wirtschaftsgeschichte der freien
Walser," Davoser Revue, XI (1935/36), 209-
216. (WW)

Lorez, Christian. Bauernarbeit im Rheinwald. Basel,
1943. (BR)

_____. "Walserisches in den Ortsnamen Grau-
bündens," Terra Grischuna, XXVIII (1969),
291-294. (WO)

Maissen, F. "Ein Kinderraub in den vier Dörfern (1689/
90)," BM (1960), 317-335. (EK)

Mayer, Johann Georg and Jecklin, Fritz. "Der Katalog des
Bischofs Flugi vom Jahre 1645," JHGG, XXX
(1900), 1-143. (KF)

Meinherz, Paul. Die Mundart der Bündner Herrschaft,
BSG, XIII. Frauenfeld, 1920. (MBH)

Meng, Johann Ulrich. "Mastrils," Bündner Gemeindechro-
nik, XXVIII (August 1964). (BG)

_____. Seewiser Heimatbuch. Schiers,
1967. (SH)

_____. Trimmiser Heimatbuch. Landquart,
1963. (TH)

Mentz, Arthur. "Schrift und Sprache der Burgunder,"
ZfdA, LXXXV (1954/55), 1-17. (SB)

Meyer, Karl. "Die Walserkolonie Rheinwald und die Freiherren von Sax-Misox," JHGG, LVII (1927),
19-42. (WR)

_____. "Ueber die Anfänge der Walserkolonien in
Rätien," BM (1925), 201-216; 233-257; 287-
293. (AW)

Meyer-Marthaler, Elisabeth. "Die Walserfrage. Der
heutige Stand der Walserforschung," ZSG,
XXIV (1944), 1-27. (DW)

Mohr, Conradin von. "Die Regesten der Landschaft Schanfigg," Theodor von Mohr, Die Regesten der

Archive in der schweizerischen Eidgenossenschaft. I, 45-59. Chur, 1851. (RS)

Mommsen, Theodor. "Die Schweiz in römischer Zeit,"
Gesammelte Schriften. V, 352-389. Berlin,
1908. (SR)

Mooser, Anton. "Die Walsersiedlungen auf dem Territorium
von Maienfeld," BM (1944), 127-129. (WM)

Moulton, William G. Swiss German Dialect and Romance
Patois. Yale University diss. Supplement
to Language, XVII, no. 4. (Language diss.
no. 34). Baltimore, 1941. (SG)

Müller, Iso. "Die Anfänge des Klosters Disentis," JHGG,
LXI (1931), 1-182. (AK)

_____. "Die Entstehung des grauen Bundes 1367-
1424," ZSG, XXI (1941), 137-199. (EGB)

_____. "Die Schenkung des Bischofs Tello an das
Kloster Disentis im Jahre 765," JHGG, LXIX
(1939), 1-138. (SB)

_____. "Die sprachlichen Verhältnisse im Vorder-
rheintal im Zeitalter des Barocks," BM
(1960), 273-316. (VV)

_____. "Die Wanderung der Walser über Furka-Ober-
alp und ihr Einfluss auf den Gotthardweg,"
ZSG, XVI (1936), 353-428. (WW)

_____. "Rätien im 8. Jahrhundert," ZSG, XIX
(1939), 337-395. (RJ)

Muoth, Giachen Caspar. "Die Thalgemeinde Tavetsch. Ein
Stück Wirtschaftsgeschichte aus Bünden,"
BM (1898), 8-19; 33-47; 74-77; 97-108.
(TT)

_____. "Register der Personen, die 1631
zu Schlans an der Pest gestorben sind," BM
(1898), 202-203. (RP)

_____. Ueber bündnerische Geschlechts-
namen und ihre Verwertung für die Bündner-
geschichte. I: Vornamen und Taufnamen als
Geschlechtsnamen. Chur, 1892; II: Ortsnamen. Chur, 1893. Beilagen zum Kantons-
schulprogramm, 1891/92, 1892/93. (BG)

365

Muoth, Giachen Caspar. "Ueber die soziale und politische
          Stellung der Walser in Graubünden," <u>JSG</u>,
          XXXIII (1908), 201-221. (<u>SPS</u>)

Nied, Edmund. <u>Heiligenverehrung und Namengebung mit Be-
          rücksichtigung der Familiennamen</u>. Frei-
          burg i. Br., 1924. (<u>HN</u>)

Niermeyer, J. F. <u>Mediae Latinitatis Lexicon Minus</u>.
          Leiden, 1954ff. (<u>ML</u>)

Oechsli, Wilhelm. "Zur Niederlassung der Burgunder und
          Alamannen in der Schweiz," <u>JSG</u>, XXXIII
          (1908), 225-266. (<u>NB</u>)

<u>Onoma</u>. Bulletin d'Information et de Bibliographie.
          Louvain (Belgium), 1950ff.

Perret, Franz. <u>Die Geschlechter der Landschaften Sargans
          und Werdenberg</u>. Bad Ragaz, 1950. (<u>SW</u>)

_____. "Die romanische Volkssprache im Sarganser-
          land," <u>BM</u> (1957), 120-126.· (<u>RV</u>)

Pieth, Friedrich. "Aus der Geschichte des Tales Schan-
          figg," <u>JHGG</u>, LXXXI (1951), 97-125. (<u>GS</u>)

_____. <u>Bündnergeschichte</u>. Chur, 1945. (<u>BG</u>)

Planta, Peter Conradin von. <u>Das alte Rätien</u>. Berlin,
          1872. (<u>DaR</u>)

_____. <u>Die currätischen Herr-
          schaften in der Feudalzeit</u>. Bern, 1881.
          (<u>CH</u>)

Planta, Robert von. "Die Sprache der rätoromanischen
          Urkunden des 8.-10. Jahrhunderts," <u>Quellen
          zur Geschichte Vorarlbergs und Liechten-
          steins</u>. I, 62-108. Innsbruck, 1920-25.
          (<u>SU</u>)

_____. "Ueber die Sprachgeschichte von
          Chur," <u>BM</u> (1931), 97-118. (<u>SC</u>)

_____. "Ueber Ortsnamen, Sprach- und
          Landesgeschichte von Graubünden," <u>RLR</u>,
          VII (1931), 80-100. (<u>OS</u>)

_____ and Schorta, Andrea. <u>Rätisches
          Namenbuch</u>. I. Zürich/Leipzig, 1939. (<u>RNB</u>)

Poeschel, Erwin. Das Burgenbuch von Graubünden. Zürich, 1930. (BB)

_____. Die Kunstdenkmäler des Kantons Graubünden. 7 vols. Basel, 1937-48. (KG)

Pradella, Johann Anton. "Verzeichniss der Landammänner von Dissentis," BM (1858), 180-183; 202-205. (LD)

Pulgram, Ernst. "Indo-European Personal Names," Language, XXIII (1947), 189-206. (PN)

_____. "Theory of Names," BNF, V (1954), 149-196. (TN)

Pult, Chaspar. "Historische Untersuchungen über die sprachlichen Verhältnisse einiger Teile der Raetia prima im Mittelalter," RLR, III (1927), 157-205. (HU)

Ribi, Adolf. "Die Geschichte Rätiens in einer Darstellung einer unveröffentlichten Chronik des 16. Jahrhunderts," BM (1938), 144-157. (GR)

Richard, Willy. Untersuchungen zur Genesis der reformierten Kirchenterminologie der Westschweiz und Frankreichs. Romanica Helvetica, LVII. Bern, 1959. (UG)

Rübel, Hans Ulrich. Viehzucht im Oberwallis. BSM, II. Frauenfeld, 1950. (VO)

Rupp, Theodor. "Gemeinde und Kirche im Prättigau in ihrer Entwicklung bis zur Reformation," BM (1950), 97-127. (GK)

Salis-Soglio, Nicolaus von. Regesten der im Archiv des Geschlechts-Verbandes derer von Salis befindlichen Pergamenturkunden. Sigmaringen, 1898. (RP)

Schatz, J. "Ueber die Lautform althochdeutscher Personennamen," ZfdA, LXXII (1935), 129-160. (LP)

Scheidl, J. "Der Kampf zwischen deutschen und christlichen Vornamen im ausgehenden Mittelalter," ZNF, XVI (1940), 193-214. (KV)

Schiess, Traugott. "Kulturzustände in Davos und Prätigau im 16. Jahrhundert." Special supple-
ment. BM, 1935. (KD)

Schmidt-Gartmann, Martin. "Einiges über die Landschaft
Davos," Wir Walser (1964), no. 1. 3-8.
(ED)

_____. "Wie die Walser nach Grau-
bünden kamen," Terra Grischuna, XXVIII
(1969), 279-282. (WG)

Schmidt, Ludwig. "Zur Geschichte der alemannischen Besiedlung der Schweiz," ZSG, XVIII (1938),
369-379. (GB)

Schönfeld, M. Wörterbuch der altgermanischen Personen-
und Völkernamen. Heidelberg, 1911. (WP)

Schorta, Andrea. "Elemente der christlichen Kultur in
den Ortsnamen Graubündens," BM (1949),
265-279. (EK)

_____. "Namenkundliches aus dem Prättigau,"
Terra Grischuna, XXII (1963), 26-28. (NP)

_____. "Namenkundliches zur Lüener Stiftungs-
urkunde vom Jahre 1084," BM (1949), 97-112.
(NL)

_____. Rätisches Namenbuch. II. Bern, 1964.
(RNB)

_____. "Romanische Ortsnamen des Prättigaus,"
Prättigauer Zeitung und Herrschaftler (1949)
Nos. 53, 56, 59, 61, 67, 70. (PZH)

_____. "Wechselbeziehungen zwischen Ortsnamen
und Personennamen in Graubünden," Studia
Onomastica Monacensia IV (Report of the
Sixth International Congress of Onomastic
Sciences). Munich, 1961. 685-691. (WO)

_____. "Zur Siedlungsgeschichte von Davos,"
Davoser Revue (1936), 222-225. (DR)

Schüle, Wilhelm. "Die Landschaft Davos im Lichte bünd-
nerischer Ortsnamen," BM (1930), 97-125.
(LD)

Schürr, Friedrich. "Die Alpenromanen," VR, XXII (1963), 100-126. (DA)

Senn, Alfred. "Notes on Swiss Personal Names," Names, X (1962), 149-158. (NN)

Senn, Nikolaus. Archiv Jenaz. Schaffhausen, 1869. (AJ)

_____, ed. Urban der kilchgenosen vnd nachge- purschafft des kilchspels zu Buchs A? 1484. Buchs, 1882. (UB)

Senn, Ulrich. "Die Alpwirtschaft der Landschaft Davos," Geographica Helvetica, VII (1952), 265- 350. (GH)

Sererhard, Nicolin. Einfalte Delineation aller Gemeinden gemeiner dreyen Bünden. ed. O. Vasella. Chur, 1944. (ED)

Simonett, Christoph. "Das Avers," BM (1955), 117-125. (DA)

_____. Die Bauernhäuser des Kantons Grau- bünden. I. Basel, 1965; II. Basel, 1968. (BG)

Socin, Adolf. Mittelhochdeutsches Namenbuch nach ober- rheinischen Quellen des zwölften und drei- zehnten Jahrhunderts. Basel, 1903. (MN)

Sonderegger, Stefan. "Aufgaben und Probleme der althoch- deutschen Namenkunde," Namenforschung (Festschrift für Adolf Bach). Heidelberg, 1965. 55-96. (AP)

_____. "Das Althochdeutsche der Vorakte der älteren St. Galler Urkunden," ZMF, XXVIII (1961), 251-286. (AV)

_____. "Der althochdeutsche Personennamen- schatz von St. Gallen," Studia Onomastica Monacensia IV (Report of the Sixth Inter- national Congress of Onomastic Sciences). Munich, 1961. 722-729. (SOM)

_____. "Die althochdeutsche Schweiz," Sprachleben der Schweiz. Bern, 1963. 23-55. (AS)

Sonderegger, Stefan. "Die Ausbildung der deutsch-roman-
ischen Sprachgrenze in der Schweiz im
Mittelalter," Rheinische Vierteljahrsblätter, XXXI (1966/67), 223-290. (SS)

_____. "Volks- und Sprachgrenzen in der
Schweiz im Frühmittelalter. Der sprach-
geschichtliche Aspekt," SZG, XIII (1963),
493-534. (VS)

Sprecher, Andreas von. "Die Ansiedelung von Germanen in
Churrätien im Zusammenhang mit der Teilung
zwischen Bistum und Grafschaft Chur durch
die Karolinger," BM (1922), 65-82. (AG)

Sprecher, Anton von. "Das Zinsbuch der Kirche Serneus
vom Jahre 1479," JHGG, LXXXI (1951), 66-
96. (ZS)

_____. "Davoser Chronik von Florian und
Fortunat von Sprecher," BM (1953), 314-
375. (DC)

_____. Stammbaum der Familie von Salis.
Chur, 1939. (SS)

_____. Stammbaum der Familie von Tschar-
ner--Bündner Zweig. Chur?, 1942. (ST)

Sprecher, J. A. von. "Die Pest in Graubünden während
der Kriege und Unruhen 1628-1635," BM
(1942), 21-32; 58-64. (PG)

_____. Kulturgeschichte der drei Bünde
im 18. Jahrhundert. ed. Rudolf Jenny.
Chur, 1951. (KB)

Staehelin, Felix. Die Schweiz in römischer Zeit. Basel,
1948. (SR)

Stoffel, Johann Rudolf. Das Hochtal Avers. Zofingen,
1938. (HA)

Szadrowsky, Manfred. "Altes Alemannentum im rätoromanischen Graubünden," ZNF, XVIII (1943),
144-161; XIX (1944), 242-258. (AA)

_____. "Rätische Namenforschung," ZFN,
XVI (1940), 97-121; 239-261. (RN)

Szadrowsky, Manfred. "Ueber walserische Sprachdenk-
    mäler," BM (1927), 49-62. (WS)

_____. "Walserdeutsch," BM (1925), 161-
    197. (Wd)

_____. "Wie sich Rätoromanisch und Deutsch
    in Graubünden mischen," Die Alpen, XIV
    (1938), 53-63; 88-96. (RD)

Theus, Arno. Systematische Untersuchung der bündn. Be-
    völkerungsverschiebungen, deren Ursachen
    und Folgen. Chur, 1938. (SU)

Thöny, Matthias. Prättigauer Geschichte. Schiers,
    1948. (PG)

Tobler-Meyer, Wilhelm. Deutsche Familiennamen nach
    ihrer Entstehung und Bedeutung, mit be-
    sonderer Rücksichtnahme auf Zürich und die
    Ostschweiz. Zürich, 1894. (DF)

Tomamichel, Tobias. Bosco Gurin. Basel, 1953. (BG)

Tschudi, Aegidius (Gilg). Grundtliche und warhaffte be-
    schreibung der uralten Alpischen Rhetie/
    sampt dem Tract der anderen Alp gebirgen
    und Schweitzerlands: nach Pliny/Ptolemei/
    Strabonis/auch an deren welt und gschicht-
    schrybern warer anzeygung . . . Basel,
    1538. (AR)

Valèr, M. Schloss und Herrschaft Tarasp. Chur, 1943.
    (ST)

Vasella, Oskar. "Bauernkrieg und Reformation in Grau-
    bünden 1525-1526," ZSG, XX (1940), 1-65.
    (BR)

_____. "Die Ursachen der Reformation in der
    deutschen Schweiz," ZSG, XXVI (1947), 401-
    424. (UR)

Vetter, Ferdinand. Ueber Personennamen und Namengebung
    in Bern und anderswo. Bern, 1910. (PN)

Waltershausen, A. Sartorius Freiherr von. "Die Germani-
    sierung der Rätoromanen in der Schweiz,"
    Forschungen zur deutschen Landes- und
    Volkskunde, XII (1900), 369-474. (GR)

Wartmann, Hermann. Rätische Urkunden aus dem Central-
archiv des fürstlichen Hauses Thurn und
Taxis in Regensburg, QSG, X. Basel, 1891.
(RU)

Weinreich, Uriel. Languages in Contact. The Hague, 1967
Fifth printing. (LC)

_____. Research Problems in Bilingualism,
with Special Reference to Switzerland.
Columbia University diss. 1952. (RP)

Weiss, Richard. Das Alpwesen Graubündens. Zürich, 1941.
(AG)

_____. "Die viersprachige Schweiz im Atlas der
schweizerischen Volkskunde (ASV)," Sprachleben der Schweiz (Festschrift für Rudolf
Hotzenköcherle). Bern, 1963. (DvS)

_____. Volkskunde der Schweiz. Zürich, 1946.
(VS)

Wiezel, Gubert von. "Historie des Klosters zu Churwalden," BM (1904), 1-5; 25-30; 45-54;
65-75. (HK)

Woolf, Henry Bosley. The Old Germanic Principles of
Name-giving. Baltimore, 1939. (GN)

Zimmerli, J. Die deutsch-französische Sprachgrenze in
der Schweiz. III: Die Sprachgrenze im
Wallis. Basel/Geneva, 1899. (SW)

Zimpel, Heinz-Gerhard. "Zur Entwicklung und zum heutigen
Stand der Walserkolonien," Beiträge zur
Landeskunde Bayerns und der Alpenländer.
(Festschrift für Hans Fehn). Munich, 1968.
123-173. (EW)

Zinsli, Paul. "Das Berner Oberland als frühe alemann-
ische Siedlungsstaffel im westlichen
Schweizerdeutschen Sprachgrenzraum,"
Namenforschung (Festschrift für Adolf Bach)
Heidelberg, 1965. 330-358. (BO)

_____. "Die mittelalterliche Walserwanderung in
Flurnamenspuren," Sprachleben der Schweiz.
Bern, 1963. 301-330. (MaWW)

Zinsli, Paul. Walser Volkstum. Frauenfeld, 1968. (WV)

——————————. "Zum Flurnamenzeugnis für die deutsche
Besiedlung der Alpen," Studia Onomastica
Monacensia IV (Report of the Sixth Inter-
national Congress of Onomastic Sciences).
Munich, 1961. 798-811. (ZF)

Zopfi, Fritz. "Zeugnisse alter Zweisprachigkeit im
Glarnerland," VR, XII (1951/52), 280-315.
(ZZ)